the handbook of learning activities for young children

By Jane A. Caballero, Ph.D

Elementary Education Department
University of Miami
Coral Gables, Florida

Art Director/Designer
Mechanical Artist

EARL DAVIS

HUMANICS LIMITED
P. O. Box 7447
Atlanta, Georgia 30309

Copyright © 1980 by Humanics Limited. All rights reserved. No part of this book may be reproduced by any means, nor transmitted, nor translated into machine language, without written permission from Humanics Limited.
Library of Congress Card Catalog Number: 80-81660

PRINTED IN THE UNITED STATES OF AMERICA
ISBN 0-89334-058-8

Acknowledgements

I would like to extend my thanks to Charles T. Caballero for his photographic and graphic assistance, M. Liz Christman-Rothlein for providing additional ideas during the compiling of this text, and Mary Louise Cole and Ronald Lewallen for their editorial assistance. My thanks also go to Alma David, Betty Rowen, and Gary Wilson for their continued support.

Dedicated to Lara

contents

Acknowledgements iii

Introduction 9

part I
getting ready
.... 11

chapter 1
competency based training   12
Competency Structure Chart 13

chapter 2
learning centers   15
Process of Developing A Learning Center 16
Classroom Flow Chart 19

part II
creating materials
.... 21

chapter 3
health and safety   22
Health Activities 22
Cooking Activities 24
Recipes 26
Safety Activities 28
The Tooth Tree Ditto Sheet 29
Bicycle Inspection Check List 34
Resources 36

chapter 4
play   37
Values of Play 37
Good Playthings 38
Types of Play 38
Puzzles 41
Play Activities 42

chapter 5
movement   43
Relays, Stunts, and Tumbling 44
Movement Activities 44

chapter 6
science   46
Science Activities 46
Simple Experiments 48
Our Senses. 50
Weather Chart Pattern. 54
Animal Ditto Sheets 55
Elementary Aerospace. 59
Aerospace Poems. 60
Resources 61

chapter 7
social studies   62
Career Education. 62
Career Activity Patterns .65
Pollution. 67
Transportation 69
Transportation Activity Pattern 70
Countries of the World .71
Field Trips. 72
Resources 73

chapter 8
math   74
Math Finger Plays 75
Math Activities 76
File Folder Games. 78
File Folder Game Patterns. 81

chapter 9
language development 85
Listening. 85
Speaking. 87
Language Experience Stories. 89
Traditional Stories. 94
Story Prop Patterns. 95

chapter 10
pre-reading   103
Pre-Reading Skills and Activities. 103
Word List 106
The Alphabet 107
Additional Activities 108

chapter 11
art 115
Drawing....117
Painting....118
Cut and Paste....121
Flannel and Bulletin Boards....123
Clay....124
Printing....126
Textile Projects....130
Photography....132
Puppetry....135

chapter 12
music 141
Traditional Songs, Poems and Fingerplays....141
Rhythm....148
Listening....149
Sight Reading....150
Creativity....156
Song, Poem, and Fingerplay Prop Patterns....157

part III
loose ends

....163

chapter 13
behavior 164
Behavior Modification....164
Establishing Rules....165

chapter 14
evaluation 167
Readiness Checklist....169

chapter 15
parent involvement 170
Rules of Parenting....171
Activities To Do At Home....172
The Eight Basic Toys....174
File Folder Games....176
Bibliography....204

Footnotes....206

introduction

This book is designed as a resource for teachers, parents, students or any adult concerned with early childhood education. It is hoped that the ideas and activities presented herein will serve in the creation of a curriculum that is both child-centered and exciting. The basic philosophy for such a curriculum is based on that of Piaget:

> "The principle goal of education is to create men who are capable of doing new things, not simply of repeating what other generations have done — men who are creative, inventive, and discoverers. The second goal of education is to form minds which can be critical, can verify, and will not accept everything that they are offered. The great danger today is of slogans, collective opinions, ready made trends of thought. We have to be able to resist individually, to criticize, to distinguish between what is proven and what is not. So we need pupils who are active, who learn early to find out by themselves, partly through their own spontaneous activity and partly through materials we set up for them; who learn early to tell what is verifiable and what is simply the first idea to come to them."[1]

Research is continuing to prove that the years before a child begins formal schooling are the most important years in his intellectual development. Freud based his theories on his findings that innate motives and the basis for behavior are established in the first years of life.

Hunt's extensive work with young children indicated that by restructuring the environment to provide more stimulation, the I.Q. of the child could be raised considerably.[2] Bloom, in his research of human intellectual development, emphasized the importance of the child's early environment by concluding that by the time the child is four years old 50% of his organized thinking patterns are established, by the time he's eight another 30% are developed with the remaining 20% developing by the time he is seventeen.[3] Considering that the majority of children in the United States do not enter a classroom until they are six years old, the urgency of making all of those adults responsible for those early years aware of the importance of a stimulating environment becomes apparent. It is clear then why education in the United States is facing such violent criticism. We simply cannot afford to wait until the child is six years old to begin his education. Education of the child, if it is to have any real effect, must begin at his birth or even before.

To face this challenge, parent involvement in early childhood education is vital. Rising to meet this challenge, Project Head Start was launched in an attempt to brighten the educational future of disadvantaged children. Parents are encouraged to become involved in the education of their children both at home and at school. One of the key emphases of education in the home is on language. Language development is equated with success. It has been found by Bereiter and Engelman[4] and others that language structure is formed early in life and is difficult to change. Programs aimed at treating cultural deprivation as synonymous with language deprivation may help the disadvantaged child catch up with their more privileged peers. Parents then are encouraged to play with their children, to make every effort to stimulate communication. Because the development of communication during these early years is seen as crucial, the parents' role in their child's future is vital.

It is increasingly evident that if education is to prepare the child to live in today's complex technological society, our schools must prepare children to become self-motivated and self-directed. Based on the philosophy of Froebel and other leaders in the field of early childhood education, the curriculum of young children should be play-oriented.[5]

Through play activities the exploring, experimental, imaginative nature of the child can be nurtured. Play is a practicing ground for skill development. Through it the seeds of knowledge are planted and beginning concepts are established. If the activities are free of detail, stimulating and, above all, available to the child, his curiosity and interest in his world should prepare him for an active participating role in society.

The play activities presented in this text are designed to stimulate the development of the child's intellect and imagination from 2-8 years old. All areas of development are encouraged: perceptual and language development, health and safety, math, art, music, reading, science, and social studies. The parent or educator who utilizes this text will find the materials used in these activities inexpensive to make and exciting to use. They are basically child-oriented, requiring little adult direction. Each chapter provides learning activities designed to lead the child into developing his own powers of thinking by presenting him with new and interesting situations. The educational objectives for each activity are stated clearly.

Piaget emphasizes that if learning is to be meaningful children must internalize new concepts in order to be able to transfer them to new situations. In order for such internalization to occur the child must be physically (concretely) involved in his world. The adult who serves to guide him must be aware of his developmental level and design tasks to meet his individual needs and interests. The activities presented in this book are easily adapted to meet the developmental task level of each child. A developmental task has been defined as, "a task which arises at or about a certain period of the individual's life, the successful achievement of which leads to his happiness and to success with later tasks, while failure leads to unhappiness in the individual, disapproval by society, and difficulty with later tasks."[6]

In summary, as long as we maintain the awareness that rates and abilities vary, we can provide enough experience to stimulate all children to develop their intellects to the fullest. If we agree that learning takes place by interacting with the environment then it is our responsibility to allow the child the maximum opportunity for such interaction in the most exciting enriched environment possible.

Jane A. Caballero, Ph.D.

part 1
getting ready

chapter I competency based training

Teacher training institutions have been forced to re-examine their programs. The research being conducted repeatedly emphasizes the importance of the early years in the child's total development. Traditionally left to the care provided in the home, the development of many young children has been stifled or retarded from the start. The demands of modern society have forced many working mothers to delegate the nurturance of their infants and/or toddlers to baby-sitters or day care centers. The quality of the child-care settings is directly related to the level of development that child can attain.

Institutions have become increasingly aware that it is not enough to ask a person to provide the correct answers to written questions on a test. The responsibilities of working with small children are deemed so important that programs are being developed that ask the applicant for child care certification to prove that she is competent. The leader in competency-based programs for child care is the Child Development Associate Program (CDA).

This program, sponsored by a Consortium of 39 agencies involved in child care, represents a national effort to improve the quality and effectiveness of care provided to young children. This Consortium has developed a process through which the Child Development Associate Credential is awarded on the basis of demonstrated competence in 6 delineated areas. At this time standards have been set for child care staff in programs for children 3 to 5 years of age. Training is individualized according to the background and needs of each CDA candidate. It must be a combination of academic training (formal college or informal workshops) and supervised field experience.

With the aid of a field trainer, the candidate develops competence in the thirteen functional areas (subdivisions of the 6 competencies). Examples of his competence in each area are organized in a portfolio as the candidate progresses through training. At the end of his training the candidate applies to Washington, D. C. (The CDA Consortium) for the assessment process to begin. The requirements for eligibility for assessment are: The applicant must be 16 years of age and must have worked with preschool children 3 to 5 years of age for at least 16 months part-time or 8 months full-time.

The activities presented in this book are correlated with the 6 competency areas of the CDA. Therefore, an overview of the CDA is included in this text. Although each activity is presented as a demonstration of the development of one functional area, it may easily be adapted for numerous other areas. For this reason, there is a blank space available for *you* to fill in as you decide how you would use the activity. The limits are set only by the imagination and versatility of the reader.

The following Competency Structure Chart provides you with the Functional Area Key Words which will be used throughout this book.

Competency Structure Chart[7]

DEFINITION OF THE CDA: The Child Development Associate or CDA is a person able to meet the specific needs of a group of children in a child development setting by nurturing children's physical, social, emotional, and intellectual growth by establishing and maintaining a proper child care environment, and by protecting good relations between parents and the child development center.

COMPETENCY AREA:

I	II	III	IV	V	VI
ESTABLISHES and maintains a safe and healthy learning environment	ADVANCES physical and intellectual competence	BUILDS positive self concept and individual strength	PROMOTES positive functioning of children and adults in a group	BRINGS ABOUT optimal coordination of home and center child rearing practices and expectations	CARRIES OUT supplementary responsibilities related to children's programs

FUNCTIONAL AREA (Key Words):

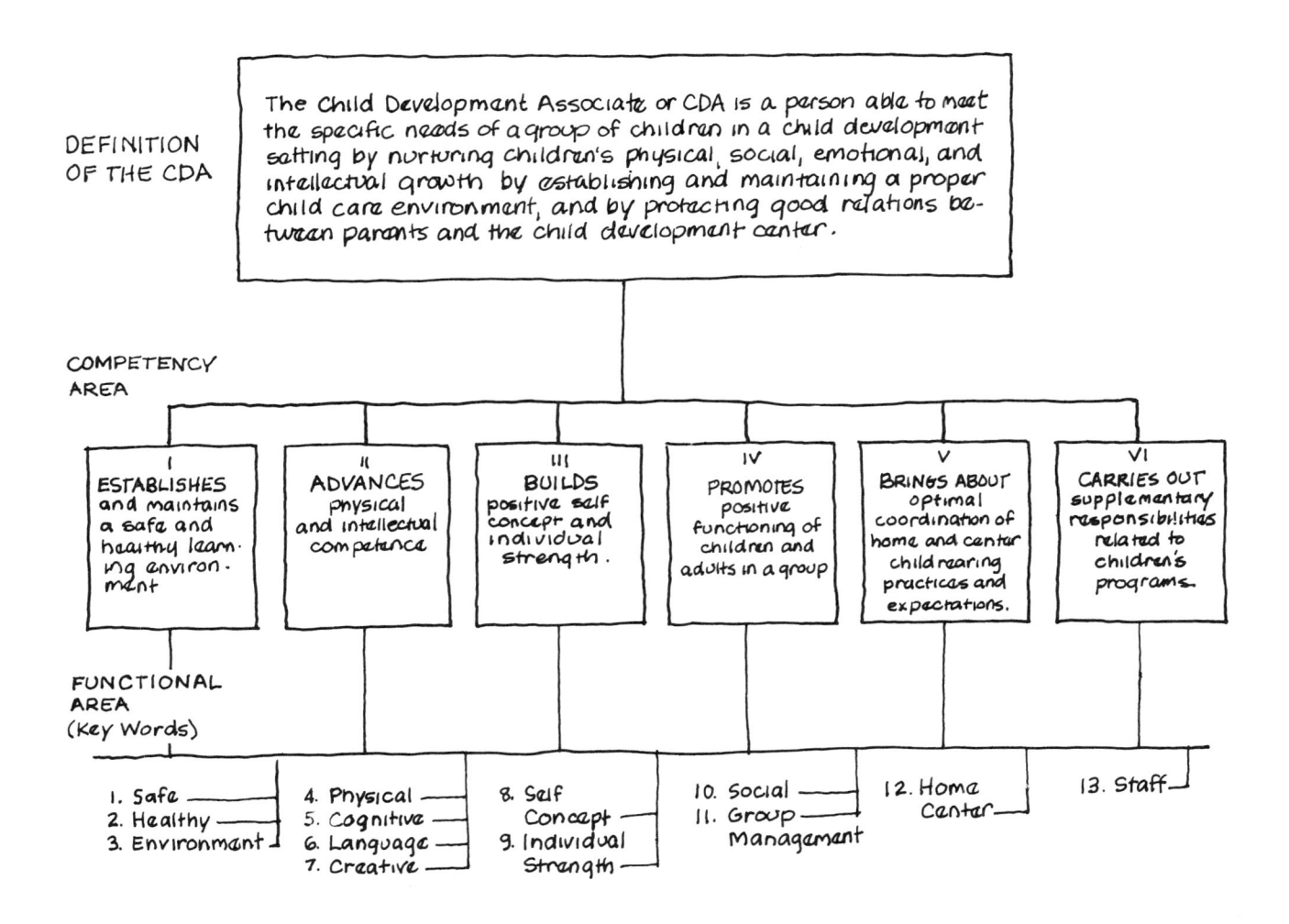

1. Safe
2. Healthy
3. Environment
4. Physical
5. Cognitive
6. Language
7. Creative
8. Self Concept
9. Individual Strength
10. Social
11. Group Management
12. Home Center
13. Staff

Reprinted with permission form CDA Consortium, The CDA Credential and the Credential Award System, 1976.

As an aid to the CDA candidate or potential child care worker, suggestions of ways to utilize the portfolio to demonstrate competence in the 13 functional areas follow. Please note the importance of explaining in writing on each item how it might be utilized to meet the competency requirement. It is also helpful to develop a portfolio check sheet to provide a record of which items have been placed in a functional area, what other competency requirements this particular item might fulfill and the date filed.

Some suggestions for examples of competence in the thirteen functional areas for the CDA portfolio are:

- Safety (center license, fire drill materials and posters, rules for the classroom or playground, safety materials or activities demonstrated in class, rules and precautions on field trips with pictures taken on a trip, accident-first aid procedures)
- Health (health forms, records, emergency cards, local health department materials such as brochures and posters, stories about health problems and procedures, cooking rules and classroom recipes, health rules such as washing before eating)
- Learning environment (room diagram showing interest centers, activities placed in centers with pictures, daily schedule, information on learning center approach)
- Physical (growth and development characteristics, gross and fine motor activities, perceptual motor development-checklists, play equipment to develop physical development skills)
- Cognitive (checklists and tests, your philosophy, curriculum units on math, science, social studies with samples of children's work, monthly activities based on seasons and teacher made learning materials)
- Language (language arts materials, how to read and tell a story, felt story, poetry, new words learned on field trips, multi-ethnic books, rules for reading, language experience approach)
- Creative (examples of children's creative stories and illustrations, music objectives and movement activities, art objectives and examples [puppetry, drawing, painting, photography, cut and paste, fabrics and fibers, bulletin boards, clay, printing, seasonal activities])
- Self concept (cultural relevance of materials, positive reinforcement techniques, self concept activities, body awareness games)
- Individual strength (written observations and records on children, mainstreaming concept, goals for individual children, case studies of children, grouping)
- Social (how children are grouped and why, goals for the particular group of children, social development principles for children of this age)
- Group management (discipline philosophy, positive reinforcement, planning and implementing for various groups)
- Home center (memos, newsletters, notes to parents, activities to do with your child at home, parent volunteers in the classroom, parent conferences)
- Staff (inservice and formal training, workshops and meetings, write-up [resume] of your qualifications and goals, memberships, and sharing and planning with co-workers)

The candidate's other major responsibility in the CDA process is to be observed by a trainer in these 13 areas. The trainer must be aware of the intern's professional growth over a length of time, be a professional in early childhood, be familiar with preschool requirements, and not presently be working in the candidate's room. Observation forms which are helpful will focus on the 13 areas noting activities demonstrated and specifying the strengths and suggestions for improvements. The intern should interact with her trainer and discuss areas for improvement.

Both the candidate and the trainer judge when the candidate is competent. The trainer observes the candidate for a period of 3 hours and records the observations on a trainer report covering all 13 functional areas. The candidate then applies to the CDA consortium for assessment.[8]

chapter 2
learning centers

There are many ways to divide the curriculum into subject areas. For the sake of clarity each subject area will be presented accompanied by ideas and activities to help the teacher get started in creating exciting and stimulating learning centers. Of course, for the learning center experiences to be meaningful the teacher who prepares them must first know what the desired objectives of that learning experience are. Each subject area presented will include some possible objectives that a teacher might have for structuring learning experiences in that area.

This brief introduction will only present a minimum amount of information. The inexperienced educator will want to do further reading and research in each area. The textbook, *Good Schools for Young Children*, will provide much of this needed information.

The educator using this textbook to create materials based on the Child Development Associate credential will also want to reorganize the material. (Refer to organization diagram chart in Chapter I.) Most of the activities presented may be used to develop individual strengths in the children as well as social skills.

WHAT IS A LEARNING CENTER?

A learning center is an area in the classroom which contains a collection of activities and materials to teach, reinforce, and/or enrich a skill or concept.

The following are key points for a learning center:

1. A learning center:
    a. must have a variety of activities for the children to do.
    b. activities and materials must cover the range from simple to difficult and from concrete to abstract.
    c. should be geared to the abilities, interests, and needs of the students within the classroom.
2. Every learning center should contain:
    a. multi-media materials to support the topic, theme, concept, or skill (slides, filmstrips, books, records).
    b. manipulative materials for exploration and discovery.
    c. directions for use of the center.

3. Every learning center needs the reinforcement of:
   a. a teacher's introduction to what the center contains and how it can be used.
   b. a classroom organizational pattern which tells children when to use the learning center.

4. For the student, the learning center is used as:
   a. a self-selected activity for independent study.
   b. follow-up for a teacher-taught lesson.
   c. an activity in place of a regular assignment.
   d. an enrichment activity.

PROCESS OF DEVELOPING A LEARNING CENTER

1. Select a subject area.
   Example: Reading, math, careers, science

2. Determine the skill or concept to be taught, reinforced, or enriched.
   Example: To teach the skill of rhyming.

3. Develop the skill or concept into a learning activity: Manipulating (cutting, pasting, matching), experimenting (observing, charting, keeping a log), listening or viewing.
   Example: Students will learn about rhyming by listening to a tape or rhymes and matching rhyming words to rhyming pictures.

4. Prepare the skill or concept into an applying activity: filling in, arranging in order, putting together, taking apart, listening, classifying, matching, tracing, writing, locating, or labeling.
   Example: Students will apply the rhyming skill to games or worksheets which ask them to fill in the rhyming words, list words which rhyme, and classify words with the same rhyming sounds.

5. Incorporate the skill or concept into an extending activity: comparing, developing your own, researching, reconstructing, finding what other, or deciding what if.
   Example: Students will extend their skill of rhyming by writing their own poem, finding out about Edgar Allan Poe, or rewriting a nursery rhyme.

6. Place all the games, worksheets, charts, etc., together in one area of the room for children to use in a self-selected manner.

THE TEACHER'S ROLE IN A LEARNING CENTER

The basic assumption when defining the teacher's role in a learning center is that a learning center does not have its own lifeline: it is dependent on the teacher as a source of energy to keep it alive and functioning. The teacher needs to be responsible for preparing, introducing, encouraging, and keeping records for the learning center as follows:

1. The teacher should prepare all the learning tools, such as worksheets and games, and collect all available resources for the center so that it contains all the necessary equipment for students to discover, learn, and apply the concept or skill for which it was developed.

2. The teacher should thoroughly introduce the learning center to the students so that they can clearly understand the answers to these questions:
   What can be done at the center?
   How is each activity, game, etc. used?
   Where are the materials necessary for production kept?
   Where are the finished products to be stored?

3. The teacher should motivate and encourage students to use the learning center by doing the following:
   Adding new activities or materials to the center
   Letting students create their own activities at the center
   Having teacher-directed lessons in small or large groups at the center
   Providing opportunities for sharing and teaching among the students who have worked at the center

4. The teacher should provide some means for record keeping and evaluating so that both students and the teacher can account for time spent and learnings accomplished at the center.

EXAMPLES OF LEARNING CENTERS

Many of the ideas and activities in this book would be very conducive to a learning center approach. Therefore, this section may prove helpful in organizing your classroom.

Learning centers seem to be a realistic way to organize the classroom so that every student may be reached. Through centers we can use the interests of each individual child to provide learning experiences on his level. Children in learning centers learn how to learn. They learn by asking questions and discovering the answers on the level that is relevant to them. Thus, real learning or "education" takes place. The teacher's responsibility is to educate students. She is to guide and direct the learning experiences of her students. She is not forced to teach the subject, but is allowed to teach the students.[9]

The following descriptions and pictures may help give both the teacher and paraprofessional some ideas in setting up a learning centered classroom.[10]

Reading Center
The Reading Center may be coordinated with the Writing Center. Word and reading games as well as books on various levels enable each student to read at his own level. The teacher is free to explain games, test word knowledge, help teach new words, and develop other reading skills.[11]

Music Center
The Music Center may contain books, rhythm instruments, and records. Music, a universal language, is an important part of the classroom learning organization. It contributes to the child's total development. In the classroom it is an emotional outlet for tension, helps to shape an integrated personality, is a direct experience, and helps to create a sense of togetherness. Opportunities are provided for musical experiences which allow each child to respond in terms of his own needs. Music materials and activities are designed to help each child discover his talents, capacities, and interests.[12]

Science Center
The Science Center can contain chairs and desks, resource books, bulletin boards with unit material displayed, various games, and science material. The child is encouraged to use the discovery method to find out about the unit at hand as well as other science concepts. He is encouraged to bring natural, animate, and inanimate objects to display. Rocks, sand, leaves, insects, and many other objects can be studied, labeled, and used in experiments.[13]

Math Center
The Math Center can contain desks and chairs, math books, dittos, papers and pencils, abacus, cuisanaire rods, chalk board, counting sticks, and numerous other math aids. The child can work at his own level and has the opportunity to choose from a variety of materials to help him. Many concrete as well as abstract problems can be solved. The child can learn to discover by doing. The child is encouraged to think for himself, correct his own mistakes, and achieve self-reward. He learns math can be fun. The aim is for him to realize that math can be used in everyday situations.[14]

Art Center
The Art Center can contain paper, colors, glue, scissors, colored paper, design blocks, paints and any other art supplies available. Art experiences allow a child to express the feelings and responses he is unable to verbalize. It is one of the most powerful tools for increasing both intellectual and emotional growth. The child is allowed to explore this area with freedom. All materials are at the child's disposal.[15]

Writing Center
The Writing Center may include desks and chairs, bulletin boards with alphabet cards, calendar with days and months noted, papers and pencils, and resource books. The child is given the opportunity to use his own vocabulary to write stories or illustrate pictures. The teacher can write down stories the child dictates to him. The child learns that words really can mean something to him. He can learn to write and read in a more meaningful fashion.[16]

Game Center
The Game Center may contain blocks, dishes, dolls and baby bed, dress-up clothes, telephones, puzzles, and other games. Freedom of choice in various game situations is available to the child so he can learn to share and get along with his peers.[17]

Social Studies Center
The Social Studies Center may contain material relating to the child's family, home, school, community, city, state, and world. The child is made aware of himself and the world in which he lives. Other cultures such as those of Hawaii and Mexico can be studied to help the child to become aware of and to understand basic cultural differences.[18]

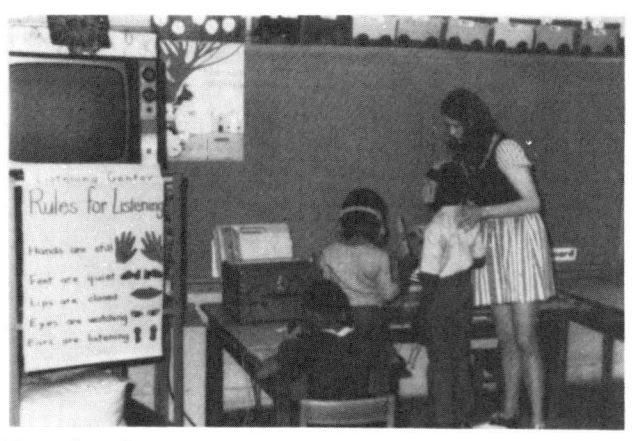

Listening Center
The Listening Center may contain a television, language master, records, record player, view master, and listening units with headphones. The independent activities are available for the child to develop various reading and listening skills.[19]

ORGANIZATION

The organization of the classroom into learning centers requires thoughtful planning. Noisy centers should be on one side of the room away from quiet ones. There should be enough space between centers to allow for free flowing of traffic and activity. The picture (pg. 19) illustrates an example of the type of floor plan each teacher must design before the room can be organized into centers successfully.

A classroom organized into learning centers requires more than physical diagrams of the planned positions of the centers. The children will need to be organized into groups and a flow chart drawn to allow for an adequate variety of experiences throughout the week. The picture (pg. 19) presents a flow chart for different children or groups that is easy for the children to follow. Colored squares are placed on the chart as indicated. Children who are "red squares" begin in the Language Arts center on Monday morning. They work at their individual or group assignment there for the allotted time and then move on to the Math Center. On Tuesday they begin at the Math Center while the "blue squares" work at the Language Arts Center. The teacher maintains a master chart so that she knows on what skills each child is working and where he plans to do group teaching.

The top picture illustrates a possible floor plan for setting up learning centers within a classroom. Be certain to place noisier centers such as music, woodworking and housekeeping away from the quieter centers. Be sure to allow adequate room for manipulation.

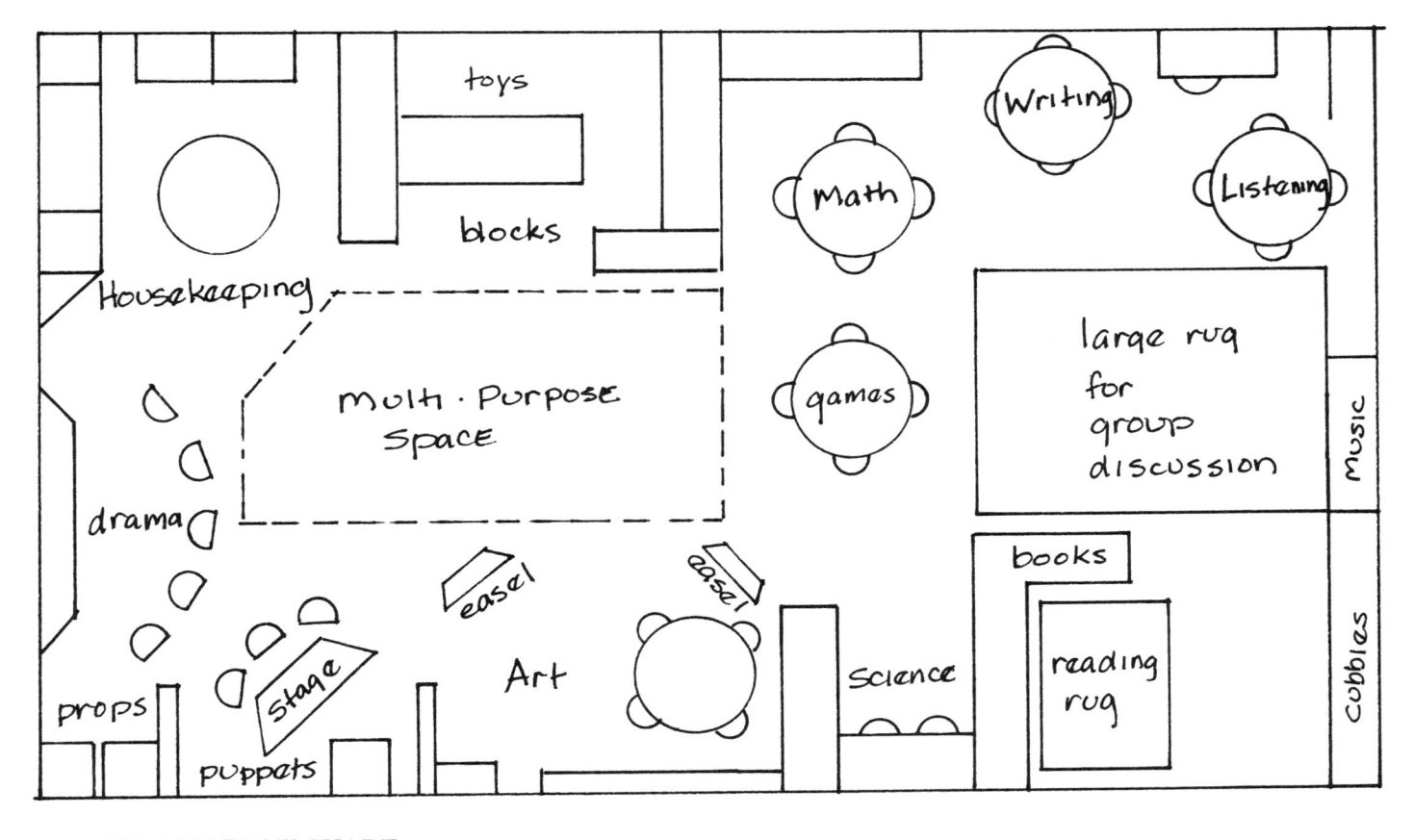

CLASSROOM FLOW CHART

time: 15 min.	mon.	Tues.	Wed.	Thurs.	Fri.
Language Arts					
Math					
Crafts					
Writing					
Listening & Viewing					

SAMPLE KINDERGARTEN SCHEDULE

8:30 – 8:45	Opening Schedule
8:45 – 9:30	<u>Whole Class Activities</u> Language Development, Social Studies, Science, Music, Art, Finger Plays, etc.
9:30 – 10:30	<u>Work Time (LEARNING CENTER)</u> Language Arts, Mathematics, Craft Projects, Pre Writing Center, Listening Station, Viewing and Library
10:30 – 10:50	<u>Clean up Time</u> Wash hands. Get ready for lunch
10:50 – 11:20	<u>LUNCH TIME</u>
11:20 – 11:40	Come back from lunch. Bathroom activities and get ready for
11:40 – 12:20	<u>Resting Period</u>
12:20 – 12:50	<u>OUTDOOR PLAY</u> · FREE PLAY AND ORGANIZED GAMES
12:50 – 1:30	<u>Story Time</u>: Films, Dance, Music, Rhythmical Exercises. FRIDAY: Sharing Time
1:30 – 1:50	<u>Summary of the day</u> · Keep work in folders, or take them home
1:50 – 2:00	Get ready for <u>Dismissal</u>

Each teacher will prefer to schedule the school day according to the previous experiences she has had. The sample schedule above provides a variety of activities with a balance of active and quiet periods.

part II
creating materials

chapter 3
health and safety

For many reasons, young children must be encouraged to learn numerous facts and practices that will enable them to make intelligent decisions related to their health. Children should be provided with numerous opportunities which will develop attitudes that motivate them to make appropriate decisions concerning healthful daily living and continue these practices throughout their lifetime. Children must be taught these skills at a young age in order that these health practices become habits. Young children need to learn habits of personal hygiene, skills in physical education, the importance of proper table manners, the identification of nutritional foods, proper care of teeth and hair, the ability to dress themselves, and the necessity of relaxation and exercise.

Teachers should stress the following practices in the classroom: cleanliness, regular medical checkups and immunizations, personal safety, adequate rest, proper nutrition, and proper exercise.

Some objectives of health and safety education include:

1. Recognizing the need for proper nutrition.
2. Learning how to act in emergencies.
3. Learning facts about body growth and the functions of the body parts.
4. Learning the importance of rest and sleep.
5. Learning about communicable diseases.
6. Learning safety regulations.
7. Learning to care for the body, especially the eyes.
8. Learning the roles of health personnel and their function.
9. Learning to exercise and participate in recreational activities.

HEALTH ACTIVITIES

1. Draw foods from the 4 basic food groups, color them and cut them out. Attach strings and hang to a coat hanger to make a food mobile.

2. Keep a record of what you eat daily. Try to make sure you choose from the 4 food groups.

3. Give the children paper plates and have them draw a well balanced breakfast, lunch and dinner.

4. For dental health make a poster on good dental health. Ask your dentist for free brochures to help you. Some rules may include: brush the whole tooth; clean the gums; eat lots of fruits, vegetables, and meat; don't eat lots of sweets; drink lots of milk; visit the dentist.

5. Examine a first aid kit with the class. Demonstrate the use for each item. Relate first aid experiences to the child. Make up situation stories such as "Lara's Puppy."

   Lara's new puppy wanted to play ball. Lara was holding the ball up and then throwing it for her puppy to retrieve. She was getting ready to throw the ball when her puppy got anxious and jumped up and grabbed for the ball. He bit her hand. Lara cried, "I better go get my mommy to fix my hurt." Her mother washed it, pressed it with a clean gauze pad until the bleeding stopped, and covered it with a Band-Aid. She then put an ice compress on it. Her mother then called the doctor to see if she needed a tetanus booster. The doctor said she didn't because she had been given one the year before.

6. Allow the children to make simple foods in the classroom.

Health Habits Game

Functional Area: Health

Purpose: The strips of paper with "good" and "bad" health habits on them are placed into the appropriate slots thus allowing the child to learn basic health habits. (Examples are: Wash before you eat, Eat lots of candy.)

Functional Area:

Purpose:

Teeth and Their Jobs Game

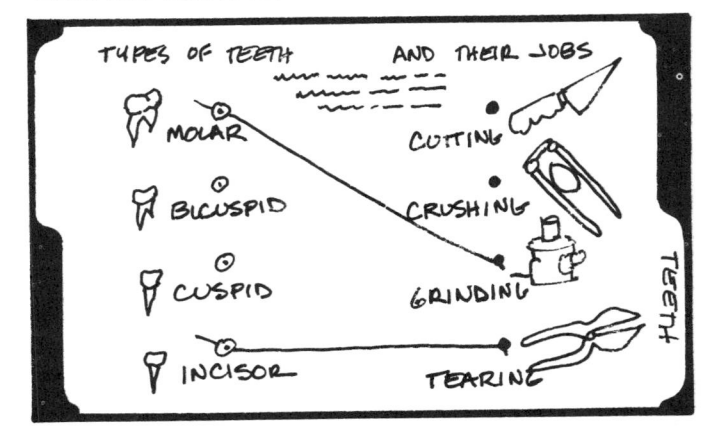

Functional Area: Health

Purpose: The child learns the various functions of the teeth by matching the string next to the tooth with its function.

Functional Area:

Purpose:

Food Group Poster

23

Functional Area: Cognitive (classification)

Purpose: The poster will help the child learn how to group the foods that he has learned about into the basic food groups.[20]

Functional Area:

Purpose:

Functional Area: Cognitive

Purpose: The children can visit a grocery store so they can learn to recognize various foods, then they can draw or cut out magazine pictures of the foods and add them to a class food market.[21]

Functional Area:

Purpose:

Cooking

Adults often hesitate to involve young children in the preparation of food. Teachers in particular, concerned with time limitations and the "mess" involved, often fail to understand the abilities of children in so far as cooking is concerned. The importance of cooking or food preparation as a learning experience for young children should not be underestimated. Many negative attitudes toward foods or toward helping others may be alleviated during cooking activities. Children who contribute to the preparation of foods often learn to enjoy new types of foods. Children who help set a table for lunch or snack may take more pride in their work.

Objectives for cooking in the kindergarten classroom include:
1. Promoting the child's sense of accomplishment.
2. Having fun thus enhancing his self concept.
3. Promoting cognitive, social, and cultural learning experiences.
4. Utilizing sensory perceptions.
5. Learning about the colors, shapes, and sizes of foods.
6. Learning about units of weight and measurement.
7. Learning proper use of kitchen tools and utensils.
8. Developing new vocabulary words.
9. Following directions.
10. Sharing in a group project.
11. Learning proper nutritional habits.
12. Observing physical and chemical changes.

In cooking, as with any activity, certain safety precautions must be observed. These include:
1. Identifying children with food allergies and making a list.
2. Using caution when serving foods which may cause choking such as nuts, celery, and popcorn.
3. Encouraging children to sit down while eating.
4. Limiting the number of children to avoid crowding and allowing each to participate.
5. Using child size furniture.
6. Using unbreakable equipment, if possible.
7. Having enough utensils for all the children. Using blunt knives for cutting.
8. Supervising cooking carefully or only allow an adult to do the actual cooking over the burners.
9. Planning the project carefully and discussing the plans with the children.
10. Fastening long hair and floppy sleeves.

11. Washing hands before beginning.
12. Allowing adequate time for exploring the foods: observing, tasting, discussing.
13. Providing recipe pictures when possible.
14. Beginning with simple recipes that require little cooking.

Folder recipes: Recipes with visual helpers can be written inside file folders.

Functional Area: Cognitive (following directions)

Purpose: The child learns to read a recipe and follow the directions.

Functional Area:

Purpose:

Recipes

The space provided below is for recording recipes you have found that work well with young children.

Recipes that Work....

The following healthy recipes are inexpensive to make and the ingredients can be found at most supermarkets. The average cost per recipe is $2.50. Each recipe will provide samples for a class of twenty-five children.

Cooking in the Kindergarten Recipe Potpourri

Apple Pudding

Ingredients:
2 c. cooked rice
2 c. apple sauce
2 t cinnamon
2 c. whipped cream (see recipe)

Mix together the first three ingredients. Add the whipped cream and serve. Makes 8 cups.

Cheese & Sprouts Sandwich

Ingredients:
1½ c. grated cheese
1 c. of alfalfa sprouts
mayonnaise

Mix together cheese and sprouts. Gradually add mayonnaise to give it the right consistency. Spread on bread or crackers and serve.

Alfalfa Sprouts

Ingredients:
1 quart size jar
1 ring top canning lid with wire mesh cut to fit into the ring top (or cheesecloth)
2 T alfalfa sprouts
water

Soak the sprouts in water over night. Drain thouroughly through wire mesh or cheesecloth and sit in a sunny window. Rinse and drain several times a day for 3 days.

Fruit Smoothie

Ingredients:
3 c of orange or other fruit juice (or 6 oz can of frozen orange juice plus 3 cans of water)
½ c. powdered milk
2 bananas (peeled)
1 apple (peeled)

Put all of the ingredients in a blender and blend well. Makes 1 quart.

Fruit Jello Cubes

Ingredients:
1 12 oz. can of frozen fruit juice concentrate, thawed (grape, orange, apple or lemon)
1½ c. water (1 12 oz. can)
3 envelopes of Knox unflavored gelatin

Soften gelatin in fruit juice. Boil water, add fruit/gelatin mixture and stir until gelatin dissolves. Cool. Pour into lightly greased 9×13 in. pan and refrigerate. Cut into squares when firm. Store in refrigerator, covered. Will maintain shape unrefrigerated for up to 4 hours.

Whipped Cream

Ingredients:
2 c. heavy whipping cream (chilled)
4 Tb. sugar
2 tsp. vanilla

Pour cream into a bowl and beat until it begins to thicken. Sprinkle sugar over cream and beat again. Add vanilla and beat until stiff. (Be careful not to over beat as it will lose its thickness)

Daily Food Guide

	Child	Preteen & Teen	Adult
Milk or Milk Products	3	4	1
Meat, Fish, Poultry, Eggs (in servings)	1	3	1 large
Green & Yellow Vegetables (in servings)	1	2	2
Citrus Fruits & Tomatoes (in servings)	1	1	1
Potatoes, Other Fruits & Vegetables (in servings)	1	1	1
Bread, Flour & Cereal (in servings)	3	4	3

1. The need for the nutrients in 1 or 2 cups of milk daily can be satisfied by cheeses or ice cream. (1 cup of milk is approximately equivalent to 1½ cups of cottage cheese or 2-3 large scoops of ice cream.)
2. The recommended daily servings of meat, fish, and poultry may be alternated with eggs or cheese, dried peas, beans.
3. It is important to drink enough fluid. The equivalent of 3-5 cups daily is recommended.

Table Setting

Functional Area: Health

Purpose: The child learns to make balanced meals with the cut outs of the various foods. (He can also learn how to set a place setting.)

Functional Area:

Purpose:

SAFTEY

Bicycle Safety
Parents' responsibility: When planning to purchase a bicycle, parents should be aware of the responsibility which they must assume. They should select the proper model and make the children aware of traffic laws. They should ask themselves: Is the child old enough to understand traffic laws and remember safety rules? Can he ride without getting hurt? Is the neighborhood safe? Are we willing to help them learn to ride safely?

Some rules of the road follow:
1. Obey all applicable traffic regulations, signs, and signals.
2. Observe local ordinances pertaining to bicycles.
3. Keep right; drive with traffic – not against it; drive single file.
4. Watch out for drain grates, soft shoulders, and other road hazards.
5. Watch for cars pulling into the traffic and for dogs.
6. Don't carry passengers or packages.
7. Be sure your bike is in proper condition.
8. Walk your bike through intersections.
9. Use red reflectors and lights if driving at night.
10. Don't hitch a ride on another moving vehicle.

School Safety
Rules should be established as needed in school. Let the children help make the rules. Try to state the rules in a positive manner.
1. Use gym equipment properly.
2. Walk in the halls and classroom.
3. Talk quietly.

Rules for camping and hiking, boating and other experiences should also be carefully thought out as a group.[22]

Name: _____

the tooth tree
Color me
HEALTHY!

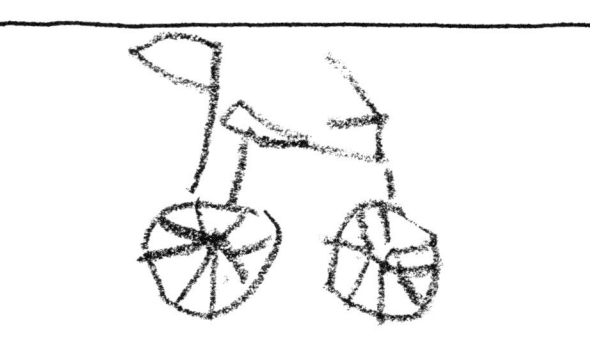

> **Ride with SAFETY**
> 1. Steer with both hands
> 2. Don't ride double
> 3. Watch for pedes-trians
> 4. Keep to the right
> 5. Don't be a show off
> 6. Obey traffic rules and signs.

> **Don't Play with Matches**

23

Functional Area: Safety

Purpose: The child will learn bicycle safety rules as he helps the teacher develop the bicycle safety rule chart.

Functional Area:

Purpose:

Functional Area: Safety

Purpose: The child learns that matches are unsafe by making his own picture on fire safety.

Functional Area:

Purpose:

The following activity patterns and ditto sheets may be copied and used to develop the functional area of your choice.

Name _____

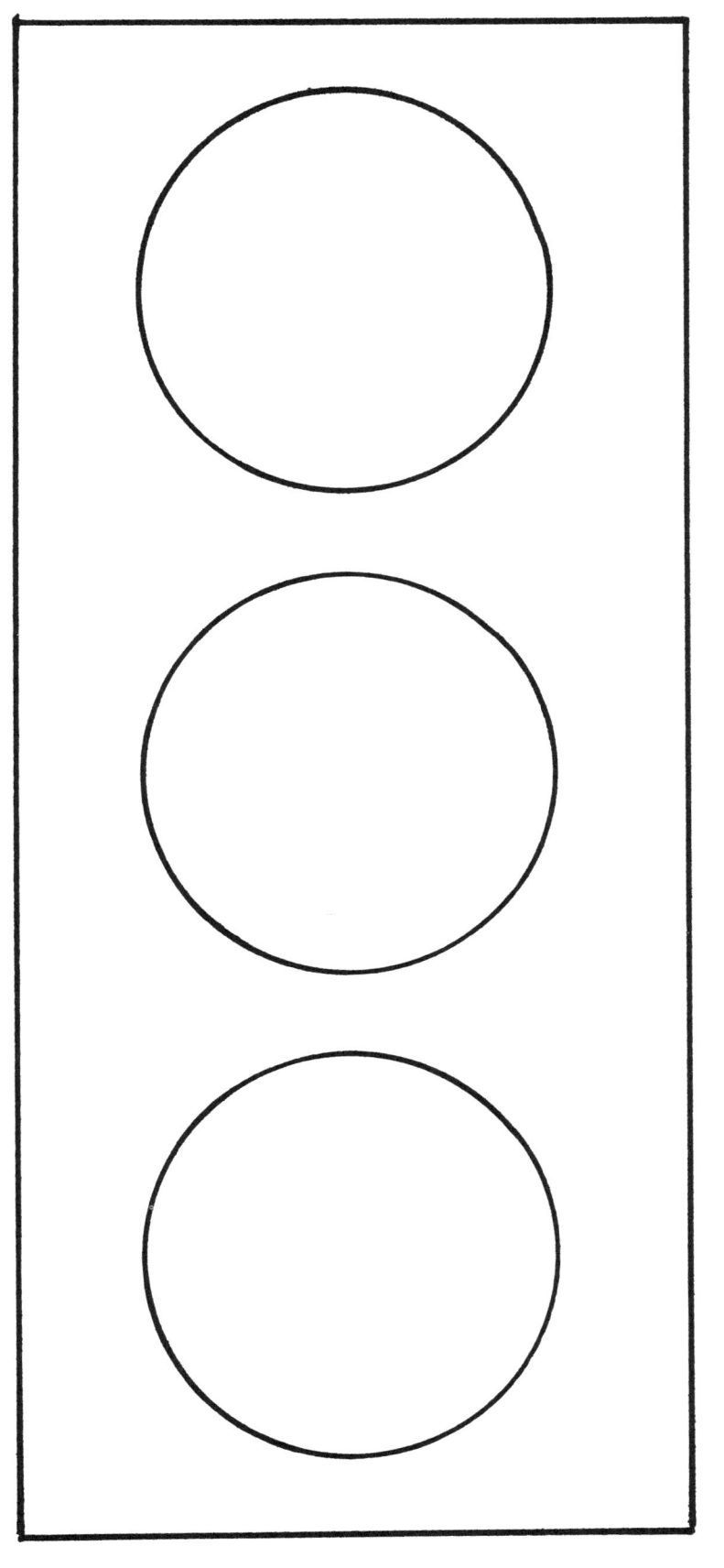

Traffic Light Poem

Red on top,
Green below,
Red means stop,
Green means go,
Yellow means wait
Even if you're late.

Paste onto tagboard. Cut out and color for room display.

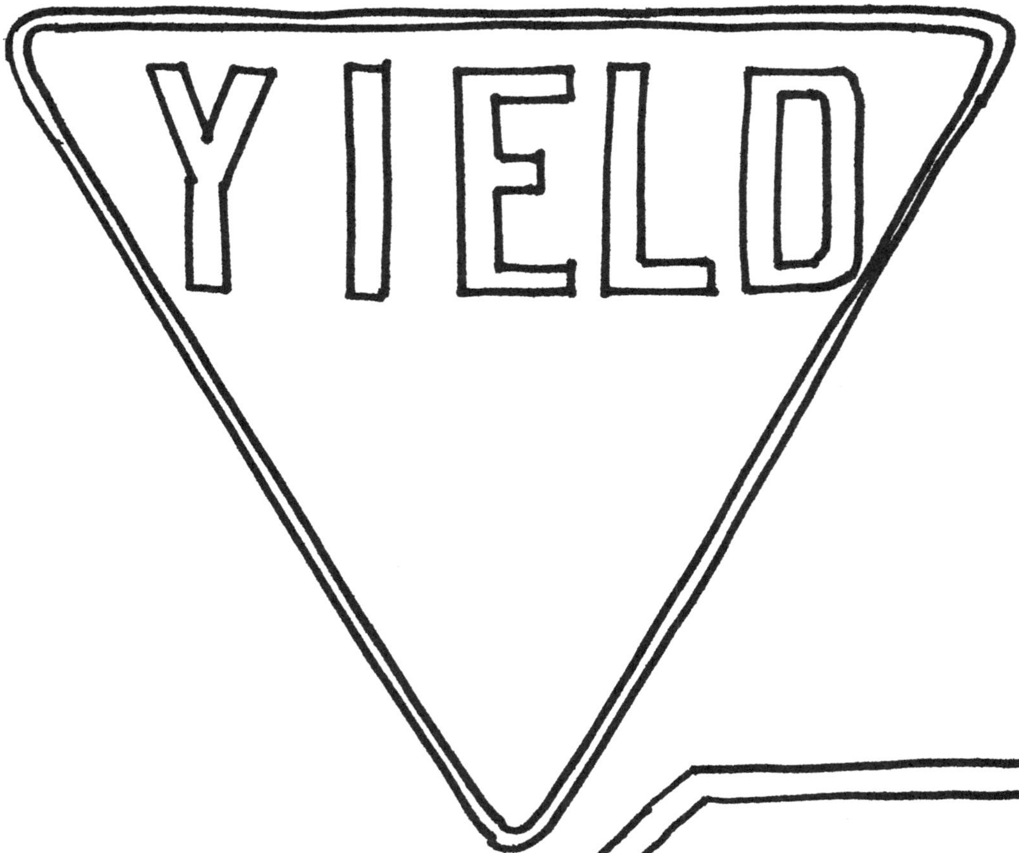
YIELD

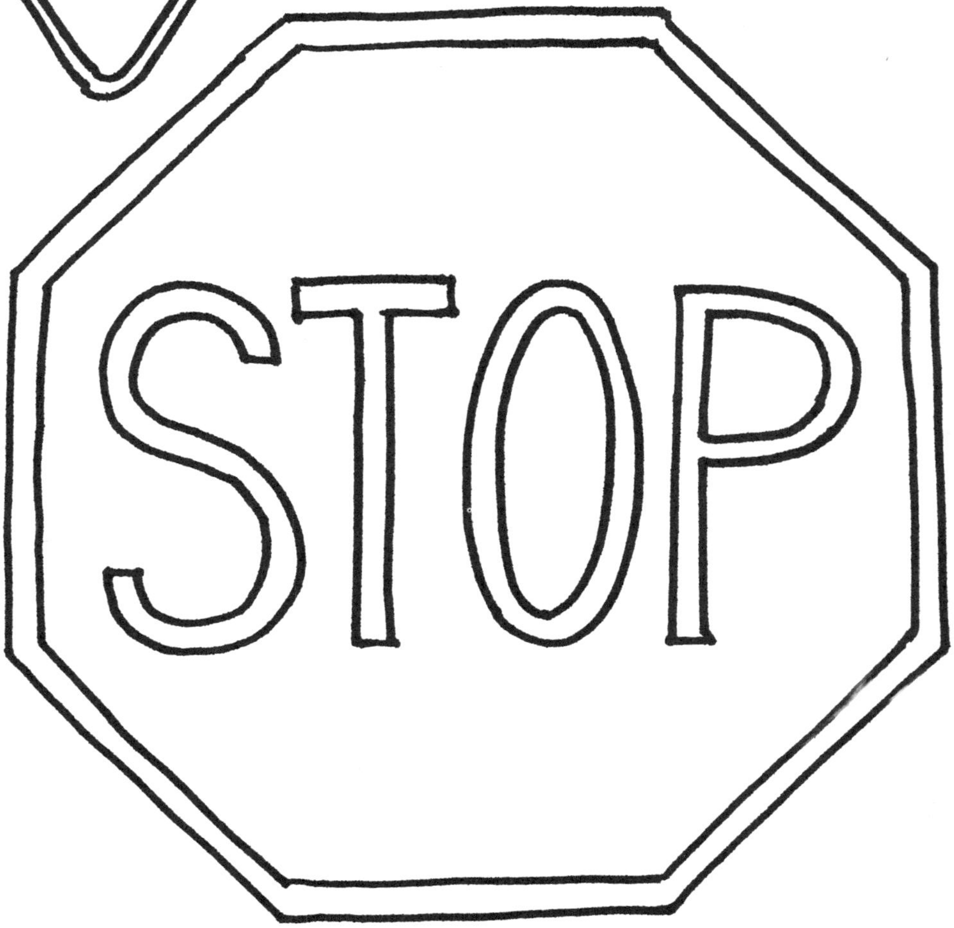
STOP

AAA Bicycle Inspection Check List

Name .... Date ....

Address ....

Phone .... School ....

		FRONT		REAR	
		Yes	No	Yes	No
WHEELS	Spokes missing or broken	( )	( )	( )	( )
	Loose spokes	( )	( )	( )	( )
	Hub bearing binds, restricting free movement	( )	( )	( )	( )
	Warped or bent rim	( )	( )	( )	( )
	Bearing play over 3/8" at rim	( )	( )	( )	( )
TIRES	Bulges or defects	( )	( )	( )	( )
	Improper inflation	( )	( )	( )	( )
	Worn tread	( )	( )	( )	( )
FENDERS	Loose	( )	( )	( )	( )
	Broken supports	( )	( )	( )	( )

		Yes	No			Yes	No
FRAME	Broken	( )	( )	**CHAIN GUARD** Missing		( )	( )
	Bent	( )	( )	**SPROCKET** Loose bearing		( )	( )
FORK	Bearing too loose	( )	( )	Bearing binds		( )	( )
	Bent	( )	( )	**HANDLEBARS** Loose		( )	( )
SEAT	Loose	( )	( )	Grip missing		( )	( )
	Improper height or angle	( )	( )	Grip loose		( )	( )
BRAKE	Insufficient stopping action	( )	( )	**WARNING DEVICE** Missing		( )	( )
	Uneven stopping action	( )	( )	Broken		( )	( )
PEDALS	Too loose	( )	( )	**HEADLIGHT** Missing		( )	( )
	Parts missing	( )	( )	Too dim		( )	( )
	Bearings bind	( )	( )	Broken lens		( )	( )
CHAIN	Too tight	( )	( )	**REAR REFLECTOR** Missing		( )	( )
	Too loose	( )	( )	Broken—		( )	( )
	Weak links	( )	( )	Speedometer Missing		( )	( )
	Rusty and not lubricated	( )	( )	Inaccurate		( )	( )

Braking Efficiency _____ feet

REMARKS: _____

_____

_____

_____

From THE HANDBOOK OF LEARNING ACTIVITIES FOR YOUNG CHILDREN, Copyright 1980 by Humanics Limited, Jane A. Caballero.

From THE HANDBOOK OF LEARNING ACTIVITIES FOR YOUNG CHILDREN, Copyright 1980 by Humanics Limited, Jane A. Caballero.

Bicycle Reference Diagram

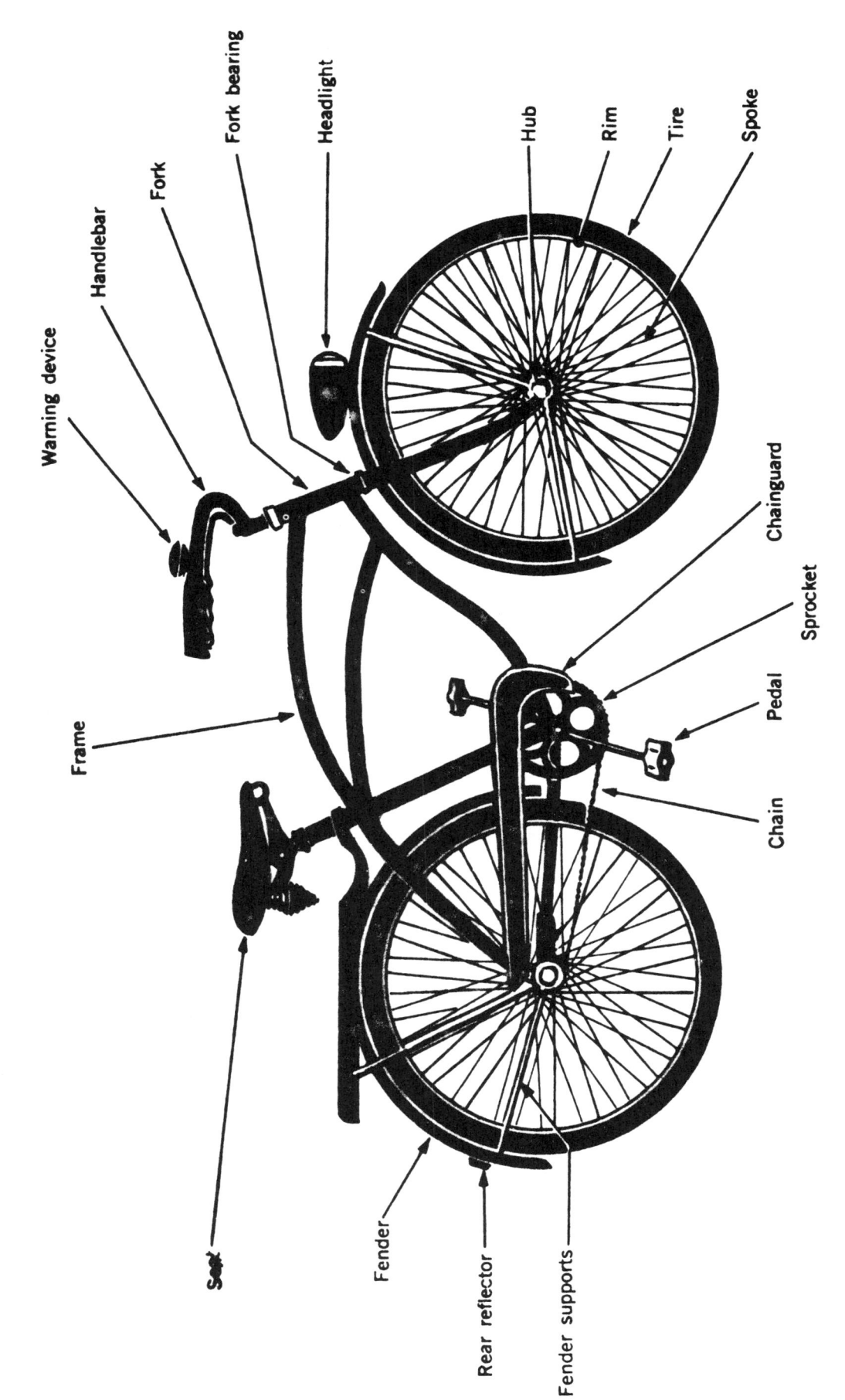

[24] Reprinted with permission from:
Pedestrian and School Safety Division, Traffic Engineering & Safety Department, American Automobile Association, Washington, D.C.

35

resources

FOOD AND HEALTH

1. *The Travelers Book of Children's Exercises.* The Travelers Insurance Co., Hartford, Conn.
2. *Dental Health Facts for Teachers.* American Dental Association, 211 E. Chicago Avenue, Chicago, Illinois 60611.
3. U. S. Department of Health, Education and Welfare, Public Health Service, National Institute of Health. Bethesda, Maryland 20014.
4. Immunization Program and Division of Health Education. South Carolina State Board of Health, J. Marion Sims Building, Columbia, South Carolina 29201.
5. *Frankie Visits the Dentist.* 1947, Georgia Department of Public Health, Atlanta, Georgia.
6. *Food Makes Us Grow.* (Reprint from "Grade Teacher.") ITT Continental Baking Co., Inc., Home Economics Department, Sally R. Watters, Director, P. O. Box 731, Rye, New York 10580.
7. *Mr. Peanut's Guide to Nutrition.* Standard Brands Educational Service, P. O. Box 2695, Grand Central Station, New York, New York 10017.
8. Green Giant Co., Consumer Services, Hazeltine Gates, Chaska, Minn. 55318.
9. Campbell Soup Co., Campbell Place, Camden, N. J. 08101.
10. Kellogg Co., Battle Creek, Mich. 49016.
11. Sunkist Growers, Inc., Dept 76–FM, Box 7888, Van Nuys, Calif. 91409.
12. *Family Nutrition Kit*, Center for Science in Public Interest, P. O. Box 3099 A, Washington, D. C. 20010 ($3.00).
13. Dept. of Health, Education and Welfare, Public Health Service, Center for Disease Control, Atlanta, Ga. 30333.
14. Dade-Monroe Lung Asso., 830 Buchell Plaza, Miami, Fla. 33131.
15. American Dental Association, 211 East Chicago Ave., Chicago, Illinois 60611.

SAFETY

1. Posters: *Education for Survival.* An Elementary School Kit on Safety and Health. Safety and Health Services. Employee's Insurance of Wausau, Wisconsin 54401.
2. Brochures and Sparkey Fire Books: National Fire Protection Association, Inc., 60 Batterymarch Street, Boston, Mass. 02110.
3. *Junior Fire Marshal.* Pacific Insurance Co., Limited, 16 N. Ala Moana Blvd., Honolulu, Hawaii 96815.
4. Fire Prevention Posters. National Board of Fire Underwriters.
5. Visit your local fire department.
6. Department of Transportation, U. S. Coast Guard Auxiliary (water safety coloring book).
7. American Automobile Association (contact your local AAA).
8. Johnson & Johnson, 501 George St., New Brunswick, N. J. 08903.
9. U. S. Consumer Products Safety Commission, Washington, D. C. 20207.
10. Aetna Life & Casualty, 151 Farmington Ave., Hartford, Conn. 06156.
11. John Hancock Mutual Life Ins. Co., 200 Berkeley St., Boston, Mass. 02117.
12. Schwinn Bicycle Co., 1856 North Kostner Ave., Chicago, Illinois 60639.
13. Florida Aids for Classroom Teachers (FACT), Florida Power & Light Co., 4200 W. Flagler St., Miami, Florida.

chapter 4
play

PLAY TODAY?
by Leila P. Fagg

You say you love your children, and are concerned they learn today?
So am I — that's why I'm providing a variety of kinds of play.

You're asking me the value of blocks and other such play?
Your children are solving problems; they will use that skill everyday.

You're asking what's the value of having your children play?
Your daughter's creating a tower; she may be a builder someday.

You're saying you don't want your son to play in that "sissy" way?
He's learning to cuddle a doll; he may be a father someday.

You're questioning the interest centers; they just look like useless play?
Your children are making choices; they'll be on their own someday.

You're worried your children aren't learning and later they'll have to pay?
They're learning a pattern for learning; for they'll be learners always.[25]

VALUES OF PLAY

Playtime aids growth
Play is a voluntary activity
Play offers a child freedom of action
Play provides an imaginary world a child can master
Play has elements of adventure in it
Play provides a base for language building
Play has unique power for building interpersonal relations
Play offers opportunities for mastery of the physical self
Play furthers interest and concentration
Play is a way of learning adult roles
Play is a dynamic way of learning
Play refines a child's judgement

Academic can be structured into play
Play is vitalizing.

If play has such positive power, why is it not valued in todays life scheme?

GOOD PLAYTHINGS

Good Playthings should have the following characteristics:

- free of detail as possible
- versatile in use (has many uses)
- involve the child in the play
- large, easily manipulated
- material warm and pleasant to touch
- durable
- work as intended
- construction easily comprehended
- sufficient quantity and roominess
- encourage cooperative play
- price based on durability and design[26]

TYPES OF PLAY

Types of play can be classified into the three following categories:

- Free or Spontaneous Play
  Objectives
  1. To provide his body with exercise it needs
  2. To encourage him to act our emotional drives
  3. To dramatize the adult roles he will later assume
  4. To learn how to participate in a group through games

- Dramatic or Initiative Play
  Objectives
  1. Investigating objects and materials
  2. Child uses imagination
  3. Child experiences role playing

- Constructive Play
  Objectives
  1. Eye-hand coordination is enhanced
  2. Gains control of large muscle and increased co-ordination
  3. Learning planning and cooperation
  4. To experience concept of space, classification and seriation

Some suggested outdoor and indoor play activities follow:

Outdoor Play Includes:

Swinging on tires, bars, swings
Climbing ropes, jungle gyms, parallel bars
Walking planks and other balance apparatus
Riding tricycles
Running, jumping, hopping, and skipping
Throwing, catching, and kicking a ball
Pulling and pushing wagons, boxes and other toys
Playing in sandbox and water
Imitating cowboys and Indians, airplanes, animals, movie and T.V. idols, and adult activities
Sliding down ropes
Jumping ropes

Indoor Play Includes:

Building with blocks
Rolling and tumbling on mats
Initiating adult roles in playing house, doctor, nurse, spaceman, grocery store clerk and other people
Looking at books and magazines
Playing with beanbags, ring toss, and bowling games
Playing with folder games and board games
Listening to records
Coloring or painting
Playing with trains, cars, buses, and other movable toys
Dramatic play with puppets, dolls and dress-up clothes
Following the leader imitating animals
Hopping, skipping, jumping, and galloping
Singing songs
Water activities
Art projects

Water Play and Sand Play

Pictured: plastic equipment which can be used for sifting, measuring, and making designs.

Sand and water are basic materials like paint or blocks that are always available. Values of water and sand play include:
— observe, analyze, hypothesize, and test without fear of failure thus achieving competence
— meet individual needs for relazation and satisfaction
— encounter basic scientific principles and knowledge about basic elements
— engage in cooperative ventures
— form attitudes of responsibility
— grow in understanding of volume and measurement and language associations
— further the development of small muscle control and hand-eye coordination

Functional Area: Cognitive (science)

Purpose: The child can learn basic scientific principles and knowledge about the basic element, water, as he plays with the water table.

Functional Area:

Purpose:

Role Play

House Keeping Center
 I. House Keeping
    a. Learning to work with kitchen utensils
    b. Learning to care for household chores
    c. Role Playing
 II. Playing in Doll Corner
    a. Learning roles of the mother and father and children.
    b. Using imagination
    c. Learning to take turns to share a piece of equipment.

Functional Area: Cognitive (Social studies-role playing)

Purpose: The child learns the role of the mother, father and children as he interacts in the housekeeping center.

Functional Area:

Purpose:

Block Building

Types of building blocks can include Tinker Toys, Lego, colored blocks of various shapes and sizes, and Lincoln Logs.

Optimal value in block building is dependent upon careful planning.

Some values of block building include:
Children:
- become aware of size, shape, weight, blaance and positional relationships
- practice measurement and beginning concepts of volume
- encounter scientific concepts such as leverage and balance
- strengthen eye-hand coordination and perception
- develop feelings of accomplishment

Woodworking

Woodworking is another valuable experience for the young child. Boys and girls enjoy making something with their own hands. Real tools are necessary. Soft wood should be provided. Careful instruction and supervision are necessary.

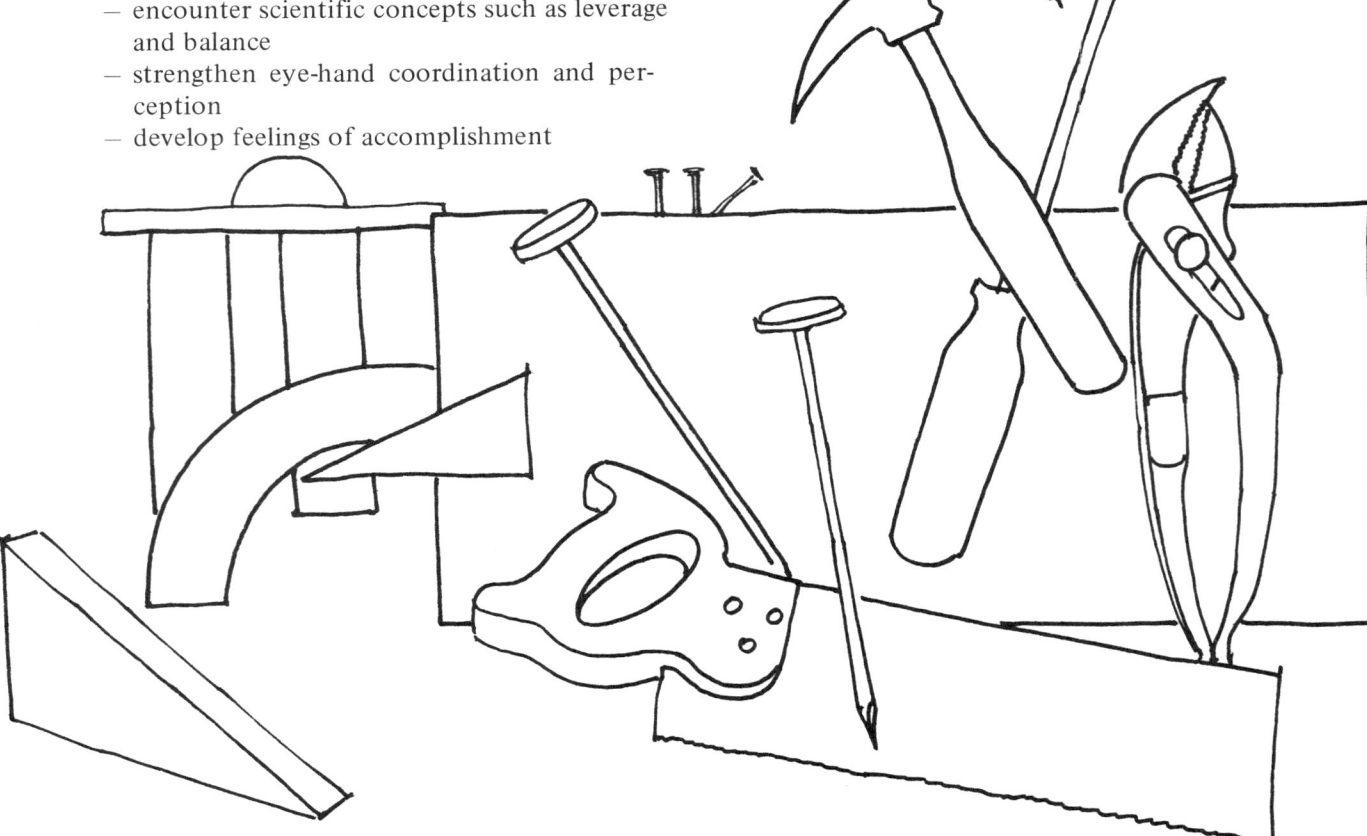

Functional Area: Creative (Block building)

Purpose: The child learns to create architectural forms as he plays with blocks.

Functional Area:

Purpose:

Functional Area: Physical (gross-fine motor development)

Purpose: The child learns to have more accurate control of his muscles as he plays with the various tools in the woodworking center.

Functional Area:

Purpose:

PUZZLES

Puzzles are probably the most popular of all table games. They develop perceptual and problem solving abilities in the children, and at the same time serve as a stimulus to learning. They have the effect of not permitting a child to reinforce a skill incorrectly by repetition. It also rewards children positively for doing the skill correctly. Through puzzles the children explore and experiment. Cognitive growth and conceptual growth can be enhanced and a variety of skills may be taught and reinforced in different subject areas: science, math, health, nutrition, etc. Puzzles prepare children in a highly motivational and independent format for the reading comprehension experience. Children are helped to develop social relationships, to use the materials with others, to take turns and to ask for what they want or need. Language growth is stimulated in many ways.

For the pre-school children puzzles are good for developing eye-hand coordination, use of small muscles, recognition of shapes and colors, use of visual memory, form, and generalizations, so important in the early phases of mental development.

Puzzles should be large and of few pieces. Wooden or hard plastic puzzles are better than rubber ones. They seem to last longer and are easier to handle. The child will play with puzzles over and over. He'll return again and again to a puzzle that he has mastered which you consider too simple for him. We tend to forget that children enjoy success as much as we do and going back to do something we know we can do is very reassuring. Practicing on known things lays the foundation for learning new things. So let your child practice on simple puzzles even after he has mastered complex ones.

Some recommendations when using puzzles follow:
— Present puzzles as enjoyable games
— Demonstrate how the pieces are placed
— Finish one puzzle before starting another
— Praise the child's successes
— Parents may help children complete puzzles
— Make your own puzzles from inexpensive materials:
      cereal boxes
      magazine pictures
      photographs
      wall posters

Functional Area: Physical

Purpose: The child learns to develop small muscles as he puts the pieces of the puzzle together.

Functional Area:

Purpose:

ACTIVITIES

Functional Area: Physical

Purpose: Small muscle control will be developed as the child traces inside a template shape.

Functional Area:

Purpose:

Functional Area:

Purpose:

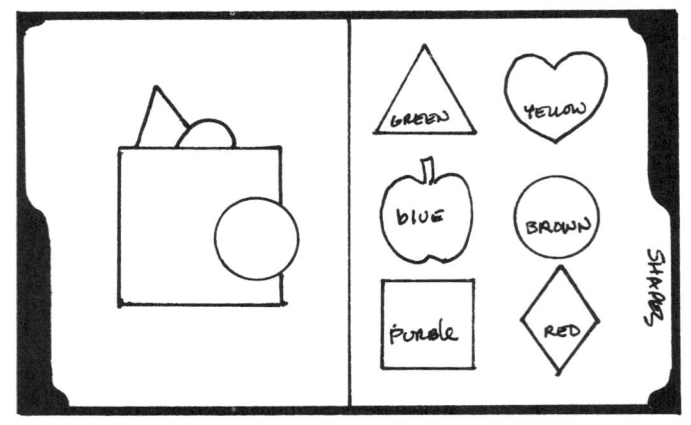

Functional Area: Cognitive

Purpose: The shapes of various colors are cut and mounted on an empty file folder and the child matches the corresponding shape to the one on the folder. Visual discrimination is enhanced.

Functional Area:

Purpose:

Functional Area: Physical

Purpose: The child learns to develop his small muscles as he practices lacing, snaping and buttoning the animal.

Functional Area: Cognitive (math-counting)

Purpose: The child learns to count the jacks as he plays the game of jacks.

Functional Area:

Purpose:

42

chapter 5
movement

Movement Education is defined as learning to move and moving to learn. It may be thought of as synonymous with Physical Education. In learning to move, the child acquires movement competency, he learns what his body can do, and he learns about himself and his environment.

The objectives of the movement education program should help each child to:

Develop and maintain a suitable level of physical fitness.
Become competent in managing body skills.
Acquire acceptable social standards and ethical conduct such as good sportsmanship and good conduct.
Learn safety skills.
Learn to derive enjoyment from recreational activities.
Develop creativity through participating in various activities.
Acquire a positive self-concept through participating successfully in physical educational activities.

To attain these purposes, the program must be carefully planned and take into consideration the child's individual needs, interests, and levels. There must be movement — this is the basis for physical education. Children learn by doing and skills are only learned through repetition. Don't make the children listen too long or let a few children dominate the activity.

Three categories of skills should be taught in the instructional program.

Locomotor: Skills used to move the body from one place to another. Examples are walking, running, galloping, jumping, hopping, skipping, and climbing.
Nonlocomotor: Skills the child does in place without moving from place to place. Examples are pushing, pulling, twisting, bending, shaking, and bouncing.
Manipulative: Skills employed when the child handles some kind of play object. Eye-hand and eye-foot coordination are enhanced as the child develops these skills. Manipulative activities are neces-

sary if the child is to play games effectively. Activities should incorporate beanbags, balls, wands, hoops, jacks, and a parachute, if possible.

In the kindergarten program attention should be focused on the learning process and the child. Play activities are highly important as children learn best when they enjoy what they are doing. Some games which may help develop motor skills are:

Farmer in the Dell	Simon Says
Duck Duck Goose	Hokey Pokey
Hot Potato	Red Light, Green Light
Musical Chairs	Mulberry Bush
Follow the Leader	

RELAYS

Relays help children learn to cooperate with others in the interest of winning, conforming to rules and directions, and using skills in situations of stress and competition. Little equipment is needed. Relays are a little beyond the capacity for most kindergarten level children, but some experiences of handling beanbags and yarn balls in relay races are valuable. Following is a sample activity. Place children in a line (side by side) and have them pass the articles down to the end, or arrange them in a circle and have them pass the beanbag around the circle. The objective of the activity is to pass well and not drop the article. The child learns to participate in the activity and to cooperate with others.

STUNTS AND TUMBLING

Stunts and tumbling are important in children's overall physical education experiences. Since the work is individual and seldom mastered quickly, the child faces his own challenge and has the opportunity to develop self confidence and courage. Social interplay is provided by partner and group stunts. Right and left, near and far, wide and narrow, up and down, forward and backward are additional concepts that may be acquired. The kindergarten program should include a progressive introduction to the basic tumbling stunts such as the forward and backward rolls and basic stands. The program should also include animal movements, balance stunts, and partner and group stunts.

RHYTHMIC ACTIVITIES

In rhythmic activities, children gain a better appreciation and understanding of the use of their bodies. The important goal for each child is to be able to keep time and move in keeping time with the rhythm. Creativity is important. The goal is to communicate through movement guided by rhythm. No matter what the approach, the child should have the opportunity to invent, fabricate, pretend, and act out his ideas. There is no right or wrong way in creativity. The teacher should guide movement patterns by suggestions, questions, and encouragement. Movement songs should be simple and tell the child what to do and how to move. Examples are: Hokey Pokey, Loobey Loo, Mulberry Bush, Farmer in the Dell, and London Bridge.

As the teacher begins using games, the directions should be given one at a time followed by the activity. For example, the first direction may be, "Take hands and make a circle." The teacher then moves among the group helping each child as needed. This is done before the next direction is given. In games which involve choices, some children may not be chosen. In order that all children may have a chance to play, ask those who haven't had a turn to raise their hands. Ask the child who is making the choice to select a child whose hand is raised.

ACTIVITIES

Beanbags and yarn balls can provide the first throwing and catching activities for younger children. They help build confidence because they tend to eliminate the fear younger children have of catching a hard object. After enough practice with beanbags and wadded up newspaper balls, use balls. Be sure to start children at a low level of challenge so all can achieve success. Most activities begin with the individual approach and move to partner activities.

Functional Area: Physical

Purpose: As the child throws the soft objects, he enhances his eye-hand coordination.

Functional Area:

Purpose:

Parachutes

Parachutes provide a new and interesting medium of physical fitness. A wide variety of movement possibilities are employed by parachute play. Locomotor skills are evident while manipulating the parachute. Rhythmic beats of the tom-tom can guide locomotor movement. Parachute play provides excellent group learning.

Functional Area: Social

Purpose: The children learn to cooperate as they manipulate the parachute.

Functional Area:

Purpose:

Body Parts Doll

Functional Area: Physical

Purpose: The child becomes aware of body positions as he moves the braded body parts of the doll. The child can then imitate the positions of the doll with his own body.

Functional Area:

Purpose:

Large Apparatus

Apparatus activities play a large role in the child's overall physical development. A wide variety of apparatus is available. Exploratory and creative activity as well as wide experience in body management should characterize the instructional approach. Climbing and hanging types of apparatus include: climbing ropes, horizontal ladders, climbing frames, and exercise bars. Floor apparatus include: balance beam, benches, tires, jumping boxes, magic ropes, individual mats, balance boards and bouncing boards.

Functional Area: Physical

Purpose: As the child climbs on the jungle gym, he develops his gross motor skills.

Functional Area:

Purpose:

Newspaper Ball and Ring

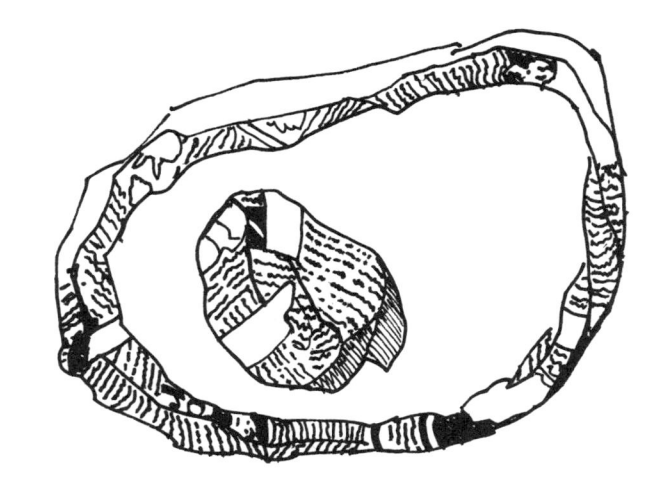

Functional Area: Social

Purpose: The child will learn to throw the newspaper ball through the ring without fear of hurting his partner. They can exchange the ring and ball thus learning the social skill of cooperation.

Functional Area:

Purpose:

chapter 6
science

Preschool children may learn a great deal about science since they are observant, interested, and easily motivated. While scientific concepts may have to be simplified and words clearly defined, most young children will relate well to the study of science. Adaptation to the level of the children with whom one is working is essential.

The scientific process begins with observations, followed by the forming of hypotheses, experiments to test these hypotheses, and the measurement of the results.

Some objectives for young children studying science include:
1. Learning about the physical world;
2. Becoming aware of the properties of objects and basic scientific laws or principles;
3. Developing the skills necessary in investigating and understanding simple yet basic scientific ideas.

The strategy for teaching science involves the following steps:

1. Permitting children to explore and experiment on their own;
2. Providing materials which encourage experimentation;
3. Asking questions which stimulate thinking and trying to understand what the child is thinking.

Children will learn best when information is given in response to their own questions. Listen to their questions, try to understand their reasoning, and then try to direct their questions so that they will be able to discover answers by themselves.

Science should be an interdisciplinary subject. At lunchtime, have the children identify the types of food they are eating, whether or not it includes all the food groups and what each item is made from. (This observation may also be good while studying the unit on nutrition.) During recess, have the children observe the types of plants, insects, rocks, and leaves that are outside. They can also observe the weather conditions.

Some areas of science that are good to explore in

the elementary school are:
1. The five senses (taste, touch, hearing, sight, smell)
2. Weather
3. Plants, rocks
4. Animals
5. Basic laws (gravity, motion, etc.)
6. Causal relationships — something happens because something else did first
7. Aerospace (earth, universe)
8. Cooking — nutrition
9. States of matter/classifying matter
10. Ecology
11. Magnets, electricity, sound, light

The following information and activities may promote the development of a meaningful science curriculum.

ACTIVITIES

Matching Leaves
Two matching leaves are located by the child. He then irons the leaves between 2 pieces of wax paper. One leaf may be glued to a piece of cardboard. The child matches the 2 leaves that look alike. Visual discrimination and awareness of the differences of leaves will result.

Functional Area: Cognitive (science)

Purpose: The child will learn to look for various leaves in nature.

Functional Area:

Purpose:

Classifying Living and Non-living

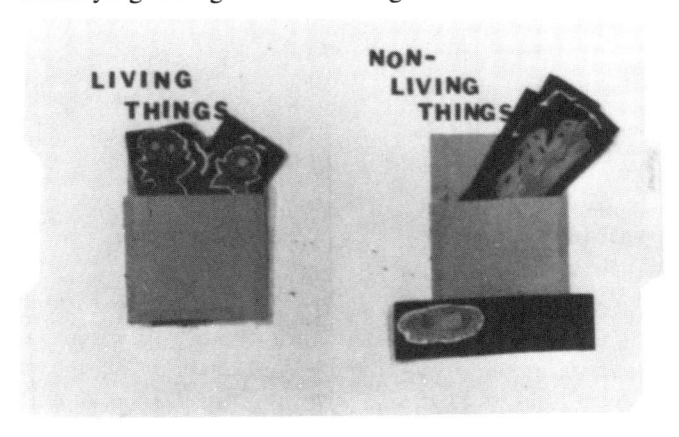

Functional Area: Cognitive (concept-picture reading)

Purpose: The pictures of living things — plants, animals, and people and non-living things — rock, pie, chair — are placed on strips of paper for the child to look at and learn to classify.

Functional Area:

Purpose:

Magnets — Classifying

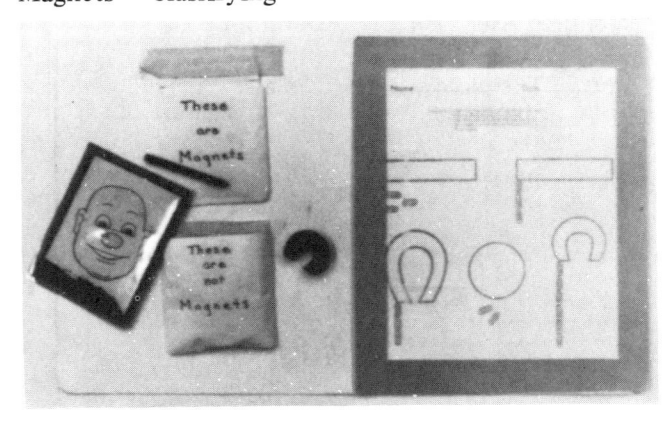

Functional Area: Cognitive (classification)

Purpose: The child will be given magnets of various shapes and sizes and non-magnets (clay, wood, nail, paper clip, etc.). They may be placed in envelopes, as noted. The child experiments with the objects, learning to classify. (Games using the magnets can be played by using self directed dittos (see photograph).

Functional Area:

Purpose:

Weather Symbols

Cut out the pictures on page 54 and adhere to a file folder. Print the following words on strips of construction paper or tagboard: cloudy, windy, warm, snowy, cold, partly cloudy, rainy, sunny. Have the children use these words to match the appropriate weather symbol.

Functional Area: Language Development

Purpose: The child will learn to associate the words with their meanings.

Functional Area:

Purpose:

Light

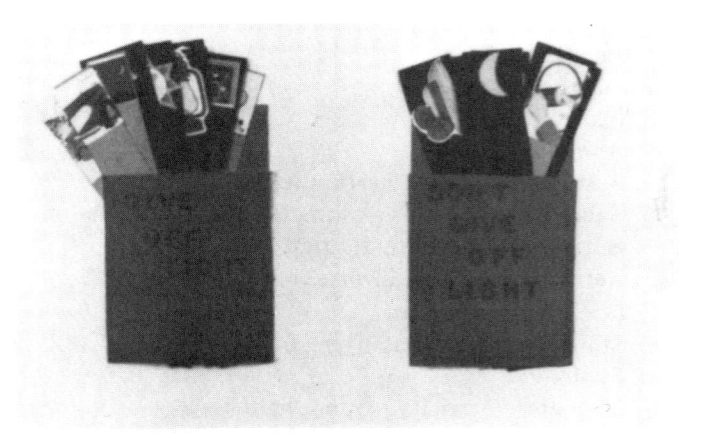

Functional Area: Cognitive

Purpose: The pictures of things that give off light — a flashlight, sun, car light — and pictures that don't give off light — car, siren, hat, guitar — are glued on strips of paper for the child to place into the correct envelope. He learns to classify the various objects according to these two criteria.

Functional Area:

Purpose:

SAMPLE EXPERIMENTS

Gravity Experiment

Problem: What is gravity?

Material: Any object which can be dropped.

Procedure: Give each child an object and have him drop it. Where does it go?

Observation: It falls to the floor.
Have each child repeat this several times. Each time the child drops the object, ask a question such as "Will it fall to the ground this time?", "Will it fall up?", "What will happen the next time you drop it?", etc.

Observation: The object falls to the floor every time. You can predict that the next time you drop the object, it will fall to the floor.

Conclusion: There is a force which pulls everything downward to the center of the earth. This force is called gravity.

Functional Area: Cognitive (science)

Purpose: The child will learn the basic scientific principle of gravity as he drops the objects.

Functional Area:

Purpose:

Thunder Experiment

Problem: What makes thunder?

Material: Empty paper bag

Procedure:
1. Blow up paper bag and hold neck tightly so air cannot escape.
2. Hit the bag with the other hand.

Conclusion: The bag will break with a loud bang.

Observation: When air rushes together it makes a loud noise. Lightning forces air apart, and when the air rushes together again it makes a loud noise. Whenever there is lightning forcing the air apart, you will then hear thunder as the air rushes back together.

Plant Experiment

Materials:
1. Flowers (white carnation) or celery
2. Food coloring
3. Tall glass
4. Knife
5. Water

Procedure:
1. Color water with food coloring.
2. Let celery stand in solution for one hour.
3. Remove and make cross cuts to show colored streaks.
4. Leave celery in colored liquid for several hours and note results.

Results:
The colored fluid travels upward from the roots leaving a telltale path.

Supplemental Information:
Plants have well defined passage ways through which liquids travel. By using colored solution we can trace these channels through the plant.

Float/Sink Experiment

Problem: Which objects float; which objects sink

Materials: Pan (with several inches of water)
Capped empty bottle	Scissors
Wooden block	Pin
Plastic block	Nail
Styrofoam	Screw
Metal spoon	Sponge
Plastic spoon	Coin
Plastic top	Toothpick

Procedure: Ask students to name an object they think will float/sink.
Have student place object on the water's surface.
Encourage verbalization.

Variations:
1. Have student sort objects into sink or float piles according to results of the water surface test.
2. Continue one step further, make a chart and divide into two sections— Sink/Float. Place a drawing and the objects name in the Float or Sink section.

Conclusion: Various objects will float and sink.

Observation: Depending upon the weight of objects, some objects will float and some objects will sink.

Functional Area: Cognitive (classification)

Purpose: The child will learn how to classify objects by the two concepts: objects that float and objects that sink. As he drops the objects into the water, he discovers if he is correct.

Functional Area:

Purpose:

49

OUR SENSES

We have five senses: hearing, feeling, smelling, tasting, and seeing which help us learn about the world. The more we use our senses, the more "aware" we become.

I. SIGHT

The eye is our most important organ for finding out about the world around us. We use our eyes to know things around us, to enjoy and take an interest in the beauty of nature and to like literature and painting. Our eyes help us carry on almost all the activities of daily life. We see the different properties of objects and learn to compare them. Objects with similar characteristics can be grouped. The grouping of objects helps us to understand them better.

The eyes can overcome great distances. Our eyes are helpers, for without eyes we could not see pictures in books or magazines. In addition, we wouldn't be able to see the beautiful flowers, trees, animals, food that we eat and people that we would like to be with.

An eye chart is used by a doctor to examine your vision and see whether or not you need glasses. There are two kinds of charts, a Snellen and an E chart. The Snellen chart is used for people who can read the letters and the E chart is for people who can't read but can show the direction in which the letter is pointing.

Eyes are like cameras. They take still and moving pictures, with or without color. Eyes set themselves for speed, distance and brightness of light.

The eye is made up of three layers. The retina, which is the inner layer of the eye is sensitive to light and color. The cornea is in front of the eye's two outer layers. It is clear or open and permits light to enter your eye. The pupil is the opening in the middle layer where it has a black spot. The iris is the thin curtain of tissue which is in the front of the lens.

Eyes have eyebrows over them and eyelashes around them. The eyebrows and eyelashes are made of little hairs. They keep dust from falling into his eyes. Eyes have eyelids, too. They are like window shades. They close over your eyes and keep out the light so you can go to sleep. They blink to keep out dust.

Sight Activities:

The following experiences can be used to help make the awareness of sight more meaningful.

1. Recognizing shapes, such as circles, triangles, or squares, in drawings could deepen the awareness of shapes.
2. Color blindness may be detected by playing the color spot test. A picture made up of spots of one color is put on a spotted background of another color. The child is to name the picture.
3. Recognizing small objects or pictures camouflaged in a larger picture will develop the "seeing" of a child.
4. Have a child describe a picture from memory.
5. Have a child put puzzle pieces together to form a picture.
6. Build-a-Letter — Use pipe cleaners or pegs to make the ABC's or numerals.
7. Figure Ground — Find the numbers and color them each with a different color.
8. Bend Light Rays Experiment — Place a pencil in a half a glass of water. Look at it from the top, bottom and sides. Result — when you look at the pencil from the side, the pencil appears to be bent or broken at the point where it enters the water.
9. Look at the objects in the Seeing box under a magnifying glass. Describe what you see.
10. Change the location of five familiar objects in the classroom and have the children find the five changes.

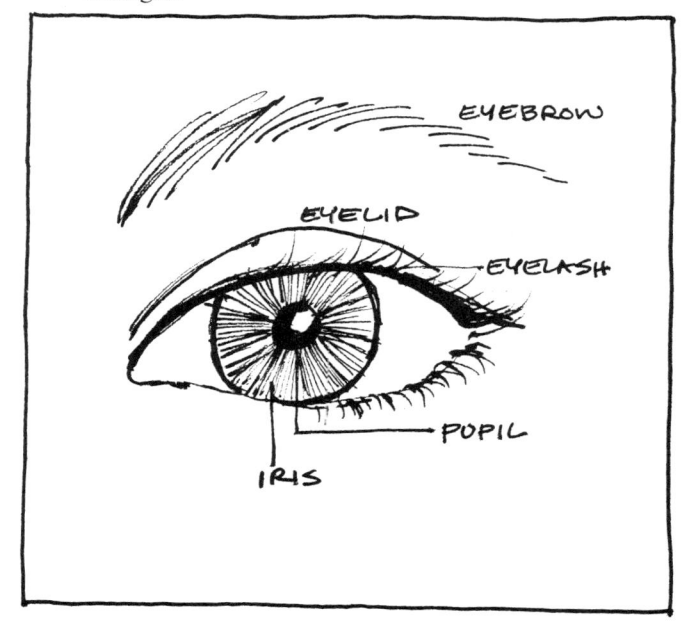

II. HEARING

The ear is a delicate organ, easily damaged by infection or injury. If any serious damage comes to the ear, a person can become partly or completely deaf.

Our ears are helpers, too. Our ears help us learn how to talk. Our ears help us to hear and listen to music, our parents, our friends, animal sounds and many things around us. We have high and low, loud and soft sounds.

All sounds are caused by something moving back and forth very fast. It is called vibration. A vibration causes sound waves in the air. When a wind blows leaves, they make a sound. We cannot see sound waves but we can see what causes them.

We have an eardrum in each ear which starts to vibrate when sound waves hit it. The eardrum causes three little bones to vibrate. The nerves in our ears pick up the vibration and carry the messages to the brain. This is the way we hear.

The parts of the ear are: eardrum, inner, middle and outer ear. Three small bones are found in the eardrum and are called the hammer, anvil and stirrup.

Everyone should take care of their ears. We should never put anything into them, nor poke at them with anything which has a sharp point because it might break the eardrum.

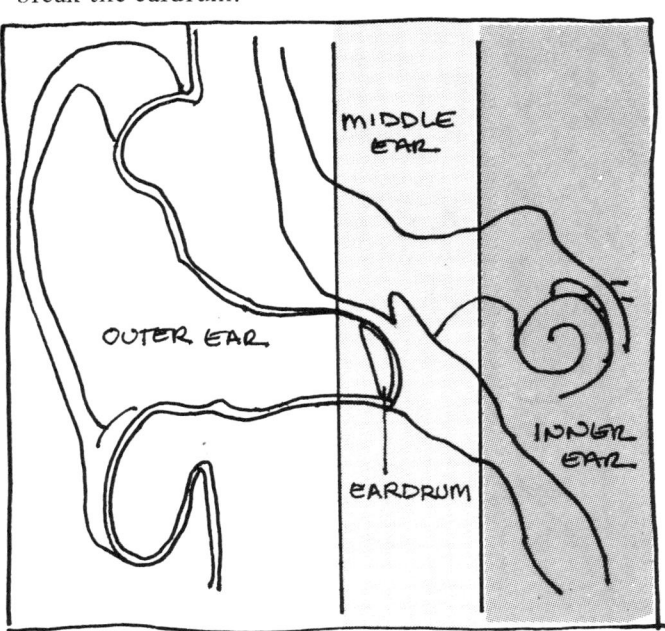

Hearing Activities:

1. The teacher plays a tape recorder with different sounds with which the children are familiar. Then the children will tell the different sounds they recognize.
2. The child will run his finger down the comb. What does he hear? What happens to the comb's teeth? Do they move?
3. Cut a big window in one side of a milk carton. Stretch a skinny rubber band lengthwise around the carton over the window. Pluck the rubber band. What do you hear? Do the same with a fat rubber band.
4. Tie a metal spoon to the middle of a long piece of string. Hold the ends of the string by your ears. Swing the spoon back and forth. Now swing the spoon so it hits a table. The spoon vibrates so it travels along the string to your ears. Try a bigger spoon and fork. What are the results?
5. Ask the children "What was the last thing you remember hearing before you went to bed last night?"
6. Each day play a record of nature sounds, such as bird calls, as the children enter the room. Discuss the sounds and see if the children can identify them.
7. Let the students feel sound by listening to familiar sounds, such as washing machines, sirens, or dogs barking, on tapes or in musical arrangements. The student can feel the sounds and express them in drawing, painting, or modeling, and have a more meaningful experience than simply identifying a sound by a limited verbal vocabulary.

III. SMELL

Smell is one of the most important senses in man or animal. Like sight and hearing, smell gives information about the environment. We can smell objects some distance away, but the nose must come into contact with odor. The sense of smell is more sensitive than that of taste. The olfactory cells are the tiny hairs on the upper part of our nose. Nostrils are the two little openings at the end of the nose. The air goes up your nose and into your head. When it gets into your head, you can smell it. Smells are difficult to organize.

There are three basic types of odors. These are: flowery, such as roses or gardenias; fruity, such as apples, oranges and lemons; and burnt odors, such as found in a well done steak or black toast. Smell helps us to distinguish one smell of food from another smell of food. It helps us learn to taste. When a person has a cold, air cannot get through his nose, and so he can't smell or taste.

Smell Activities:

1. Take a lemon and close your mouth. Hold the lemon in front of your nose. Breathe in through your nose. Can you smell the lemon? Now hold your nose so that you cannot breathe through your nostrils. Hold the lemon in front of your mouth. Breathe in through your mouth. Can you smell the lemon?
2. The teacher blindfolds a child and puts an object under his nose and asks him to determine what it is. For example: food, flowers, soap, perfume, cinnamon, stone, etc.
3. Burn incense in the classroom, varying the scent from day to day.
4. Smell jars: Smelling various familiar liquid solutions, foods or spices, may also give a student a deeper experience in the use of this sense. A solution such as ammonia or smoke (a match or small piece of burning paper), a food such as peanut butter or mayonnaise, and a spice such as garlic or cinnamon, could be put in a closed jar. When the lid is removed the child could sniff and see if he can identify the smell.

IV. TASTE

Our tongue is a helper which helps us tell one food from another. The taste buds are bumps on your tongue which are *sweet* up front, *bitter* in the back, *salty* and *sour* on the sides. The front of the tongue is small and pointed and has fewer taste buds. The back of the tongue has bumps which are larger and rounder.

Food seems tasteless to a person when a bad cold has shut off the passages of his nose. One can't talk very well and doesn't seem to sound right. When you have a cold, air cannot get through your nose. Then you cannot smell or taste. We learn to organize foods and drinks by the way they taste.

Taste Activities:

1. Apple and onion activity — Blindfold a child. Hold an onion under his nose and put a piece of apple in his mouth. He will think he is eating an onion. Then he can hold his nose while you give him either an apple or an onion. He will have to tell what he ate without using his sense of smell.
2. We have four taste buds. Blindfold a child and ask if the food is sweet, salty, sour or bitter by using and not using the sense of smell.

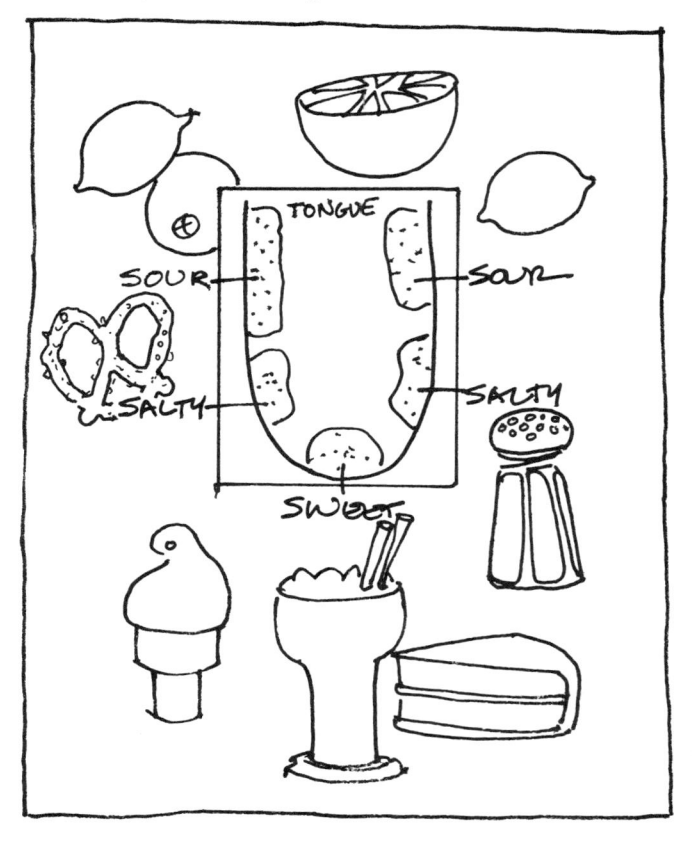

3. The "Notables Candy Cards" — The child writes on a sheet of candy with a caramel food coloring pen. Later, he can eat it if he wishes. However, you can't eat the paper envelope!
4. To help develop precise vocabularies, suggest that the children taste and describe contrasting substances such as carrot and celery, marshmallow and corn chips, popcorn and crackers.
5. Without the children's knowledge, sweeten some water with an artificial sweetner (a substance not familiar to them). Have them taste water. Then allow them to watch you place ordinary water in a glass and add a sweetner to it. Have them taste the water prepared, then ask them to describe any difference between it and the water tasted before. This is a test of the effect of the other senses on the sense of taste.

V. TOUCH

Touch is the sense which gives us notice of contact with an object. We learn the shape and hardness of objects through this sense. Touch gives a person some of his most important knowledge of the objects in the world around him. When a person touches an object, he receives feelings of warmth, cold, pain or pressure.

The feeling of pressure has the biggest number of sense organs. It is highly developed on the tip of the tongue and is poorest on the back of the shoulders. The tips of the fingers and the end of the nose are other sensitive areas. The nerve endings form small discs, just inside the living layer of the skin. These nerve endings are around each of the hairs in your skin and help your sense of touch.

Touch is pain, pressure, smooth, soft and hard. The senses are in your muscles and bones. When you climb a tree, these senses help you decide what to do and how much force to apply. When you drink something hot or cold, you feel the temperature in your mouth and throat. If you swallow something very hot, you will feel pain. If you miss a meal or two, your empty stomach will cause you hunger pains. When the amount of water in your body is low, you will feel thirsty.

We can feel with any part of our bodies. We can find out about objects by feeling similarities. Different parts of our bodies are more sensitive to touch than other parts. We can organize the things we feel by the way they feel.

Touch Activities:

1. Trace different shapes of objects, numbers or letters. Then color the designs. Cookie cutters may be good to use.
2. Awareness of texture and the vocabulary needed to describe it can be further developed in subsequent lessons by having the children touch wet and dry, sponges, hard stones, soft putty and aluminum foil.
3. To increase his awareness of the sense of touch, he could put his hand in a grab-bag of familiar objects and just feel to see if he can identify the common object he probably sees everyday. Some easy objects to use in this experience could be a rubber band, paper clip, eraser, or key.
4. Objects with a distinct texture, such as sandpaper or glass, or a distinct temperature, such as ice or an iron (a toy iron could be used for this demonstration) could be displayed. The child could tell what he thought it felt like, then touch it to see if he was correct.

Please note:
The following pages contain activity patterns and ditto sheets which may be copied and used to develop the functional area of your choice.

Weather Symbol Game Pattern

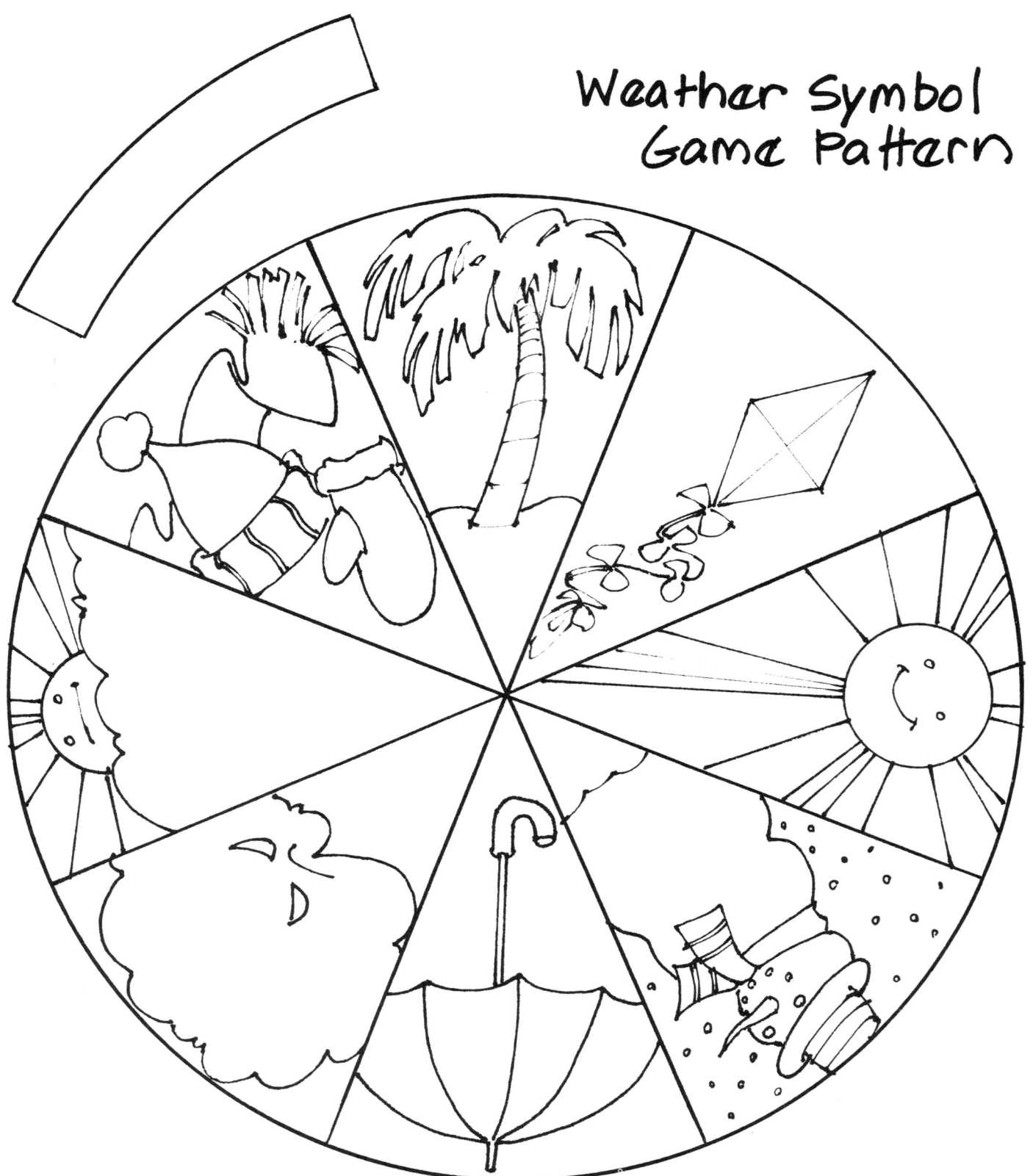

Trace eight name tags and fill in with weather descriptions, (hot, sunny, snowy, rainy, cloudy, partly cloudy, cold). Paste weather circle and name tags onto tag board. Cut out circle and eight tags. Color.

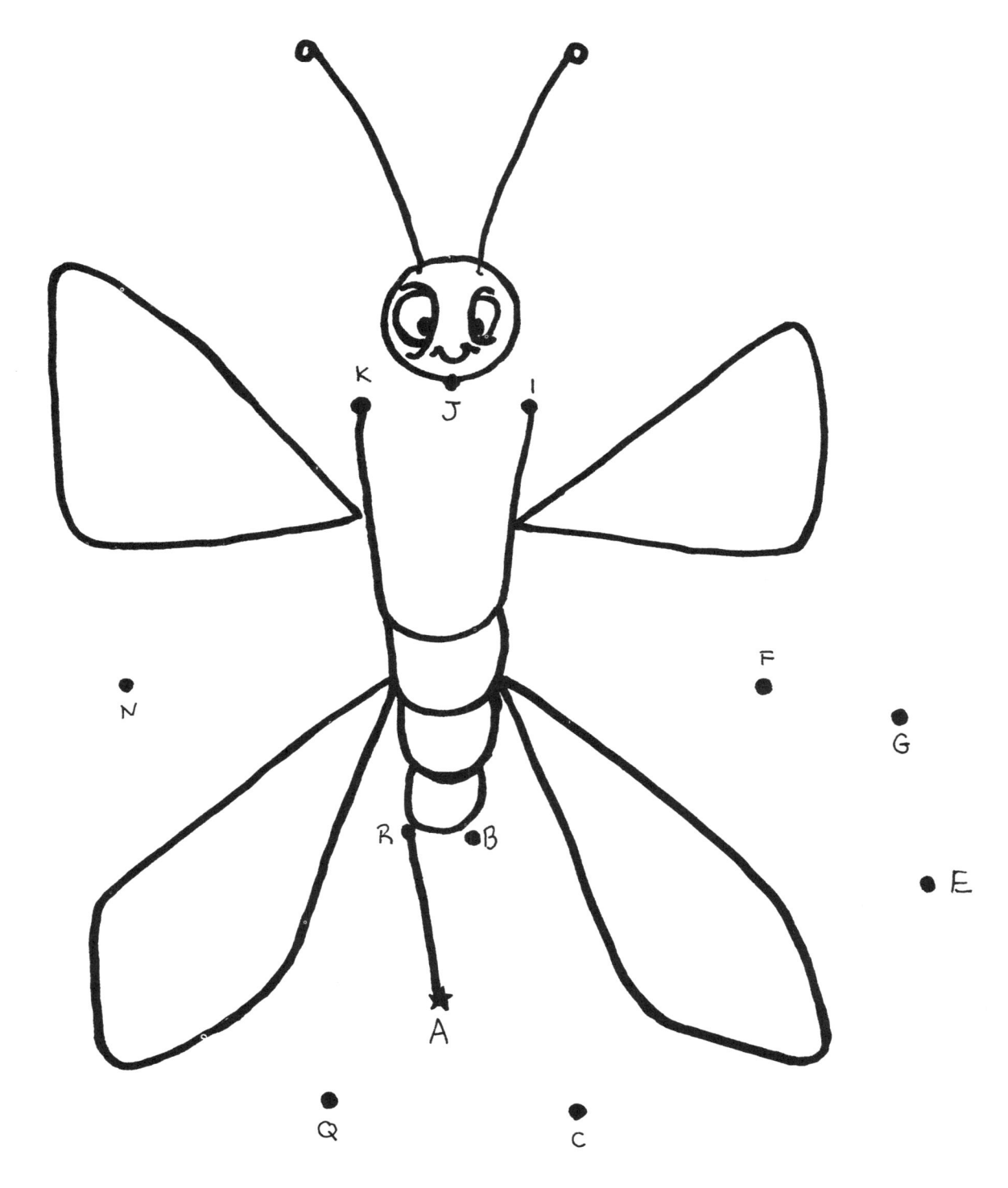

Name: _____

Butterflies

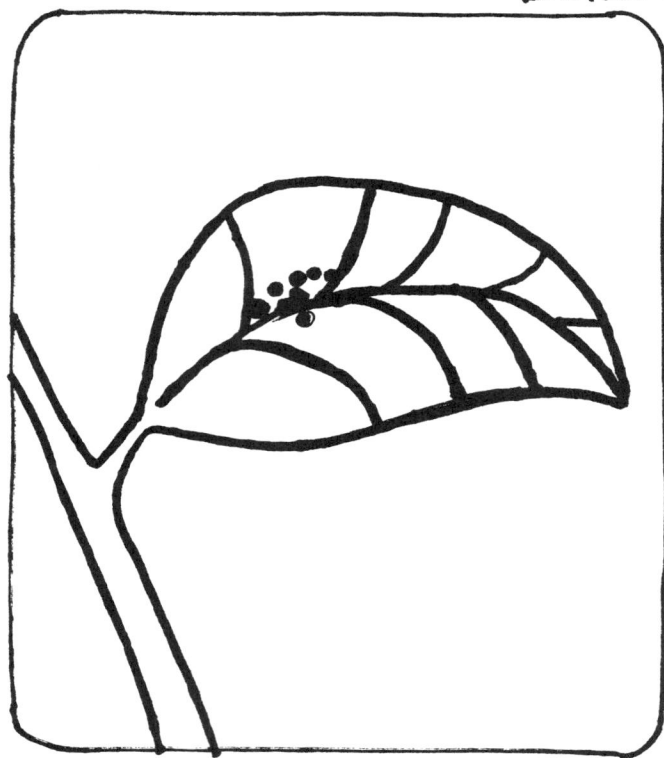

1. A butterfly lays her eggs on a leaf. An egg hatches...

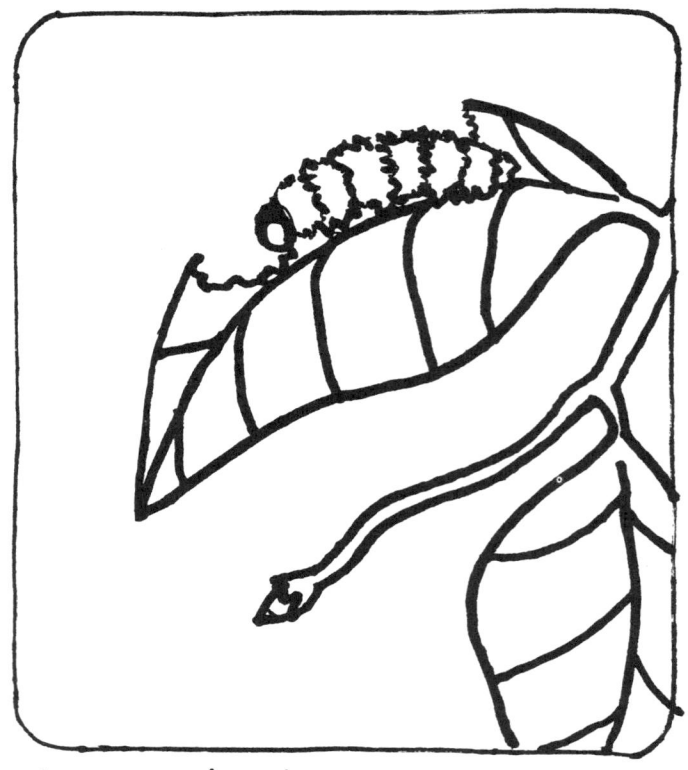

2. ...and out comes a caterpillar. He fattens himself by eating the leaves,

3. and then spins a cocoon around himself.

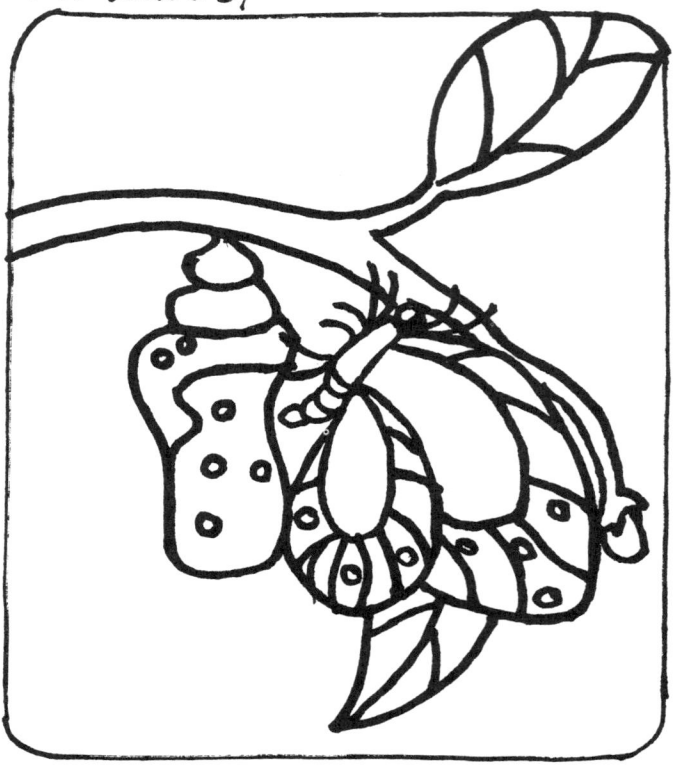

4. Weeks later the cocoon opens and out comes a new butterfly!

Name _____

Birds

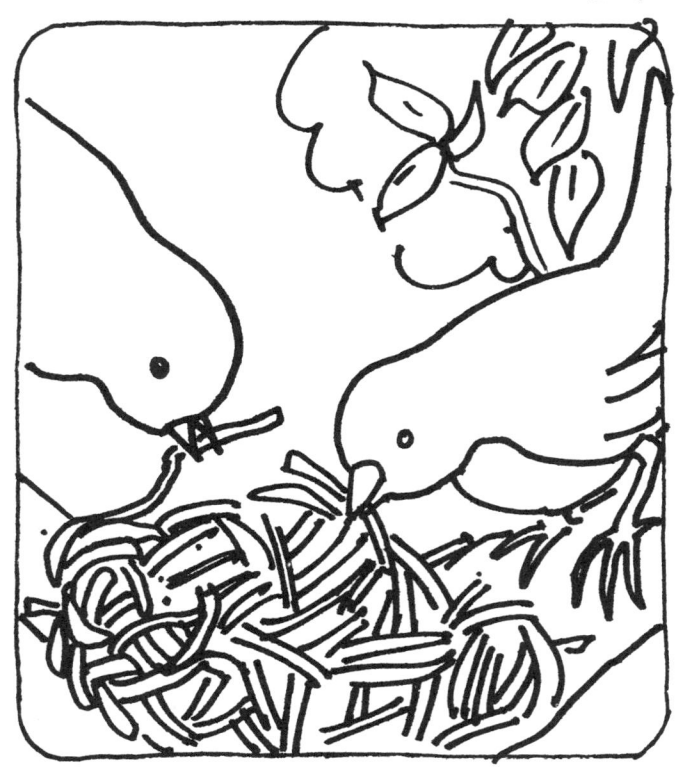

1. Building a nest.

2. Watching over the nest.

3. Feeding the baby birds.

4. Baby birds leaving the nest.

Name _____

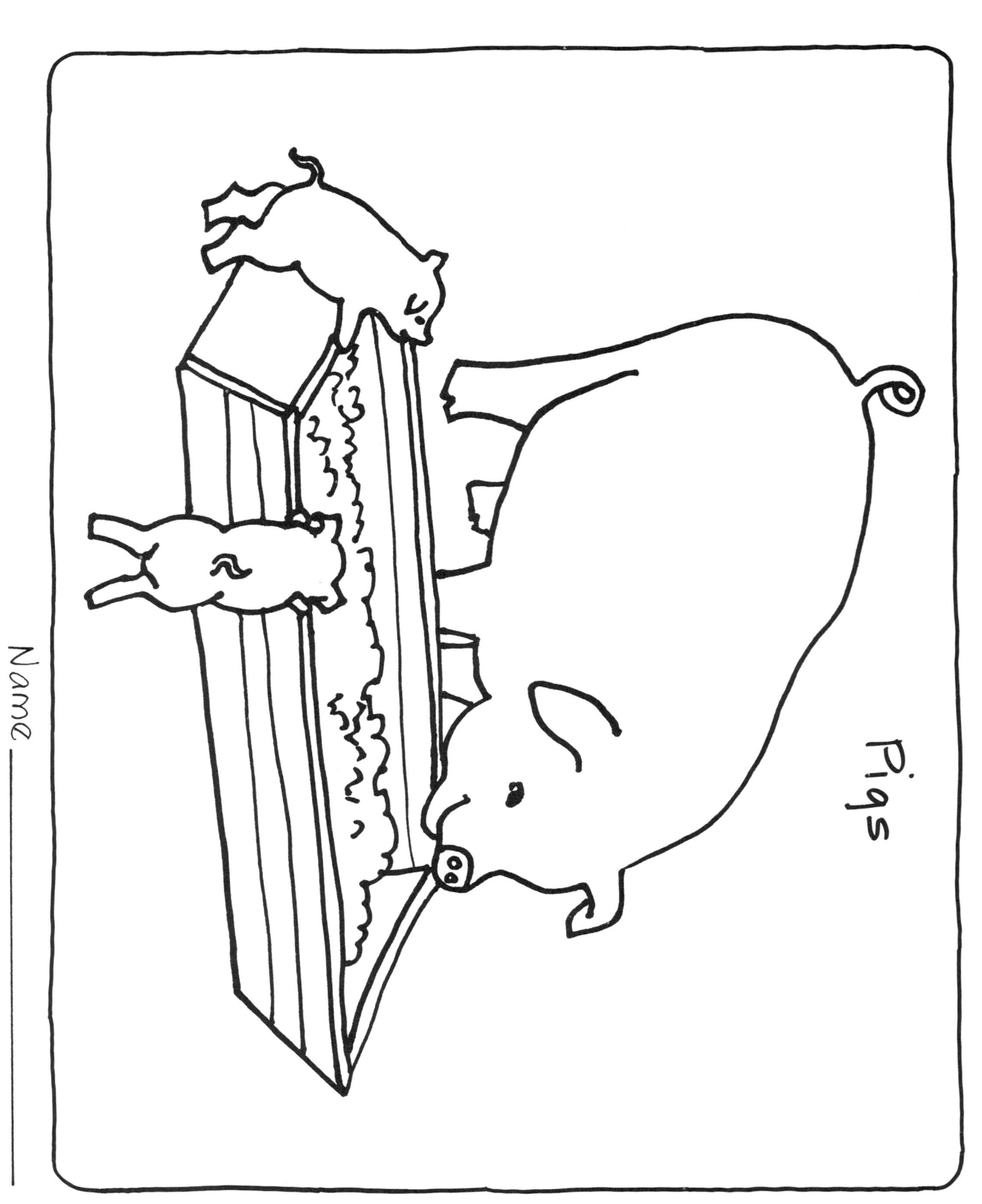

Name _____

Pigs

From THE HANDBOOK OF LEARNING ACTIVITIES FOR YOUNG CHILDREN, Copyright 1980 by Humanics Limited, Jane A. Caballero.

ELEMENTARY AEROSPACE

Air travel, rockets, spacemobiles, and even a walk on the moon are a part of our children's life, so we must prepare them for this complex world at an early age. Aerospace education must be introduced in preschool. We must get to our children while they are young, while they are still highly motivated and eager to learn. The achievements of the space age seem to baffle us but not our children; they seem to understand the NASA projects and eagerly seek more information.

We as teachers seem to concentrate our science lessons on earth, water, and air. We talk about our home — Earth — as a geographic ball, but do we relate it to the unvierse? We discuss water's evaporation and demonstrate how objects float and sink, but do we try to present the vast oceans and their many resources that have not yet been released? We show the motion of air with our pinwheels, but do we discuss how an airplane flies? Our children cannot imagine a world without aerospace.

The National Aeronautics and Space Administration Office of Public Affairs has done much to foster the education of our youth. Many excellent resources are available: posters of our solar system, rockets, satellites, planets, moons, written publications, colorful pictures, and teaching guides. Another resource, *Aerospace Projects for the Elementary School*, by Dr. J. Caballero is available from Humanics Limited, 801 Peachtree Street, Atlanta, Georgia 30309.

Following an interdisciplinary approach, I have adapted my aerospace education to the kindergarten and first grade classroom. The children responded with great enthusiasm and hopefully their interest will remain keen for later careers. Several activities combining aerospace with language arts, art, math, and music are described.

Use these suggestions to get started integrating aerospace education into your curriculum. We have the children's interest and enthusiasm now; we simply cannot miss this opportunity.

Language Arts
1. The child will develop a vocabulary related to the planets and space by having stories dictated to him. A sample vocabulary could include space, rockets, moon, planets, skylab, astronaut, stars, sun, and solar system.
2. The child will learn to converse as an astronaut by acting out the part and talking to the earth station.
3. The child can develop this vocabulary further by making a "pictionary" or television with his space terms and illustrations.

Art
1. The child will be able to paint or draw pictures of the planets, rockets, moon, astronauts, sun, and stars after seeing pictures and posters and having discussions about them.
2. The child will learn to build rockets and launching pads with blocks after studying their construction.
3. The child will learn to make paper mache planets and the moon with its craters and mountains after studying their shapes and surface texture. Toy astronauts and rockets will adadd to this demonstration.
4. The child will learn to help make a large rocket out of a cardboard box after studying and seeing their construction. He will be able to paint the outside after seeing pictures and posters of rockets.
5. The child will learn to make small paper rockets and learn to fly them.

Math
1. The child will be able to develop size relationships by comparing sizes of the planets as seen on charts or models.
2. The child will learn how the Earth and other planets revolve around the sun by acting out the movements of the plants. A globe may be the Earth and paper mache spheres may be made to represent other planets and the sun.
3. The child will learn to count backwards by learning the rocket count-down poem:
    I'm a little rocket
    Pointing to the moon
    5 4 3 2 1
    Blast off! Zoom!
(The child may squat with arms pointed above head then jump as he comes to the end of the poem.)

Music
1. The child will learn to feel weightlessness by pretending that a blown-up balloon is an astronaut and tossing it around.
2. The child will learn numbers and space terms by dramatizing and singing finger plays and songs.[28]

Skylab

Skylab is a space station.
It is in space.
It is where astronauts refuel, rest, and eat.
Astronauts will stop at skylab when they are on a long space trip.

Rockets

Rockets go into space.
Astronauts ride in rockets.
Rockets blast off. Fire makes them go.
Rockets have been to the moon.

The Sun

The planets go around the sun.
The sun gives us heat and light.
The sun is firey hot.
The sun looks red, yellow, or orange.

Astronauts

Astronauts fly rockets.
They explore space and the moon.
Astronauts wear space suits when they go into space.

Space

The moon and the planets are in space.
Space is black.
Space is cold.
There is no oxygen in space.
Astronauts ride rockets into space.
Space is endless.

resources

PLANTS

1. Cotton pamplets and charts. National Cotton Council of America, P. O. Box 12285, Memphis, Tennessee 38112.

2. Trees-colored comic magazines. International Paper Co., Southern Kraft Division, Mobile, Alabama.

3. Trees-posters American Forest Products Industries, Inc., 1835 K St., N.W., Washington, D. C. 20006.

4. Forest Service, U. S. D. A., P. O. Box 2417, Washington, D. C. 20013.

ANIMALS

1. *Animals in Your Classroom, What Do You Know About Animals?, Teaching with Toads and Turtles, Ponds Alive, You and Your Dog.* American Humane Education Society, 180 Longwood Ave., Boston, Massachusetts 02115.

2. *Care of the Cat, Feeding of Cage Birds.* Angell Memorial Animal Hospital, 180 Longwood Ave., Boston, Massachusetts 02115.

3. *How Are Birds Alike and Different?*, Discovering Birds. Basic Science Program, 1965. Scott Foresman and Co., Atlanta, Georgia.

4. National Wildlife Federation, 1412 16th St., N. W., Washington, D. C. 20036.

5. American Gas Ass., 8501 East Pleasant Valley Rd., Cleveland, Ohio 44131.

AEROSPACE

Extensive resource materials are available from NASA and the FAA. Information may be received by requesting order blanks and listings of materials.

1. Department of Transportation, Federal Aviation Administration. Aviation Education Programs Division, Office of General Aviation Affairs, Washington, D. C. 20591. (*A Trip to the Airport, Flight to Grandmothers, Some Aviation Workers.*)

2. National Aeronautics and Space Administration, John F. Kennedy Space Center, Florida 32899. ("Activities for the Elementary Classroom," numerous fact sheets, charts, brochures.)

3. *A Book of Satellites for You*, Franklyn M. Branley, Kessler, Thomas Y. Crowell Co., New York. (one of a series)

4. *Aerospace Projects for Young Children.* Dr. Jane Caballero, Humanics Ltd., 1182 West Peachtree Street, Atlanta, Georgia, 30309

5. Centuri Engineering Co., Box 1988, Phoenix, Arizona 85001.

6. Delta Dart Project, Midwest Products, Co., 400 S. Indiana St., Hobart, Indiana 46342. (inexpensive kits available)

7. *History on Stage, 30 one act classroom plays*, Barbara Friedman and Jennifer Philps, The Instructor Publications, Inc. Dansville, New York 14437.

8. U. S. Department of Commerce, U. S. Government Printing Office, Public Documents Dept., Washington, D. C. (weather information)

chapter 7
social studies

Social studies deal with the physical environment and its effect on man. Areas which may be included in early childhood education are: our environment and pollution, field trips, map skills, career awareness and role playing. One area which is receiving considerable attention is career education. The United States Commissioner of Education has called for an increase in career exploration programs beginning with the early childhood level and continuing into adulthood.

Children begin career exploration at a very young age. It often begins by playing "when I grow up" games. Children often role-play their father's work or their mother's work. Despite children's lack of information, they are often observed pretending they are "at the office," or "in the shop," or "at the store." These interests are characteristic of young children. Therefore, some provision of learning activities in career exploration can serve a developmental need of children.

One approach to providing career awareness to children is through a learning center approach. This allows the children to learn naturally, to have more free choice and to participate actively. These learning centers should contain as many real materials as possible.

One type of learning center would include prop boxes or boxes containing as many items related to a particular career as possible. An example would be to have a baker's prop box. This box would include an apron, baker's cap, rolling pin, mixing bowls, measuring spoons, baking pans, etc. — as many real materials as possible. Allow the children to play and create spontaneously with these materials.

Some suggested occupations are:

nurse	bus driver	poultry farmer
nurse's aid	waitress	telephone operator
doctor	bank teller	beautician
druggist	postman	artist
dentist	teacher	astronaut
veterinarian	mechanic	policeman
secretary	printer	pilot
carpenter	reporter	fireman

A second kind of career learning center is one in which a set of objectives and directions are established. This center provides more structure than the prop boxes discussed previously. This center also consists of many real objects, manipulative materials, games, tapes, and pictures which represent a particular career. However, the child follows the directions and progresses through a planned sequence of activities which ultimately leads to an awareness of what it is like to be people in various careers. An example of this would be to step into the role of a physical therapist, a veterinarian, a nurse, etc. Children get a "feel" for a career. They learn personal things about the person in the job. They learn new vocabulary. They formulate interests in various careers.

The process of developing such a career learning center is a personal one. However, the following simple model for development may be helpful.

1. Pick an occupational cluster (i.e., medical services, transportation, city workers, business and office)
2. Select a variety of occupations within a cluster (i.e., if medical services is chosen, choose a variety of occupations related such as physical therapist, nurse's aid, pharmacist, ambulance driver, etc.)
3. Pick the worker
4. Learn about the job
    a. interviews
    b. pictures
5. Be aware of grade level and ability of children with whom you will be working
6. Decide on materials and develop them
    a. games
    b. manipulatives
    c. costumes, badges, etc.
    d. slides
    e. books
7. Place materials in a box in a convenient area such as the housekeeping center
8. Place directions and objectives in a prominent position so the child knows what he is to do and what he will learn
9. Assist children as they work
    a. consult with child
    b. observe the child
    c. plan with children
10. Continually evaluate and make necessary changes

Children who are involved in career awareness learning centers will develop various concepts such as:

Why do most people want to work?
What are some kinds of work?
How do workers help other people?
Why do people need to work?
How do people learn to work?

With careful planning, career exploration can be used as a vehicle of growth in social interaction, positive self-concept, language skills, mathematics, music, art, woodwork, science, as well as economics.

Career exploration certainly has a place in today's curriculum. It gives children an opportunity to explore various careers and, as a result, it prepares them for future career decisions by helping them acquire values, attitudes, and knowledge concerning the world of work.

The following pictures are taken from teacher-made career centers. These are examples of kits which are related to the medical services — the physical therapist and veterinarian.

The following are some materials suggested for developing career prop boxes:

POST OFFICE
  Index card file, stamp pads, stampers, crayons, pencils, Christmas stamps, old envelopes.

SHOE SHINE KIT
  Small cans of clear (natural) polish, sponges, buffers, soft cloth.

CLEANING SET
  Small brooms, mops, cake of soap, sponges, toweling, plastic spray bottle, plastic basin, clothes line, clothes pins, doll clothes to wash.

FIREMAN
  Hats, raincoats, boots, short length of garden hose.

FARMER
  Shovel, rake, hoe, seeds.

PLUMBER
  Wrench, plastic pipes, tool kit.

HOUSE PAINTER
  Paint brushes, buckets filled with water.

GAS STATION ATTENDANT
  Shirt, hat, tire pump.[29]

Additional Social Studies Activities

1. Watch construction workers operate.
2. Look at and discuss pictures of men and women at work.
3. Tell about pollution.
4. Help prepare the snack and lunch.
5. Use a doctor's stethoscope to hear a heartbeat.
6. Read books about people in other lands.
7. Show native costumes of different people.
8. Visit community workers at their jobs: Barber, banker, cleaner, fireman, policeman, mailman, etc.
9. Divide up jobs in the classroom.
10. Prepare food from different lands.
11. Construct different kinds of homes and discuss them.
12. Discuss different ways to travel.
13. During a unit on nutrition, emphasize what you should eat.
14. Invite a foreign person to do a dance or discuss their country.
15. Visit the post office and discuss the experiences.
16. Dramatize the home situation in the housekeeping center.
17. Visit the farm and discuss the animals and foods that are grown.
18. Emphasize daily social activities such as sharing, taking turns, and cleaning up.
19. Observe different holidays and discuss their importance.
20. Invite people to visit the classroom and discuss their daily work.

Specific information and directions for a few activities will follow.

Career Awareness Game

The child places the symbols in front of himself. He looks at the community helpers on the folder then associates the symbol with the community helper. For example, the milk bottles are placed next to the milkman.

[30]

Functional Area: Cognitive

Purpose: The child will learn the association between various community helpers and symbols associated with their roles.

Functional Area:

Purpose:

Community Helpers Game Pattern

Paste Pattern onto tag board. Cut out & color.

Community Helpers Game Pattern Con't

POLLUTION

There are nearly 4 billion people on the earth. Every one of them need to breathe, drink, and eat to survive. But we are not taking care of our air, land, food, or water. We need to learn how to take care of our environment. We must not *pollute* our environment.

Our four major problems are air pollution, water pollution, waste pollution and noise polution.

Air Pollution

We must have air if we want to live. We pollute our air with car fumes called carbon monoxide. We burn fuels and they pollute the air. Chemicals, smoke, dust, and many other things pollute the air. It makes our clothes dirty and is making our life shorter. What can we do? We can use an anti-pollution system for our car. We can make factories be more careful. We can do many many things to keep our air clean.

Concept: Air pollution is a part of man's total effect on his environment. This project will make children aware:
1. Of air pollution and their role in helping to solve the problem.
2. Of what is in the air that plants, animals, and people breathe.

Materials: Steel wool; plate; baby bottle; water

Procedure: Air contains oxygen. Push a wad of steel wool all the way down in the bottom of a baby bottle. Fill it about half full of water and shake well until steel wool is very wet. Pour off water. Get a plate and add water one inch deep. Now, put the bottle, mouth down, into the plate and let the bottle stand for a day and night. Water will rise in the bottle. See how rusty the steel wool has become. The steel wool combined with oxygen in the air inside the bottle to form rust. The water then rises to take the place of the oxygen in the air that was used up by the steel wool.

Follow-up: When air has lots of smoke, soot, and other gases, we say that air is polluted. Children can make an experiment chart showing different ways that air is polluted in their town.

Waste Pollution

Litter can cause diseases. It can burn, cause health problems, and hurt our eyes by having to look at it. We must learn how to throw away things properly. We should learn to recycle trash or do away with it properly.

We must learn to make our world more beautiful because it is the only world that we have.

Concept: Awareness of litter and how it affects our environment.

Materials: Cotton rag, rubber band, paper, sandwich, aluminum pie tin, or other objects, pliers.

Procedure: Burn the above over an aluminum pie tin, holding them with a pair of pliers. Is the smell pleasant? Have the children noticed anyone burning anything in their neighborhood? Does it look or smell good?

Follow-up: Draw pictures of an area before and after clean-up. Have the class keep a certain section of the playground clean.

Water Pollution

We must have water to drink, to grow our food, to wash and to play with. Water is limited. Sewage treatment must be better. We must re-use our water because it is limited on the earth. We must be more careful and not waste our water.

Concept: In a polluted environment the number of different kinds of organisms which can survive is drastically reduced.

Procedure: Observe two small streams — one which is polluted and one which is not. Lift small rocks or submersed sticks and wash or scrape attached and crawling organisms into a pail of water. Organisms may be observed alive. Make observations and notes of the streams characteristics and any signs of pollution.

Follow-up questions: What are examples of *organic wastes*? (sewage, drainage, dead animals) of toxic wastes? (oil, copper, mining wastes)

Noise Pollution

We want to listen to more beautiful sounds. High noises may cause us to lose our hearing. We must not forget noise pollution can cause us to have nervous breakdowns, ulcers, and heart problems. We must try to prevent noise pollution.

Concept: Living things react to their environment. The lesson will make children more aware of beautiful and pleasant sounds, and of the obnoxious sounds around them.

Materials: Record player, soothing and loud records

Procedure: Ask the children to put their heads down on their desks with their eyes closed. When everything is quiet, slam the door, drop a book, etc.
Ask the children — what happened when you heard a certain noise — how did it make you feel — Did you feel like telling me to "STOP IT."

Follow-up: Discuss different kinds of sounds such as:
Sounds We *Like* to Hear: Birds singing, pleasant voices, soft music.
Sounds We *Don't* Like to Hear: Shouting, fussing, crying, brakes screeching, airplanes taking off and landing.
Sounds That *Help* Us: Horns blowing, sirens, telephone ringing.

A unit on pollution will help the child become more aware that it is important for him to learn to be neat and clean. Various free resource materials can be obtained.

Functional Area: Cognitive (Social studies)

Purpose: The child will be reminded about how pollution can affect his life as he sees these posters created by the teacher.

Functional Area:

Purpose:

TRANSPORTATION

Airplanes
Many people ride in airplanes because they go faster than trains or cars. They can eat and sleep on airplanes. They can fly around the world in just one day and one night. Airplanes carry mail and cargo. Sometimes they fly over forests looking for forest fires. Sometimes they spray the farmer's fields to kill insects. Sometimes important pictures are taken from the air. A terminal is a building where people wait for airplanes. Hangers are buildings where airplanes are kept. A wind sock is used to tell the direction from which the wind is blowing. Runways are long paved roads from which airplanes take off and land. The control tower has radios and radar for helping guide airplanes. Pilots fly airplanes.

Freight Trains
Freight trains are pulled by diesel engines. Sometimes trains carry cars, food, clothing, and many other things for people many miles away. People and mail can also travel on trains. Passenger trains have dining and sleeping cars.

Ships
Very big ships may be called ocean liners. They carry mail and people. They take trips around the world. Some ocean liners have shops where people can buy things. Movies, garages, swimming pools, and other large things may be on ocean liners. Steam makes electricity that runs these ships. Some ships carry wood, wheat, oil, and other things. These ships are called freighters. A port is where ships get close to the land. A ship that goes below the surface of the water is a submarine.

Streetcars
The streetcar is a lot like a bus. Many people ride streetcars in San Francisco. A conductor opens the door of the streetcar and takes our fare. Streetcars are run by electricity. A long pole above the car joins it to the electric wires. Streetcars run on tracks.

Trucks
Trucks are used to haul goods over the highways day and night. A truck driver must always be careful while he is driving his truck. Truck terminals are places where trucks load and unload the goods they carry.

Cars
Cars are operated by their own power. Gasoline makes cars go. Ford led the car industry in America. It was called the horseless carriage. The first car in the U. S. was made in 1892 by Charles and Franklin Duryea of Springfield. It was a 2-cylinder buggy. Then followed Elwood Haynes, R. E. Olds, Henry Ford. By 1912 cars were popular. Some new cars are run by electricity.[32]

Functional Area: Cognitive

Purpose: The functions of various modes of transportation can be reinforced as the teacher reads the short stories to the child.

Functional Area:

Purpose:

The Little Train
Once upon a time there was a little black engine. He was very lonely because he didn't have any cars to go on his *long, long* trips with him. Then one day as he was going along the track, he saw a little blue car. The little blue car said, "Oh, Mr. Engine, may I hook on to you so I can go on a long, long trip?" The little black engine said, "Sure you can go with me." Then the little train went down the *straight, straight* track and over a *tall, tall* mountain. As they were going along, they saw a little green car. The little green car said, "Oh, Mr. Engine, may I hook on to you so I can go on a *long, long* trip?" The little black engine said, "Sure you can go with us." Then the little train went down the *straight, straight* track and under a *low, low* bridge.

Repeat the story substituting the following:
yellow — through a long, long tunnel
brown — beside a short, short house
purple — around a dense, dense forest
green — behind a big, big depot
red — between a big, big building
orange — in front of a small, small farm [33]

The train can be used to practice color concepts, numbers, and directions. Allow the children to pin the cars on his shirt and act out the story using classroom furniture as the props. See pattern on page 70.

The Little Train Story Pattern

Functional Area: Language

Purpose: The vocabulary words in *italics* in the story will be learned by the children as they act out the movements of "The Little Train."

Functional Area:

Purpose:

From THE HANDBOOK OF LEARNING ACTIVITIES FOR YOUNG CHILDREN, Copyright 1980 by Humanics Limited, Jane A. Caballero.

COUNTRIES OF THE WORLD

Puzzle of the United States

Maps should be introduced to young children. A map of the classroom, school, neighborhood and community could be made. Then city, state, country and world maps could be presented. Puzzles of various places will help the child become more aware of the environment.

Children can make their own puzzles by drawing or finding magazine pictures or old maps and cutting them up. Mounting the pieces on cardboard and covering in clear contact will help preserve the pieces.

Functional Area: Cognitive (concept development)

Purpose: The pictures on the puzzles will reinforce concepts that have been developed as the child completes the puzzle. (Animals seen and identified on a field trip and maps of the state or country)

Functional Area:

Purpose:

The Little Dutch Children

The Dutch children live in Holland. The Netherlands is another name for Holland and it means "lowlands." Holland was once covered by the sea. It was reclaimed but one half of it is below sea level. Tulips are grown a lot in Holland. Fishing is very common. Polderland is the drained area that is good for farmland. A dike is made of sand and sod and is wide enough for roads. A dike keeps water from flowing overland. The people wear wooden shoes. They have clean houses since they take their shoes off inside. Farming is important and cows and sheep are raised. Cheese and butter provide much of the food. The people wear bright clothes. They ride bicycles a lot and even have separate streets for bicycles. The canal waterways freeze in winter and people skate on them. Shipping and building and importing are the main industries. The windmill gives power and is the national monument.

The Dutch Children　　Traditional

Oh, the children of Holland wear wooden shoes,
With a klip, klop, klop, klip, klop.
They can run, jump and walk just as fast as they
　choose,
With a klip, klop, klip, klop, klop.

To the windmill they go for the meal and the flour,
With a klip, klop, klip, klop, klop.
In the fields they tend great flocks of geese by the
　hour,
With a klip, klop, klip, klop, klip.

Oh, I think t'would be quite hard to walk, don't you?
With a klip, klop, klip, klop, klop.
Oh, I really don't see how the Dutch children do,
When they walk with a klip, klip, klop.[34]

Children will enjoy learning about other cultures and their own unique identity will be better understood.

Functional Area: Self concept

Purpose: The child will learn about children of other cultures thus helping him learn about his uniqueness and self identity. (The above facts were learned by 6 year old children after studying a unit on Holland.)

Functional Area:

Purpose:

FIELD TRIPS

Field trips are important for children. They provide experiences for them to relate classroom concepts to the "real" world. Children need to feel, touch, see, and hear the world. Classroom experiences can't always provide these experiences.

Good field trips add to all areas of the curriculum: science, social studies, art, math, music, and language. Trips should not be very far, crowded or dangerous. The teacher should be familiar with the location so she can provide preliminary experiences and instructions to the children. The children should be allowed to take their time in order to gain the most from the experience. Remember children will want to explore and use all their senses to assist them in learning.

The teacher should also provide follow-up activities to reinforce and clarify the field trip experience.

A trip to the zoo provides many experiences for the child. One follow-up activity is developing the pictures taken of the animals. The children choose their favorite animal and draw a picture of that animal. The picture is mounted on cardboard, covered with clear contact paper and cut into pieces. The puzzle pieces provide a fun but meaningful experience for the child. Visual discrimination and fine motor development are also enhanced.

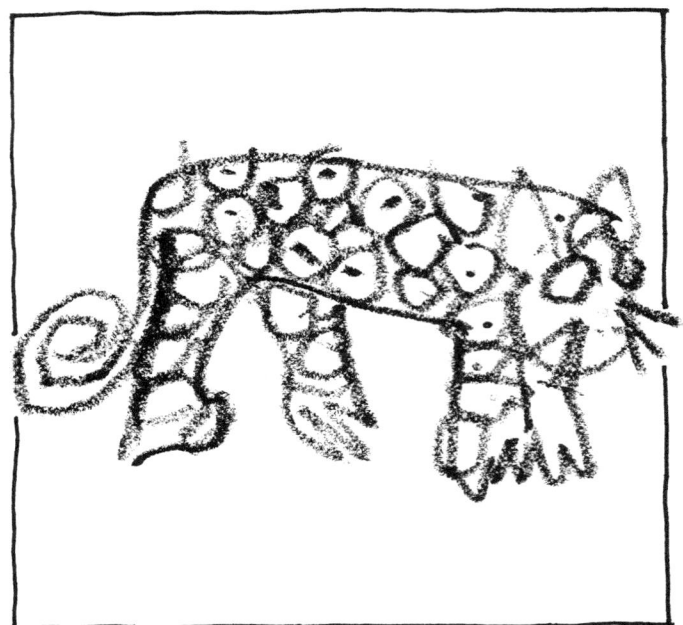

resources

TRANSPORTATION

1. *The Railroad.* Santa Fe System Lines. Neely Printing Co., Inc., Chicago, Illinois.
2. *Union Pacific Railroad.* Public Relations Dept., 1416 Dodge St., Omaha, Nebraska 68179.
3. Trans-Atlantic Passenger Steamship Conference Kits. Educational Department, Box 525, Dansville, New York.
4. *How We've Moved Our Things and Ourselves.* Posters: The Basic Social Studies Program for Primary Grades — At Home, At School, In the Neighborhood, In City, Town, and Country. Scott, Foresman, and Co., Atlanta, Georgia.
5. *Transportation Since 1775.* American Petroleum Institute, Education Department, 1271 Avenue of the Americas, New York, New York 10020.
6. Department of Transportation, Office of Public Affairs, Washington, D. C. 20590.
7. United Airlines, P. O. Box 66100, Chicago, Illinois 60666.

COMMUNICATION

1. *Communication*, reprint from the World Book Encyclopedia. Field Enterprises Educational Corporation.
2. Visit or contact your local post office and telephone company for charts and information.
3. Southern Bell, 666 NW 79th Ave., Room 616, Miami, Fla. 33126.

AMERICAN HERITAGE-PRESIDENTS

1. Portraits of the Presidents of the United States, The Constitution, record of the Declaration of Independence. Book Enterprises, Inc., New York, New York 10017.
2. Weekly Reader's and other monthly publications will contain materials relating to Washington, Lincoln, and the government.
3. Contact your local Air Force office and your state capitol.
4. (President book) John Hancock, Mutual Life Insurance Co., Boston, Mass. 02117.

ENVIRONMENT

1. United States Environmental Protection Agency, Washington, D. C. 20460.
2. McDonald Corporation, 1 McDonald Plaza, Oak Brook, Ill. 60521.
3. The Garden Club of America, Conservation Committee, 598 Madison Ave., N. Y. 10022.
4. American Petroleum Institute, Education Division, 1271 Avenue of the Americas, N. Y. 10020.
5. Continental Can Co., 633 Third Ave., N. Y. 10017.
6. (Career education) Dept. of Justice, Federal Bureau of Investigation, Washington, D. C. 20535.

chapter 8
math

The following objectives may be helpful in planning a math program for early childhood education:

1. Prepare for math experiences.
2. Relate abstract numbers to concrete experiences.
3. Build math concepts and skills.
4. Develop needed motor skills.
5. Develop vocabulary.
6. Provide opportunities to discover and explore.
7. Promote understanding.
8. Relate math experiences to curriculum.
9. Develop good attitudes and work habits.
10. Promote emotional and social growth.

Suggested number experiences are:

- Observing and describing sets of objects, models, and pictures.

- Comparing sets of objects (more, less same).

- Ordering sets of objects (longer, smaller, same, first, second, third, next, middle, last, between, before, bottom, top).

- Joining and removing sets of objects (add, subtract).

- Recognizing and comparing geometric shapes (line, square, triangle, circle, rectangle, diamond, hexagon).

- Associating numbers with sets of objects and shapes (one-to-one correspondence).

- Recognizing and reading numerals (0 to 12).

- Counting numerals (0 to 10)

- Counting to 10 (vary according to source by rote and with objects).

- Similarity with the clock face, calendar, denominations of money (penny, dime, quarter, half dollar), liquid measure, and ruler.

- Cut of geometric shapes.

- Locate similar shapes in classroom; name objects

- Locate order of children.

- Locate objects in room and describe using directional vocabulary.

- Draw sets of various objects and give numeral name.

- Draw sets of a given number of objects – 6 balls, 4 cats, etc.

- Count various abstract objects.

- Use abstract numbers

- Write numbers on ditto guide and writing paper.

- Arrange number cards in order.

- Count using tongue depressors, blocks, etc.

- Make sets of ten or less and give number name.

- Count feet, eyes, people in room, etc.

- Count other objects in class – children, girls, boys, blocks, ropes, milk, pencils, paper, windows, desks, chairs, erasers, clap of hands, number of times a child jumps rope, etc.

- Follow directions – bring 7 pencils, put the book on the bottom shelf, put 10 chairs in the circle, etc.

- Read stories with mathematical vocabulary – The Three Bears, Ten Little Indians, The Three Pigs, Baa Baa, Black Sheep, etc.

- Finger games – Ten Soldiers, Blackbird, This Old Man, He Played One, etc.

- Pat blindfolded child and ask how many times he was touched.

- Set table for certain number of children.[35]

Math concepts for the preschool may include:

circle	short	above
heart	little	below
square	tall	beneath
rectangle	fat	over
triangle	thin	under
diamond	thick	fifth
round	skinny	count rote
straight	slender	one to ten
crooked	more than	count rationally
corner	less than	from one to
edge	fewer than	ten
two	some	past
bottom	none	future
size	as many as	on
amount	enough	in
weight	pair	around
length	all	beyond
temperature	empty	today
large	full	tomorrow
small	up	yesterday
big	down	tonight
morning	evening	afternoon
beside	far	time
between	hot	first
next to	cold	second
in front of	warm	third
behind	cool	fourth
front	short	weekend
back	long	
near	medium	

MATH FINGERPLAYS　　　Traditional

10 little androids all in a row
They bow to their leader, just so.
They march to the right, they march to the left.
They stand up straight all ready to go,
But here comes Lord Barth with a lazer gun.
Zap, Zing. You ought to see those androids run!

Dive little tadpole, one. Dive little tadpole, two.
Swim little tadpoles. Oh, oh, oh. Or I will catch you.

Five eggs and five eggs, that makes ten;
Sitting on top is the Mother Hen.
Cackle, cackle, cackle; what do I see?
Ten fluffy chickens, as yellow as can be.

1, 2, tie your shoe; 3, 4, touch the floor,
5, 6, stir and mix; 7, 8, sit and wait.
8, 10, count again. 1, 2, 3, 4, 5, 6, 7,,8, 9, 10.

Here is the beehive, but where are the bees?
Why hidden inside where nobody sees.
Watch, and you'll see them fly out of their hive –

One, two, three, four, five. BZZZZZ Ouch!

Once I saw a ant hill, with no ants about;
*So I said, "Dear little ants, won't you please
    come out?"*
Then as if the little ants had heard my call —
One, two, three, four, five, came out.
And that was all.

One, two, three, and four.
I can count even more.
Five, six, seven, eight.
My fingers My lady fingers stand up straight.
Nine and ten are my thumb men.

I have five fingers on each hand.
Ten toes on both my feet.
Two ears, two eyes, one nose, one mouth,
    with which to gently speak.
*My hands can clap, my feet can tap, my eyes
    can brightly shine.*
My ears can hear, my nose can smell.
My mouth can speak a rhyme.

This old man, he played one,
he played nick-nack on my thumb, etc.

Two little astronauts are going to the moon.
Two little astronauts hope they'll get there soon.
The first one said, "Oh, this is such fun."
The second one said, "We'll see the sun."
Then – 10, 9, 8, 7, 6, 5, 4, 3, 2, 1, ZOOM!

One little, two little, three little astronauts,
Four little, five little, six little astronauts,
Seven little, eight little, nine little astronauts,
Ten little astronaut men.

Two little black birds sitting on a hill;
One named Jack and the other named Jill;
Fly away Jack; Fly away Jill;
Come back Jack; Come back Jill;
Two little black birds sitting on a hill;
One named Jack and the other named Jill.[36]

ACTIVITIES

Pints and Quarts
The pints and quarts can be made in proportion to one another. The child can learn that two ½ pints equal 1 pint and 2 pints equal 1 quart as he places paper symbols together. (see page 80)

Functional Area: Cognitive (math)

Purpose: The child can use the 2 pints and 1 quart (made out of construction paper) to discover the concept: 2 pints = 1 quart.

Functional Area:

Purpose:

Cardboard Telephone
A cardboard telephone may be made for the child. He can attach the dial with a brad thus allowing the dial to move. He can practice dialing important numbers.

Functional Area: Cognitive (math)

Purpose: The child will develop numeral recognition.

Functional Area:

Purpose:

Math Puzzles
Many types of puzzles can be made to introduce number concepts to children. Animal shapes can be

cut into pieces. A numeral on top can aid the child in locating puzzle pieces. Sets with corresponding numerals can provide enjoyable learning experiences.

Functional Area: Cognitive (math)

Purpose: The child will practice numeral recognition 0-10 as he locates the puzzle pieces.

Functional Area:

Purpose:

Paper Plate Clocks

Functional Area: Individual strength

Purpose: The child will make paper plate clocks and use this concrete experience to help him develop the concept of time.

Functional Area:

Purpose:

Kite Bulletin Board

Functional Area: Individual strength

Purpose: The child can make his own kite and add to the bulletin board entitled "MARCH WINDS BLOW 5 LITTLE KITES ALL IN A ROW"[37]

Functional Area:

Purpose:

77

Many construction paper games and activities can be made with the child to give him concrete experiences. The concept of "one dozen" can be done by cutting a rectangle and drawing twelve egg shapes. The child can use cardboard eggs and place them into the carton as he counts to twelve.

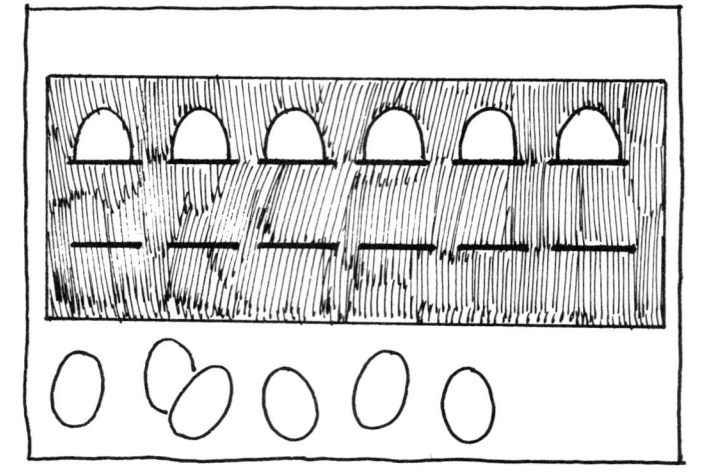

Functional Area: Cognitive (math)

Purpose: The child will learn the concept of "one dozen."

Functional Area:

Purpose:

FILE FOLDER GAMES

Games using file folders can be an inexpensive but effective way to make games for children. Any concept can be illustrated. The folder can be covered in clear contact paper for protection.

Buried Treasure
When playing Buried Treasure, the child throws a die and moves the fish the correct number of spaces. He must say the numeral he lands on to remain on the space. The first child to reach the end wins the game.

Functional Area: Cognitive (math)

Purpose: The child will practice counting as he plays the games.

Functional Area:

Purpose:

Snake Puzzle
The child places the snake pieces on the board with the corresponding shape, color, and number.

Functional Area: Self concept

Purpose: The child will enjoy the success he feels as he completes this easy snake puzzle.

Functional Area:

Purpose:

Raindrop Game
The child places the raindrops on the board in numerical sequence. The correct placement of some numerals reinforces the correct placement. The child can count in sequence after he is finished to determine if he has placed the numerals correctly.

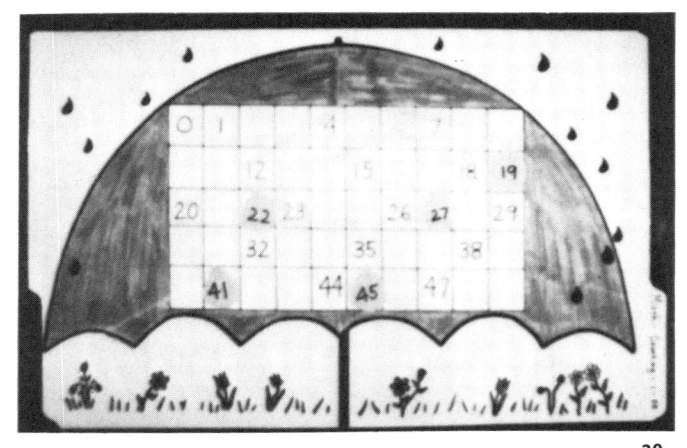

Functional Area: Cognitive (math)

Purpose: The child will practice numerical sequence as he plays with the game.

Functional Area:

Purpose:

Math Garage Game
The child counts the number of dots on the garage and then matches the corresponding numeral car. The car and garage may be color coordinated for an easier task.

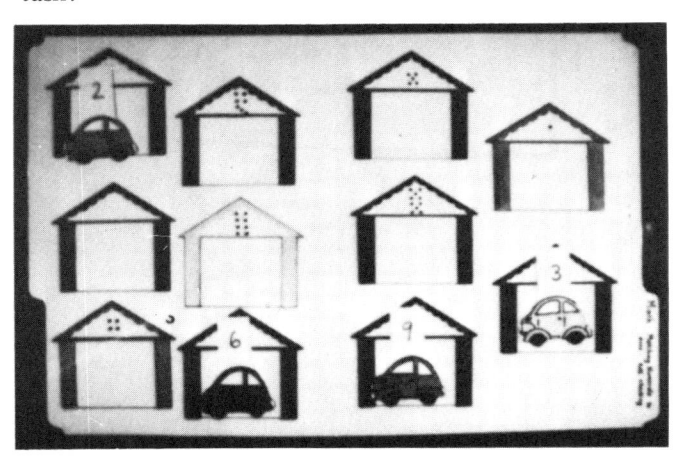

Functional Area: Physical

Purpose: The child practices small muscle development as he places the cars in the appropriate garages.

Functional Area:

Purpose:

Worm Game
Math problems and solutions are written on the worm in order that as the child pulls the worm out of the apple first a problem appears and then the answer.

Functional Area: Individual strength

Purpose: The child practices basic math facts as he plays with the worm combination individually.

Functional Area:

Purpose:

Pints and Quarts
Cut out 2 pints and 1 quart. Place the 2 pints on the quart to show equivalency.

Snake Puzzle

1 2 3

4 5 6

7 8 10

9

Paste pattern onto tag board.
Cut out and color

RAINDROP GAME

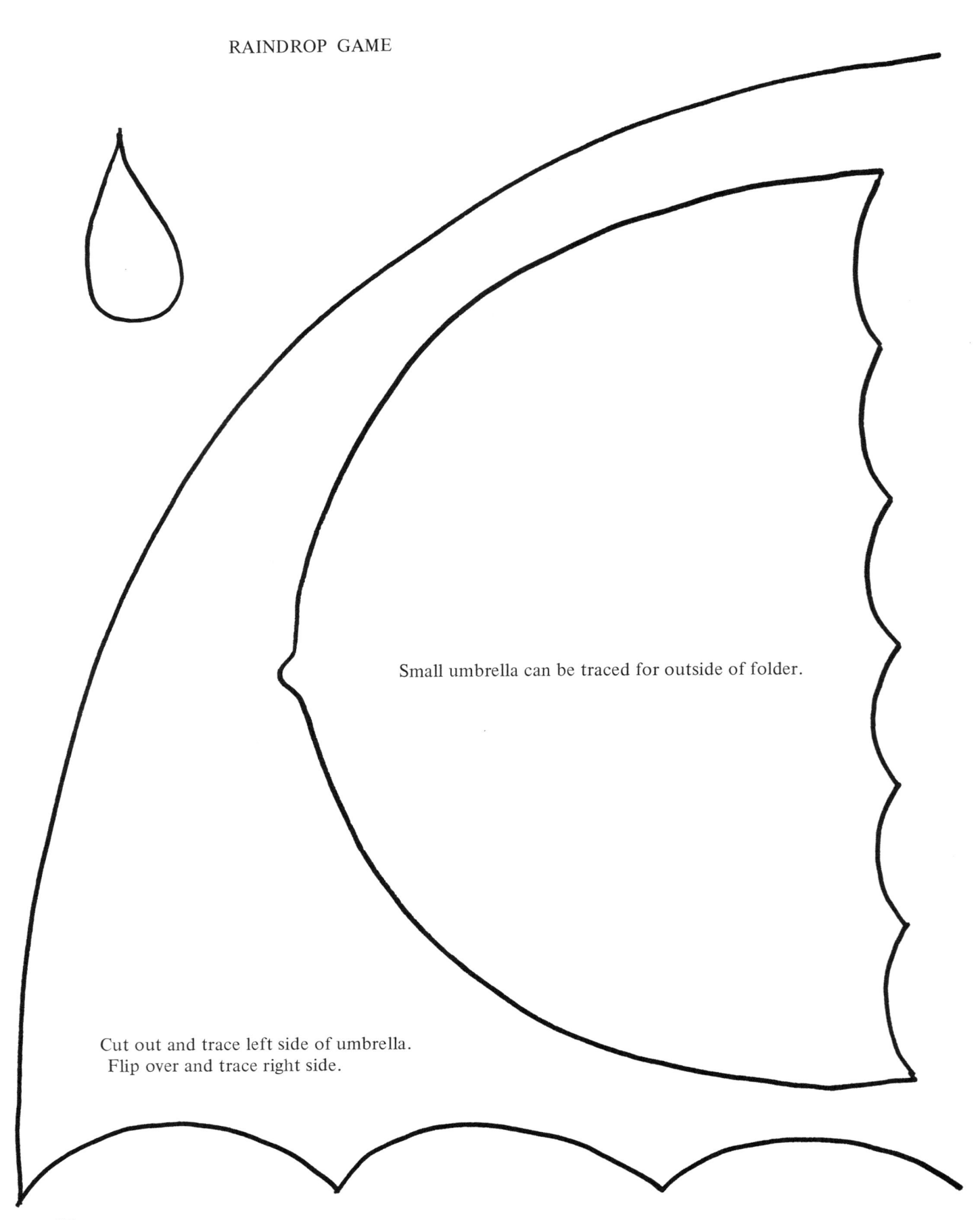

Small umbrella can be traced for outside of folder.

Cut out and trace left side of umbrella.
Flip over and trace right side.

To play the MATH GARAGE GAME trace and cut out cars numbered from 1-10 and garages dotted from 1-10. Each child is to match the number on the cars with the corresponding dots on the garage.

83

Worm Game

cut here

1+0
1

1+1
2

1+2
3

1+3
4

4-4
0

4-3
1

4-2
2

4-1
3

Paste pattern onto tag board. cut out and color

chapter 9
language development

Proverb —*Nature gave us two ears and only one mouth so that we could listen twice as much as we speak.*

Basically, there are four forms of communication: 1) listening, 2) speaking, 3) reading, 4) writing. These forms of communication are developmental. Therefore listening is very important because it is a prerequisite for speaking, reading, and writing.

There are many purposes for listening. Some of these purposes are:
- a child listens to enjoy
- a child listens to appreciate
- a child listens to communicate ideas
- a child listens to learn
- a child listens to evaluate

In the classroom, it is important that a child be given as many listening experiences as possible. The following listening ideas may be helpful.

LISTENING EXPERIENCES

Listening walk — take children out of doors to listen for sounds — birds, trucks, wind, insects, noises in the environment, etc.

Use of records — listen for directions of movement and/or exercises. listen to story or musical records. dreative body interpretation to different tempos of music.

Rhythm instruments — use instruments to repeat certain rhythmic patterns.

Tape recorder — use to record familiar sounds or children's noises. Replay and have children identify whose voice it is or what sound is made.

Pattern clapping — one child taps or claps a pattern and then other children reproduce the same pattern. Rhythm sticks, notes struck on the piano, or foot taps on the floor can be used for variations.

Sound box — Have one child select an object from the sound box while the others have their eyes closed. Leader makes a sound with the object and then conceals it. Children try to identify what object in the sound box made the noise. (Objects can include a bell, whistle, cricket, horn, etc.)

Chanting — chant a train sound, louder or softer as the train approaches or goes away.

Rhyming — Children can create their own rhyming words or verses. Children can supply the ending rhymeswords to Mother Goose Rhymes.

Musical Scales — Children sing "up, up, up" as c, e, and g are struck on the piano, rising as they do; when the notes are reversed they sing "down, down, down." Children raise or lower their arms as "the music tells them" while the notes of the octave are played.

Sound Discrimination — Children tell which sound is louder after hearing the sound of a bid Indian drum and a small toy drum and the ring of a large bell and a very small bell.

Teacher Made Learning Tapes
On the tape, pronounce words in pairs, including some that rhyme and some that do not. In the taped directions, ask the child to circle yes on the answer sheet if the words rhyme, and to circle no if the words do not rhyme.

An answer sheet as shown below can be made

```
Name _____
Please circle correct answer.

1. yes  no      6. yes  no
2. yes  no      7. yes  no
3. yes  no      8. yes  no
4. yes  no      9. yes  no
5. yes  no     10. yes  no
```

On the tape, pronounce pairs of words with the same initial consonant sounds and some with different consonant sounds. Ask the child to listen to the two words and then circle D if the words do not begin with the same sound or S if the words do begin with the same sound.

An answer sheet as shown below can be made.

```
Name _____
Please circle correct answer.

1.  S   D        4.  S   D

2.  S.  D        5.  S   D

3.  S   D        6.  S   D
```

The rules for listening will help remind the child certain physical activities must take place if he is to learn by listening. He can easily remember what to do by looking at the pictures.

RULES FOR LISTENING

Hands are still.

Feet are quiet.

Lips are closed.

Eyes are watching.

Ears are listening.

LANGUAGE DEVELOPMENT

Language development comes from language use and imitation. A child's language development starts at birth. The sounds he hears begin the learning process. This continues with the child making sounds. At about 4 or 5 months, the child has mastered the babble stage and here he begins to imitate the sounds he hears. By the time the child is 1 year old, he is producing sounds to which speakers of his language attach meaning. For example: "Ma-ma" and "Da-da."

By the time the child reaches 2, he will have added words that represent things he sees and things that he sees being done. He later begins to put words together into phrases. By the time the child reaches Kindergarten, he should be able to speak in sentences.

Growth in vocabulary — Findings from an early study, done by Madorah Smith, have been widely used. She found the vocabulary to consist of:
- Age 3 — 896 words
- Age 4 — 1540 words
- Age 5 — 2072 words
- Age 6 — 2562 words [44]

The Templin Study provides a sequence in the child's ability to pronounce the consonant sounds:
- Age 3: m, n, ng, p, f, h, w
- 3.5: y
- Age 4: k, b, d, g, r
- 4.5: s, sh, ch
- Age 6: t, th, v, l
- Age 7: z, zh, j [45]

Language Competence
A. If possible, a 5 minute taped interview with each child, asking a number of simple questions.
   Note: Absence of particular parts of speech
   Repetition of certain words
   Misuse of certain words
   Juxtaposition of words (i.e., Adjective after noun, etc.)
B. Say: "I am going to read some words. From each group of words, there is one missing. I want you to help me think of what word might fit with the words I read."
   1. The _____ has a new toy (get response, then put in alternative such as boy, girl)
   Say: "I think a lot of different words might fit in here, but all I needed was one. Let's try some more." (If necessary, tell child where in the sentence the word is supposed to go.)
   2. Mother wrote on a _____.
   3. Please, raise your _____ before you speak.
   4. You need _____ nails to pound into the boards.
   5. The ball is _____.
   6. Albert is a _____ boy.
C. Say: "I want to see how many words you can tell me. Please say out loud all the words you know. I am going to count them, and for every 10 you say I will give you a gold star." Make sure the child understands. Allow 2 minutes to complete the task.
   Try to make the atmosphere as relaxed and normal as possible.

Language Experience Stories
The following steps may be helpful in guiding the child toward creating his own stories:
1. The teacher may start a conversation with a particular child and state that she would like to work with him.
2. Provide paper, pencils and crayons, pictionary or other materials.
3. Topics for the story would be discussed and the particular subject would be decided on. (The sample stories that follow are on a unit on American Heritage. Other subjects could be follow-up stories on field trips, stories about family, etc.)
4. The teacher will talk about the topic with the child.
5. The child will then talk about the topic.
6. The child should be close to the teacher so he can see her form the letters, words, and sentences.
7. The child should be allowed to state a complete sentence and the teacher should write the sentence in the child's own words.
8. The teacher should say each word and each sentence. Limit the number of sentences to three or four.
9. Let the child read the story as you assist him.
10. Ask questions about the words and the story.
11. Talk about specific words, let the child illustrate his story and let him read it to the class.
12. Help him make up a title for the story.
13. Read the story the following day and encourage the child to do so.
14. The stories may be kept together and bound into a book.

Sample Stories

George Washington

Washington was our first President. He cut down the cherry tree but he told his daddy. He was a true and honest man.

Washington was our first President. His home was Mount Vernon. He was a patriot in the war for independence against England.

Our Flag

June 14 is the birthday of the flag. There were thirteen stars and thirteen stripes on our first flag because there were thirteen states. Washington helped to plan it and Betsy Ross made the first flag. We now have fifty stars because there are fifty states. The stars are white on a field of blue and the stripes are red and white.

Indians.

Indians used buffalo for food and skins. They lived in pueblos and tepees. The Indians taught Americans how to plant corn and pumpkins in their gardens.

Functional Area: Language

Purpose: The child's use of words will be enhanced as he tells the teacher his stories about American Heritage and she writes them down.

Functional Area:

Purpose:

Lincoln

Lincoln lived in a log cabin. He was our President in 1864. This was during the Civil War. He was assasinated.

Indians

Indians used buffalo for food and skins. They lived in pueblos and tepees. The Indians taught Americans how to plant corn and pumpkins in their gardens.[46]

TRADITIONAL STORIES

Traditional stories that help the children develop their language will follow.

Acting out these stories can enhance the childrens enjoyment and understanding of them. Some of the props needed for "acting out" can be found in the classroom. Others have to be made. For patterns for making props please see pages 95 thru 100.

THE ELEPHANT WITH THE BIG ROAR

There was an elephant named Mike, as noisy as could be. He roared and bellowed and shouted. "No one's as loud as me! And all the animals ran off whenever Mike came by because he roared so loudly. And then he'd wonder why.

"There's no one I can play with," said the elephant one day. "I guess I'll always be alone, because they're scared away." And then he raised his head and roared. "Hey! where is everyone?" But no one answered him at all, when all his roars were done.

Big Mike was very sad indeed. It wasn't fun at all to be alone and never play, or hear a friend's voice call. But one day as he jogged along, he heard a sudden cry. "Help! Help! Please save me! Please save me!" And big Mike ran there to try.

There, smack in the middle of a deep old jungle pond, a log was floating by. And a mouse was hanging on. Big Mike jumped in, waded out and pushed the log ashore. "There, fellow, you're okay," said Mike. And then he gave a roar.

The mouse took off without a backward look. "Now that just wasn't nice of him, after all the work it took! I guess I'll never have a friend, no matter how I try." And then that great big elephant sat down and had a cry.

Much later he heard music, and birds began to sing. And all the animals around came up and formed a ring. There were leopards and striped tigers, and monkeys everywhere. And rabbits and gay chipmunks and apes with long hair. But none of them were frightened now. They danced with glee. And right in front, the little mouse as bold as he could be. They all had drums and whistles to make an orchestra. "What's this?" roared Mike the elephant, not believing what he saw.

"Well," began the little mouse, "you see we've not departed. We know by now you're not so fierce, but really gentle-hearted. I am such a little thing. But you saved my life today. And from now on, big elephant, you can't scare us away."

"Well, bless my soul!" said Mike. "I really meant no harm. It's just because I am so big my voice does cause alarm. But from now on, I'll change it. I think I'll join the band." And then the great big elephant got to his feet to stand.

He raised his trunk to trumpet, and all soft notes came through. "Hurrah!" cried all his brand-new friends, "Now we can play with you!"

The elephant was happy. He'd never roar again. He'd learned — to think of others is the way to make a friend.

Functional Area: Social

Purpose: The child will learn how to get along with others as he identifies with the characters in the story. Having a pleasant voice and helping others are reinforced.

Functional Area:

Purpose:

THE BIG, BIG, TURNIP

A farmer once planted a turnip seed. And it grew, and it grew, and it grew. The farmer saw it was time to pull the turnip out of the ground. So he took hold of it and began to pull.

    He pulled and he pulled and he pulled and he pulled
    But the turnip wouldn't come up.

So the farmer called to his wife who was getting dinner.

    Fe, fi, fo, fum, I pulled the turnip, But it wouldn't come up.

And the wife came running and she took hold of the farmer, and they pulled and they pulled and they pulled and they pulled. But the turnip wouldn't come up. So the wife called to the daughter who was feeding the chickens nearby.

    Fe, fi, fo, fum, We pulled the turnip, But it wouldn't come up.
    And the daughter came running. The daughter took hold of the wife.
    The wife took hold of the farmer. The farmer took hold of the turnip.
    And they pulled and they pulled and they pulled.
    But the turnip wouldn't come up.

So the daughter called to the dog who was chewing a bone.

    Fe, fi, fo, fum, We pulled the turnip, But it wouldn't come up.
    And the dog came running. The dog took hold of the daughter. The daughter took hold of the wife. The wife took hold of the farmer. And the farmer took hold of the turnip. And they pulled and they pulled and they pulled.
    But the turnip wouldn't come up.

So the dog called to the cat who was chasing her tail.

    Fe, fi, fo, fum, We pulled the turnip, But it wouldn't come up.
    And the cat came running. The cat took hold of the dog. The dog took hold of the daughter. The daughter took hold of the wife. The wife took hold of the farmer. The farmer took hold of the turnip. And they pulled and they pulled and they pulled and they pulled.
    But the turnip wouldn't come up.

So the cat called the mouse who was nibbling spinach nearby.

    Fe, fi, fo, fum, We pulled the turnip, But it wouldn't come up.

And the mouse came running.

"That little mouse can't help," said the dog. "He's too little."

"Phooey," squeaked the mouse. "I could pull that turnip up myself, but since you have all been pulling I'll let you help too."

So the mouse took hold of the cat. The cat took hold of the dog. The dog took hold of the daughter. The daughter took hold of the wife. The wife took hold of the farmer. The farmer took hold of the turnip. And they pulled and they pulled and they pulled and they pulled, and UP came the turnip.

And the mouse squeaked, "I told you so!"

Functional Area: Language

Purpose: The child will learn the sequence of the story and be able to follow along easily, thus developing language skills.

Functional Area:

Purpose:

THE MYSTERIOUS SOUP

Once upon a time there was a very old lady who lived in a little house near the beach. She would sit in her house and knit with her cat, Fluffy, and her dog, Snoopy, near her. She would look out of her window at the beach that was to one side of her house. One morning as she sat knitting with Fluffy and Snoopy she heard a ring at the door.

The old lady opened the door and a man stood there. He said, "Will you give me something to eat?"

The lady said, "I would be happy to if you will be kind enough to dig some vegetables in the garden."

The man frowned and said, "I didn't ask for work, I asked for food," and he walked away.

This made the lady feel bad, because she was too old to dig many vegetables. So she sat down to knit again.

Now the man was very hungry and he made up his mind he would think of a way to get some food. He went back to the door and knocked. When the lady came to the door, he said, "Would you like to know how to make a delicious soup out of stone?"

The woman just couldn't believe it. "That's impossible," she said, "how could anyone make soup out of a rock?"

So the man asked her to put some water in a pot and he would go find a stone. They put the pot on and he put a clean rock in it. They waited until the water started to boil, and then the man said, "The soup is coming along fine, but if there were an onion in it, that would give it a better flavor."

The lady said, "That sounds fine. Why don't you dig one out of the garden?"

So the old man hurried out to the garden and dug up an onion, and they put the onion in the pot.

Then the man said, "The soup is coming along fine, but if there were a carrot in it, that would give it a better flavor." And the old woman said, "that sounds fine! Why don't you dig one out of the garden?"

So the old man hurried out to the garden and dug up a carrot and they put it in the pot.

Soon the man said, "The soup is coming along fine, but if there were a potato in it, that would give it a better flavor." And the old woman said, "That sounds fine! Why don't you dig one out of the garden?"

So the old man hurried out to the garden and dug up a potato and they put it in the pot.

Then the man said, "The soup is coming along fine, but if there were a tomato, some stringbeans and turnips in it, that would give it a better flavor." And the woman said, "That sounds fine! Why don't you get some out of the garden?"

And the old man hurried out to the garden and dug up a tomato, some stringbeans and turnips and they put them in the pot.

Finally the soup was done and the man said, "I think I'll take the rock out now."

The woman was so pleased, she set the table with her nicest dishes. They both were so happy as they sat down to eat the soup, because they both got what they wanted. The man got some food and the lady got her vegetables dug up in the garden. The lady thought, "What a mystery it is how this man can make soup from a rock!" And the man thought, "How lucky I am to get some food without working!"

Functional Area: Health (food recognition)

Purpose: The various vegetables found in the garden will be recognized by the child as he acts out the story. (Plastic vegetables, pictures of vegetables or the real vegetable may be used. The characters may be acted out by the children.)

Functional Area:

Purpose:

THE BEAR HUNT

Take a seated position in front of the audience so they can all see you. Narrate the following:

Would you like to go on a bear hunt? O.K., let's go! Watch me and do all the things I do and repeat after me all the things I say. Here we go! We're going on a bear hunt, every body march. (Make a marching sound by slapping your knees with your hands, alternating.)

I see a river — a great big river. We can't go around it. We can't go under it. We can't go over it. I guess we'll have to swim it. (Pretend to swim by rotating your arms. Then resume marching.)

I see a tree — a great big tree. We can't go around it. We can't go under it. We can't go over it. I guess we'll have to climb it. (Pretend to climb, using just your arms. When you reach the top, look around, shading your eyes. Climb down and resume marching.)

I see a wheat field — a great big wheat field. We can't go around it. We can't go under it. We can't go over it. I guess we'll have to go through it. (Make the sound of walking through wheat by rubbing your hands. Resume marching.)

I see a cave — a great big cave. We can't go around it. We can't go under it. We can't go over it. I guess we'll have to go in it. (Feel in front of you as though in the dark.) It sure is dark in here. I feel something. (Go through the motions.) It's big. It's fuzzy. I think it's a bear. It is a bear! Let's get out of here fast.

(At this point, retrace all the motions hurriedly. Of course, you'll get through first.) I beat you home. And now you've been on a bear hunt.

Functional Area: Cognitive (pre-reading skill: sequence)

Purpose: The child learns to recall the sequence of the story as he participates in acting out the motions.

Functional Area:

Purpose:

THE PUMPKIN MAN

Materials Needed: Flannel Board
    Parts of Man: Shoes, legs, stomach, shoulders, arms, hands, head (Jack-O-Lantern)

STORY:
There was an old, old lady who lived all alone in the woods, and she wanted someone to come and visit her. While she waited, she spun cloth —

Children: "And still she sat (Hands folded)
          And still she spun (Hands roll)
          And still she waited for someone to come."

Then one dark, dark night when the old lady was sitting spinning, she heard a sound at the door and she said, "Come in." Then s-q-u-e-a-k went the door and in came two big shoes and set themselves down. She thought,
    Oh, how strange to see those big shoes on the cold, cold floor
    But still she —

Soon she heard another sound outside and she said, "Come in." Then s-q-u-e-a-k went the door, and in came two short, short legs and sat themselves down on the big, big shoes on the cold, cold floor. She thought,
    Oh, how strange to see those short, short legs
    In those big, big shoes
    On that cold, cold floor
    But still she —

Before very long she heard another sound outside and she said, "Come in." Then s-q-u-e-a-k went the door, and in came a fat, fat stomach and sat on those short, short legs. And she thought,
    Oh, how strange to see that fat, fat stomach on the short, short legs on those big, big shoes on the cold, cold floor.
    But still she —

And while she was looking she heard another knock and said, "Come in." Then s-q-u-e-a-k went the door and in flew two broad, broad shoulders and sat themselves down on the fat, fat stomach. And the old woman thought,
    Oh, how strange to see those broad, broad shoulders
    On the fat, fat stomach
    On the short, short legs

In those big, big shoes
On that cold, cold floor
But still she —

And as she was spinning she heard another sound so she said, "Come in." Then s-q-u-e-a-k went the door and in jumped two long, long arms and hung themselves onto the broad, broad shoulders and she thought,
Oh, how strange to see those long, long arms
On the broad, broad shoulders
On that fat, fat stomach
On the short, short legs
In those big, big shoes
On that cold, cold floor
But still she —

And in just a few minutes she heard another sound, so she said, "Come in." In came two fat, fat hands and fastened on to those long, long arms, so she thought,
Oh, how strange to see those fat, fat hands
On those long, long arms
On the broad, broad shoulders
On that fat, fat stomach
On those short, short legs
In those big, big shoes
On that cold, cold floor.
But still she —

And the old woman was beginning to be a little afraid, but when she heard another sound she said, "Come in." And in rolled a round, round head and sat itself down on those broad, broad shoulders, and she thought,
Oh, how strange to see that round, round head
On the broad, broad shoulders
On the long, long arms
On the fat, fat hands
On the fat, fat stomach
On those short, short legs
In those big, big shoes
On that cold, cold floor.

So she said, "Where did you get such big, big feet?"
And someone said, "Much walking, much walking."
And she asked: "Well, where did you get such short, short legs?"
And someone said, "Much running, much running."
Then she asked, "Where did you get such broad, broad shoulders?"
And someone said, "Carrying brooms, carrying brooms."
Then she asked, "Where did you get such long, long arms?"
And someone said, "Swinging an axe, swinging an axe."
And she asked, "Where did you get such fat, fat hands?"
And someone said, "Threshing wheat, threshing wheat."
Then she said, "Well, where did you get such a round, round head?"
And someone said, "A pumpkin shell, a pumpkin shell."
Then she asked, "Well, what did you come for?
And someone said, "Y–O–U!!!"

And that is the story of the man with the
Round, round head, and the fat, fat hands
On those long, long arms,
On those broad, broad shoulders,
On that fat, fat stomach,
On the short, short legs,
In those big, big shoes
On that cold, cold floor![47]

Functional Area: Self Concept

Purpose: The child will recognize body parts thus helping him associate his body part with the Pumpkin Man's.

Functional Area:

Purpose:

The following patterns may be colored, covered with clear contact paper and cut out. With a small piece of sandpaper glued to the back, they will stick to a flannel board.

The Elephant with the Big Roar
(Prop Pattern)

Paste the following patterns onto tag board. Cut and color.

95

The Elephant with the Big Roar (con't)

The Big Big Turnip

The Big Big Turnip (con't)

The Big Big Turnip (con't)

99

The Pumpkin Man

legs (cut out two)

fat fat stomach

shoes (cut two)

100

From THE HANDBOOK OF LEARNING ACTIVITIES FOR YOUNG CHILDREN. Copyright 1980 by Humanics Limited, Jane A. Caballero.

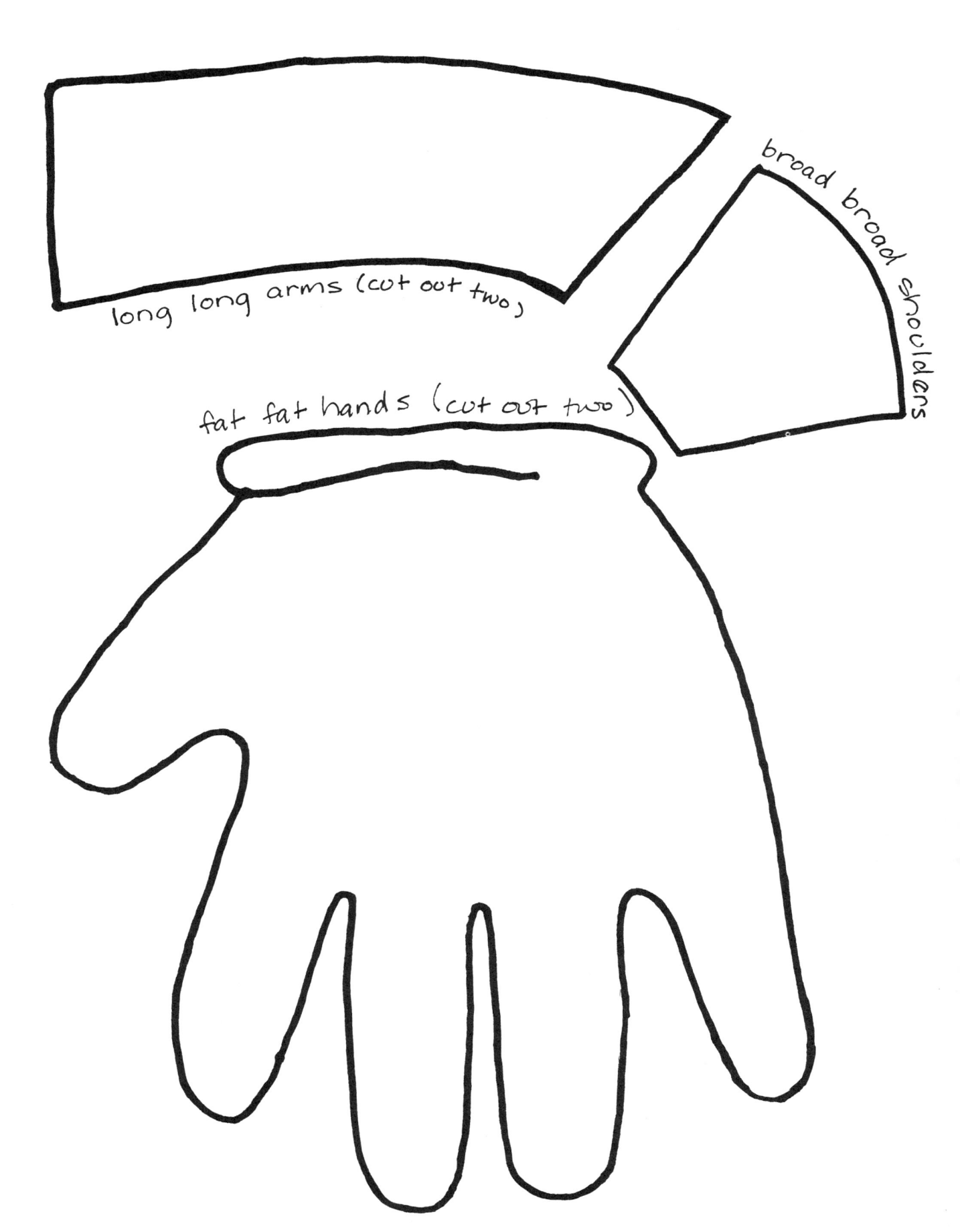

long long arms (cut out two)

broad broad shoulders

fat fat hands (cut out two)

The Pumpkin Man
(con't)

chapter 10
pre-reading

Pre-reading or reading readiness is an important part of any reading program. No formal reading should be attempted until this area has been fully covered. Pre-reading is usually started in Nursery School; therefore, the kindergarten teacher should be fully trained and well aware of the skills and procedures involved.

The objectives of Pre-reading are as follows:
1. To lay a good foundation for formal reading
2. To introduce reading as a fun subject
3. To create an interest in reading
4. To teach and develop the skills of pre-reading

SKILLS

There are eight pre-reading skills:
   a. Visual perception
   b. Auditory perception
   c. Visual-auditory sequencing and memory
   d. Perceptual motor skills
   e. Listening and speaking vocabularies
   f. Concepts
   g. Readiness for books
   h. Names of letters

a. **Visual Perception**
Aim: To help children realize the differences in letters and words
   eg: between o and a
                 v and w
                 it and if
                 am and an

Activities:
1. Ask children to cross out the word that is different in each row.

cat	hat	cat	cat
man	man	mat	man
look	look	look	long
ball	bat	ball	ball

2. Ask the children to circle the letter that is like the first one.

m	b	s	y	m
t	t	v	x	l
b	g	b	c	a
g	r	g	d	e
p	sp	y	p	q

The similarity between certain letters and words may be very confusing to some children and teachers will find that the teaching of this skill must continue even when the child can read some books.

b. Auditory Perception
Aim: To help children to differentiate between various sounds and to associate certain symbols with sounds
   eg.   between d and b
         got and goat

Activities:
1. Let children listen for sounds in the environment eg: bird — car horn
2. Let children realize the different pitches of sound eg: loud — soft
3. Teach children about rhyming words

c. Visual-Auditory Sequencing and Memory
Aims: a) To get children to realize that there is a certain sequence in which letters appear in a word
       b) To help children realize that not all letter sequences make words

Activities:
1. Let children reproduce sounds in a certain order.
2. Give verbal directions for them to carry out.
3. They should learn to repeat addresses, phone numbers and birthdays.

d. Perceptual Motor Skills
Aims: a) To get children's eyes to follow a line of symbols and make the return sweep to the next line of symbols
       b) To improve coordination skills in writing and tracing

Activities:
1. Let children trace letters.
2. Let children copy letters.
3. Let children complete a shape such as incomplete square.
4. Let children connect dots.
5. Let children practice turning pages of books.

e. Listening and Speaking Vocabularies
Aims: a) To develop adequate listening and speaking vocabularies to help them understand words and sentence structure
       b) To help children understand the meaning of words

Activities:
1. Encourage children to be attentive.
2. Give them directions to follow.
3. Let them express their thoughts in sentences.
4. Let them tell about personal experiences.
5. Encourage good enunciation.
6. Let them tell stories from pictures.
7. Let them name common objects.
8. Play games such as "Simon Says."
9. Read stories to them.
10. Use simple riddles.
11. Use the telephone.
12. Let each child add a sentence to an unfinished story.

f. Concept Development
Aims: a) To help children to form mental images of various words
       b) To increase his experiences

Activities:
1. Naming common objects in the classroom, home, and neighborhood.
2. Learning the names of colors.
3. Describing objects.
4. Increasing his experiences with short walks or trips.
5. Teaching the meanings of up, down, over, under, before, etc.
6. Teaching about the weather.
7. Teaching some nursery rhymes.
8. Teaching the days and months.

Test:
1. Give a ball to each child and ask him to follow the directions.
   a) Make the ball go up.
   b) Make the ball go down.
   c) Put the ball on the table.
   d) Hold the ball in your hand.
   e) Put the ball under the table.

2. Direct the children to label one ball *big* and one ball *little*.

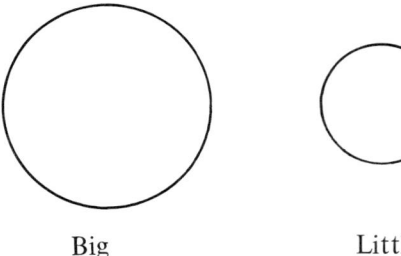

   ◯   ◯

   Big   Little

g. Readiness for Books
   Aims: a) To teach the front and backs of books
          b) To teach that words are written from top to bottom and from left to right
          c) To teach that pages are numbered in order
          d) To teach that words represent talk written down
          e) To teach children to take care of books

Activities:
1. Let the children look at pictures in books.
2. Show the front and the back of a book.
3. Teach the children how to hold the book properly.
4. Have each child make a book called "All About Me."
5. Use a calendar to show and name the days.
6. Let children practice writing their own names.

h. Names of Letters
   Aims: a) To teach the names of letters individually and in order
          b) To teach the upper and lower case letters

Activities:
   Make alphabet cards

Test:
1. Direct children to circle all the "b's"
   ball   bone   rib   rubber
   bat   bite   comb   baby
2. Direct the children to circle all the letters in their name.
   a b c d e f g h i j k l m n o p q r s t u v w x y z[48]

Name _____

ball   rib
bat   comb
bone   rubber
bite   baby

105

WORDS

The following lists of words may be helpful in making many of the activities suggested in this book.

Synonyms

find	—	locate	over	—	above
hot	—	warm	fast	—	rapid
all	—	everything	before	—	ahead
happy	—	glad	begin	—	start
big	—	large	far	—	distant
new	—	recent	let	—	allow
can	—	able	old	—	ancient
dish	—	plate	now	—	immediately
drink	—	beverage	find	—	locate
tiny	—	small	buy	—	purchase
laugh	—	giggle	came	—	arrived
cry	—	weep	close	—	shut
neat	—	tidy	speak	—	talk
finish	—	end			

Homonyms

bear	—	bare	red	—	read
here	—	hear	right	—	write
night	—	knight	ate	—	eight
blue	—	blew	you	—	ewe
be	—	bee	pale	—	pail
tail	—	tale	sale	—	sail
no	—	know	mail	—	male
buy	—	by — bye	meet	—	meat
to	—	two — too	him	—	hymn
for	—	four	break	—	brake
stare	—	stair	son	—	sun
wear	—	ware	deer	—	dear
some	—	sum	see	—	sea

Antonyms

behind	—	ahead	glad	—	sad
up	—	down	open	—	shut
bottom	—	top	hot	—	cold
boy	—	girl	laugh	—	cry
light	—	dark	buy	—	sell
go	—	stay	clean	—	dirty
full	—	empty	big	—	little
all	—	none	after	—	before
take	—	give	awake	—	asleep
play	—	work	found	—	lost
now	—	later	over	—	under
long	—	short	best	—	worst
in	—	out	always	—	never

Rhyming Words

sand	—	band	flower	—	shower
cat	—	hat	free	—	bee
most	—	host	bump	—	jump
year	—	hear	run	—	fun
horn	—	torn	park	—	dark
chair	—	pear	shells	—	bells
pain	—	chain	funny	—	bunny
fan	—	pan	car	—	star
reach	—	peach	cake	—	rake
house	—	mouse	top	—	mop
train	—	rain	sand	—	band
rub	—	tub	boat	—	coat
cook	—	book	tall	—	ball
sun	—	run	light	—	night
round	—	sound	purse	—	nurse
sit	—	fit	paste	—	taste
duck	—	truck	coast	—	toast

Compound Words

salesman	something	flagpole
toothbrush	anyway	snowman
herself	airport	blowout
football	himself	baseball
dollhouse	sandbox	whenever
into	upon	airplane
himself	without	anyone
outside	doorway	anything
somebody	inside	

Word Families Or Spelling Patterns

- an	- am	- it	- ill	- et	- ing
man	dam	bit	Bill	bet	sing
can	ham	fit	dill	get	ring
Dan	jam	hit	fill	jet	ding
fan	ram	pit	hill	let	king
man	Sam	sit	kill	met	ping
pan	yam	wit	mill	net	wing

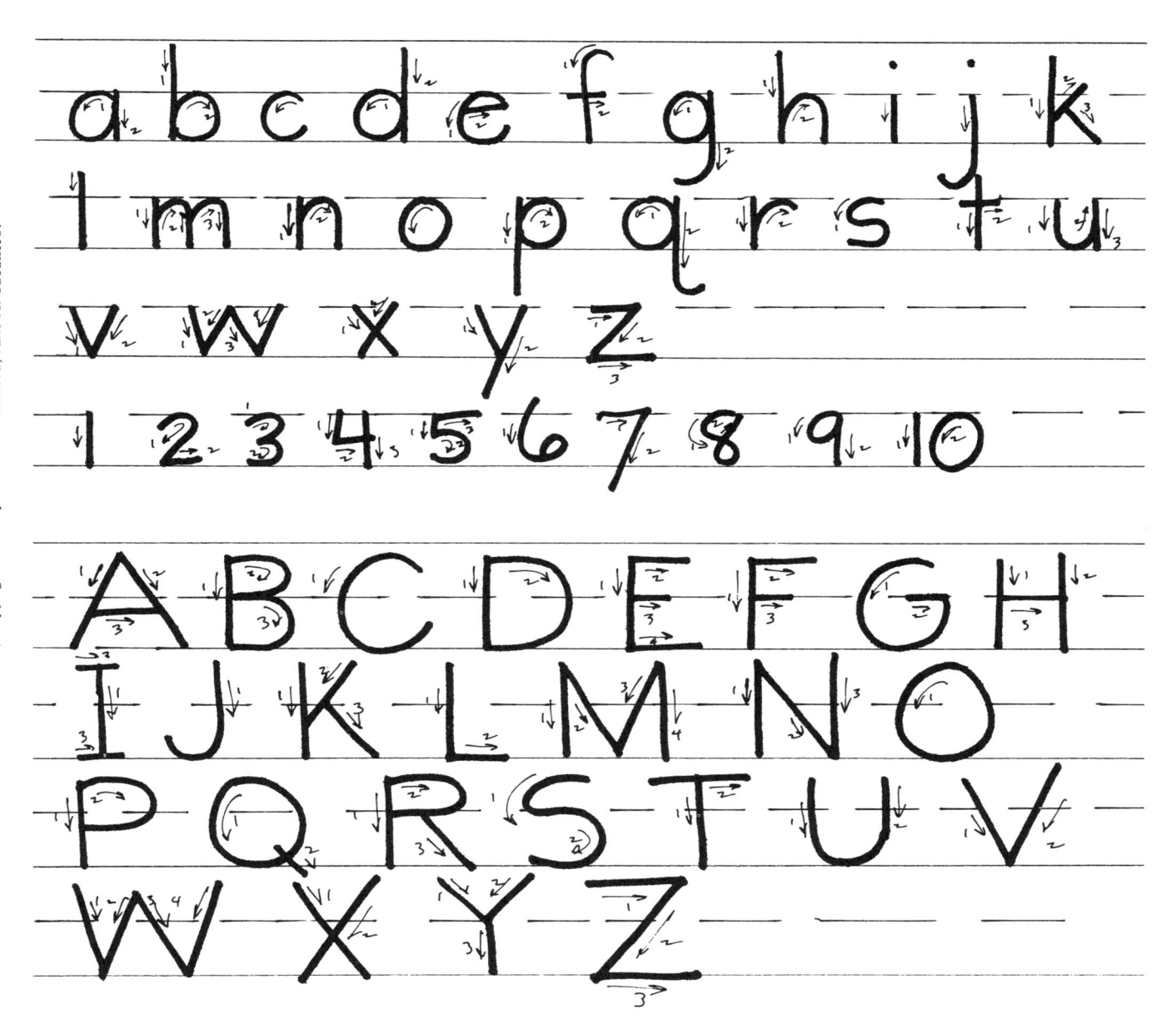

Functional Area: Cognitive

Purpose: Letter recognition will be encouraged as the child practices the letters correctly. (Good examples to follow are necessary as he begins developing his writing skills. The top and base lines may be reinforced with a colored pen to help the child see them so he can better coordinate his muscles. The child needs to learn muscle control by practicing the basic strokes before he proceeds with letter writing. He should practice similar letters together so reinforcement of the strokes is accomplished.)[49]

Functional Area:

Purpose:

107

Labeling

Functional Area: Language

Purpose: Labels on objects in the room will help the child develop extra vocabulary words.

Functional Area:

Purpose:

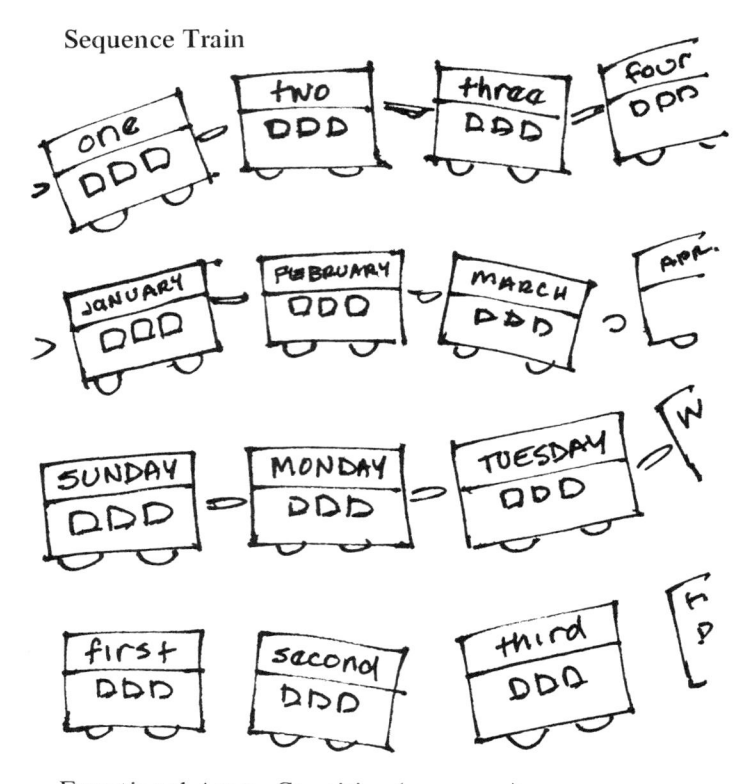

Sequence Train

Functional Area: Cognitive (sequence)

Purpose: The engine contains the initial word and the child places the following cars in sequential order. The correct number is on the back of the cars to make it self-correcting. Sequencing of days, months and word numbers cars may be added.

Functional Area:

Purpose:

Beginning Letter Game

Read the phrase outloud and tell which letter the words begin with. Younger children should have the words read to them and then asked which letter the words begin with. The beginning letter should be on the back of the card so the game can be self-correcting. The set should contain 26 alphabet cards.

seven silly seals

big blue berries

an adorable aunt

Functional Area: Language

Purpose: Initial letter sounds will be reinforced as the child plays the game.

Functional Area:

Purpose:

Stand-Up Word Game

The students will be given a letter. The teacher or other students will call upon some of the letters to stand. A word will be made as the letters line up.

Functional Area: Cognitive

Purpose: The child will learn to spell various words.

Functional Area:

Purpose:

Letter Blend Game

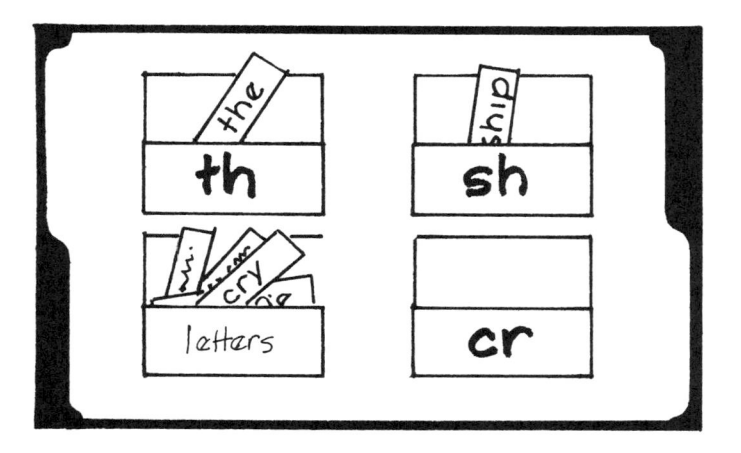

Functional Area: Cognitive

Purpose: Children will think of words with various blends and write them on cards. Then they can place the cards into the appropriate pockets.

Functional Area:

Purpose:

Word Family Game

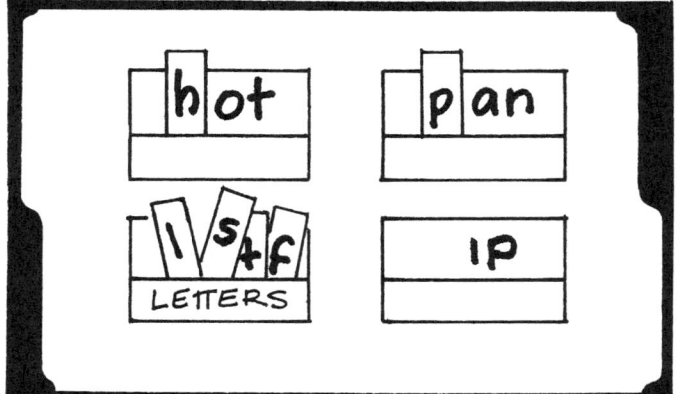

Functional Area: Cognitive

Purpose: The child will discover new words as he plays with the word family chart.

Functional Area:

Purpose:

Mailbox

Functional Area: Creative (basic art skills)

Purpose: The child can learn the colors of the mailbox, develop, cut and paste skills and learn the shape of the mailbox when he makes this small mailbox. (Patterns may be distributed, if the children are very young.)[50]

Functional Area:

Purpose:

Initial Letter Sound Game

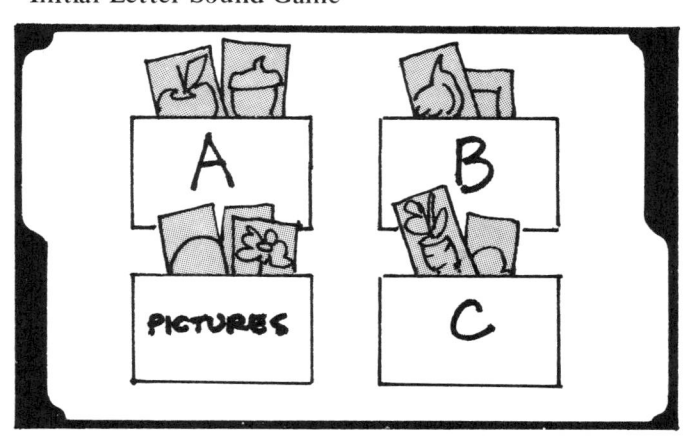

Functional Area: Individual strength

Purpose: The child has extra reinforcement of the initial sounds ABCD as he plays the game. He looks at the picture and decides what letter the picture begins with. He puts it in the envelope denoting that sound and can turn the card over for a self correcting activity.

Functional Area:

Purpose:

Visual Discrimination Game

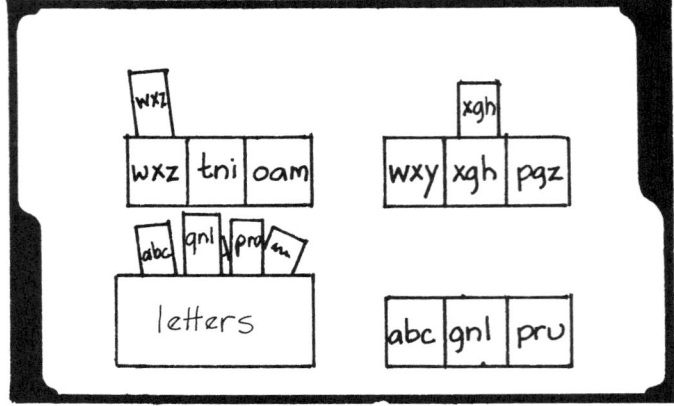

Functional Area: Physical (visual discrimination)

Purpose: The child has practice in visual discrimination as he places the cards in their corresponding envelope (A red line at the bottom of the card and envelope assist the child in directionality. Substitute symbols, letters, words, etc. on the cards.)

Functional Area:

Purpose:

Upper and Lower Case Match Game

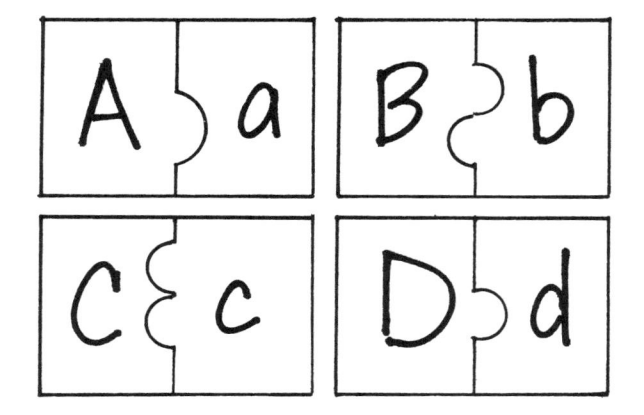

Functional Area: Physical

Purpose: The child matches the card with the upper case letter to the card with the lower case letter. The cards may be color coded for the initial step, then they may be changed to all one color. The manipulative skills are enhanced as he places the puzzles together. (Words can be written on the card; then it may be cut in half to make the game more difficult.)[51]

Functional Area:

Purpose:

Word Family Game

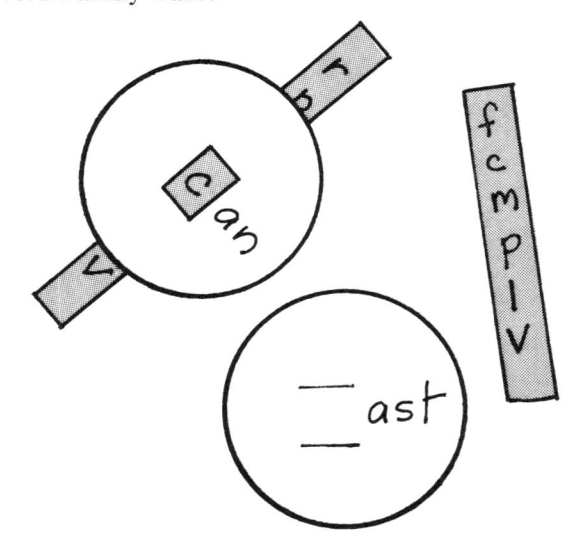

Functional Area: Cognitive

Purpose: As the child slowly pulls the strip through the ball, he sees various words that are formed thus reinforcing the word family concept. (Various math combinations that total the same sum or difference may be substituted.)

Functional Area:

Purpose:

Writing Letters

Functional Area: Physical

Purpose: Writing letters to his friends (with teacher assistance) will help the child develop writing skills. (They may be mailed in a class mailbox made out of a coke carton with 24 dividers)

Functional Area:

Purpose:

Addressing Envelopes

Functional Area: Cognitive

Purpose: The child can learn how to address envelopes and learn the different costs of postage as introduced by the teacher. (A visit to the post office will reinforce this and the postman may stamp the envelopes for the children to see.)

Functional Area:

Purpose:

Rules for Reading

Functional Area: Cognitive

Purpose: The rules for reading chart will help the child take pride in his books by learning that they are valuable and must be cared for so they will last.[52]

Functional Area:

Purpose:

Opposite Games

Functional Area: Physical

Purpose: Figure ground discrimination is reinforced as the child locates and crosses the strings. (The child reads a word and locates its opposite. The string is wrapped around the brad.)[53]

Functional Area:

Purpose:

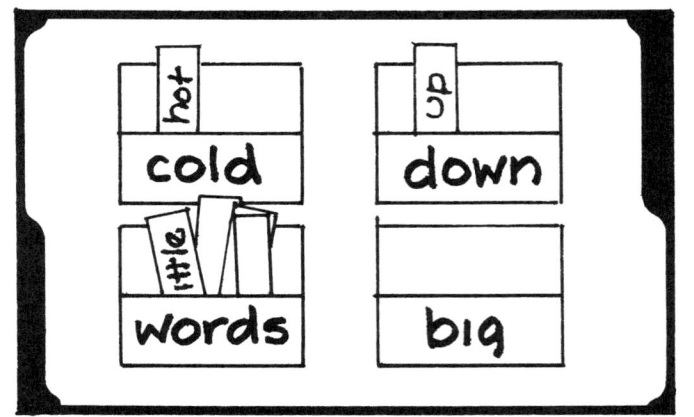

Functional Area: Cognitive

Purpose: The child can develop the opposite concept as he plays the game with his teacher.

Functional Area:

Purpose:

Rhyming Games

Functional Area: Cognitive

Purpose: The child says the word on the window and then thinks of its opposite. The antonymn of the word is stated and the window is opened for the child to see if he was correct. (The teacher may say the word to the child if necessary.)

Functional Area:

Purpose:

Functional Area: Cognitive (rhyming words)

Purpose: As the child says a word by looking at the printed word or the picture he locates another word that rhymes with it. He can place the words in the envelopes to keep them in order. (Symbols on the back of the cards make the game self correcting.) (Extend vocabulary to meet child's level.)

Functional Area:

Purpose:

W	O	R	D -	O
go	by	it	jump	let
hot	do	fun	hit	but
at	all	if	big	to
blue	a	an	in	for
I	is	be	black	let

Functional Area: Cognitive (reading)

Purpose: The child will reinforce his recognition of sight words. (The game is played similar to Bingo. Cards with basic words can be made and any number of children can play.)

Functional Area:

Purpose:

Make one Wordo card for each child. Put the words in varying order.

54

chapter II
art

Objectives of art may include:
1. Visual and tactile perception
2. Motor skill development: eye-hand coordination and large and small muscle development
3. Self expression
4. Creativity
5. Awareness of art history
6. Development of a feeling for art-aesthetic judgment

For children, art is not only a form of expressing one's feelings; but also a way of communicating ideas. Most children's art compositions relate to their experiences; how much they have observed and what is important about a particular experience. A young child's work is not an objective representation but an emotional reaction to his environment. Therefore, the teacher can learn a great deal about children through their art. Their artistic development can be easily observed. The teacher may be able to recognize the different developmental levels of the child and thus be able to guide him, individually, toward maximum creative development. Lowenfeld, noted art educator, has identified the stages of artistic development into the following categories. The scribbling stage is from approximately 2-4 years old. The child is only concerned with up and down motion. The color is unimportant. Soon he'll name the scribblings. To adults the names might have no correlation with what is on the paper, but the child sees otherwise. The pre-schematic stage is from the approximate ages 4-6. Creation becomes conscious during this stage. The child controls his scribbles and begins naming them. He may exaggerate important parts in the drawing and use "unreal" color, size and proportion. The schematic stage is from the approximate ages 7-9. Representation with no intentional experiences is exhibited. More realism is apparent. The child discovers that he is part of the environment. The child draws through symbols. The next stage is the gang stage from the ages 9-11. The child finally becomes aware of reality and begins drawing what he sees.[55]

Therefore, the teacher plays a vital role in the child's artistic development and expression. She should

115

understand the stages of development and help children express themselves creatively. She should have an understanding of human growth and development so she can anticipate, understand and cope with the behavior of the child. She should know how to plan individual art activities and use better and clearer terminology.

The value of art activities for the young child lies primarily in the process of creation rather than in the finished product. This sense of accomplishment derived from successful manipulation of art media can help build self-confidence, a feeling of "I did this by myself. I enjoyed doing it. I'm pretty good." This is especially true if the child's creation is valued for itself and not compared to someone else's which might be more "artistic" or representative, or to a model which an adult has in mind. Through experimentation and practice with some guidance, the child learns the possibilities, limits, and a beginning control of the media he uses. These learnings are important in themselves, and also as foundations for later learning.

We must learn to respect children's art work. It has a distinct charm of its own. Children have a difficult time feigning the enjoyment of art, so we must be aware of a child who doesn't enjoy art and evaluate how *we* are presenting it. Remember children are not concerned with using color imitatively as it appears in nature, and they do not draw things the way they look to adults. Therefore, there is no place for stereotypes, mimeographed outlines or coloring books. Every activity should be a creative experience which requires original thinking, planning, and doing. Children should be encouraged to create at their own speed and verbalize about what they are doing.

Remember all children have the potential for creative expression. It is the responsibility of parents and teachers to provide opportunities for this potential to develop as fully as possible. We must provide experiences in working with various drawing media such as pastels, charcoal, crayons, and tempera paints to encourage skill development as well as awareness of color. Children can work with fabrics and fibers learning simple dye and batik techniques, and how to make weavings and collages. Photography can be used to emphasize sequencing and awareness of the surroundings. Cut and paste activities can encourage manipulative skill development and compositions. Children should help construct bulletin boards. This experience will provide them with knowledge about the subject of the board as well as compositional knowledge. Puppet making can encourage creativity and help children to learn to express themselves. Printing techniques such as finger printing, vegetable, sponge and cardboard printing encourage children to discriminate between thick and thin as well as to learn the art of printmaking. Clay can allow for self expression and success. It stirs the imagination and its resistance is challenging. Communication and sociability can be encouraged as children work together. The manipulation of the media encourages creativity. The following list of projects may be adapted to meet your students' needs.

Painting (tempera)
    color wheel, blends, projects: blob, blow (with straws), string, tissue paper

Painting (water color)
    washes, finger prints

Drawing (charcoal, pencil, India ink, pastels, crayons, felt pens)
    lines: expressive, contour & gesture; crayon resist, still life, body completion, face, perspective

Clay (modeling, ceramics)
    pinch, coil, slab techniques, wedging, firing, glazing processes

Printing (finger, leaf, cardboard, linoleum, vegetable)
    vocabulary, techniques

Cut and Paste (shapes, expanding, fastening, cutouts, symmetrical, sculpture)
    murals, mosaic, flowers, paper mache, miscellaneous projects

Puppets (stick, sack, paper mache, plate, sock, fold paper, hand puppet)
    language objectives, puppet stages

Photography (media experience with visuals and equipment)
    family tree, slides, color blend, flip book, frame/mount, opaque/transparent

Visual File (utilizing magazines, personal photographs)
    classification of pictures, collages

Fabric/Fiber (batik, tye dye)
    yarn, material collage, weaving

Bulletin Boards (guidelines, suggestions, flannel boards)
   seasonal, subjects, rules, people, 3-D boxes

Lettering Techniques
   cutting, forming, writing

Art Appreciation (the child should be familiar with an overview of artists, art periods, and special topics which can enhance his awareness of this aspect of art.)

Evaluation of the art program must be carefully considered. Considerations should include:
1. The quality of each pupil's personal artistic expression;
2. The quality of each pupil's reaction to the work of others;
3. The quality of each pupil's behavior as exhibited during his participation in all types of art activities.

The teacher should realize that he will most likely be wrong in his appraisal of the child's patterns of behavior and his ability to produce and appreciate art. The most effective way of developing as a teacher of art is growth through teaching practice. Efficiency of art teaching and the teacher's professional growth go hand in hand. Learning to understand children is made easier through the arts. It provides an excellent means for observing the behavior of children; and because the free creative expressions of children are projections of their personalities, art products offer revealing insights into the more complex factors of the children's organizations. Sometimes we need to examine how we feel about what we saw, or how someone we're trying to draw might feel.

We must remember that the central purpose of the art program is to provide children with a vehicle to wholesome personality development and enriched living. But the deepest educational insight will be achieved only when the subject matter and the technique are developed from the most direct experiences possible.

DRAWING

A line is a mark made by a moving point. Some materials that you can experiment with may include: white drawing paper, oak tag, construction paper, felt tip pens, pen and ink, conte crayon, pencil, chalk, crayon, charcoal, yarn and string.

Sample activities may include:
1. Drawing lines: expressive — play a musical selection and draw any desired subject; texture — close, detailed lines; directional lines — draw 1, 2, or 3 directions to show variety and texture; contour — one continuous line that creates a boundary between a space and its background.
2. Cut out part of a human body from a magazine (one half of the figure may be desirable). Glue it on paper and let the child draw the rest of the person. Body awareness is emphasized.
3. Look at an object, person, or still life. You may want to draw the face of the person or do a gesture drawing. A gesture drawing is a quick drawing of a person showing the action or movement.
4. One and two-point perspective drawings may be introduced.
5. Experiment with crayon resist. Color on a paper with random color — press hard. Paint on top with black tempera, India ink or black crayon. Scratch through with a pointed object. A paper clip may be used if young children are doing the activity.
6. Draw a picture with glue and place yarn or string on top.

Crayon Resist Drawing

The following is an example of crayon resist drawing. The child colors the entire piece of paper with different crayon colors and then covers the paper with a layer of black tempera paint. The paint dries and the child can scratch in a design with any pointed instrument. Young children enjoy this type of activitey because it is a completely different way of drawing.

CRAYON RESIST

Functional Area: Creative

Purpose: The child is free to draw any picture.

Functional Area:

Purpose:

Drawing with Yarn

PAINTING

Color Wheel:
The child learns the concept of primary, secondary and intermediate colors through the creation of the color wheel. Making a color wheel lets the child experiment with color combinations and demonstrates the formation of specific colors through mixing. Vocabulary words including hue, primary color, secondary and intermediate colors, neutral, blend, intensity, warm and cool colors can be introduced to the students.

Tissue Paper Painting
This is yet another method of painting when regular materials are not accessible. The child simply arranges tissue paper pieces on a paper and then applies small amounts of water to soak the pieces, then the tissue paper is lifted off and the coloration remains as a finished product. As in regular painting, colors can be mixed by overlapping and colors may run together to create an interesting effect.

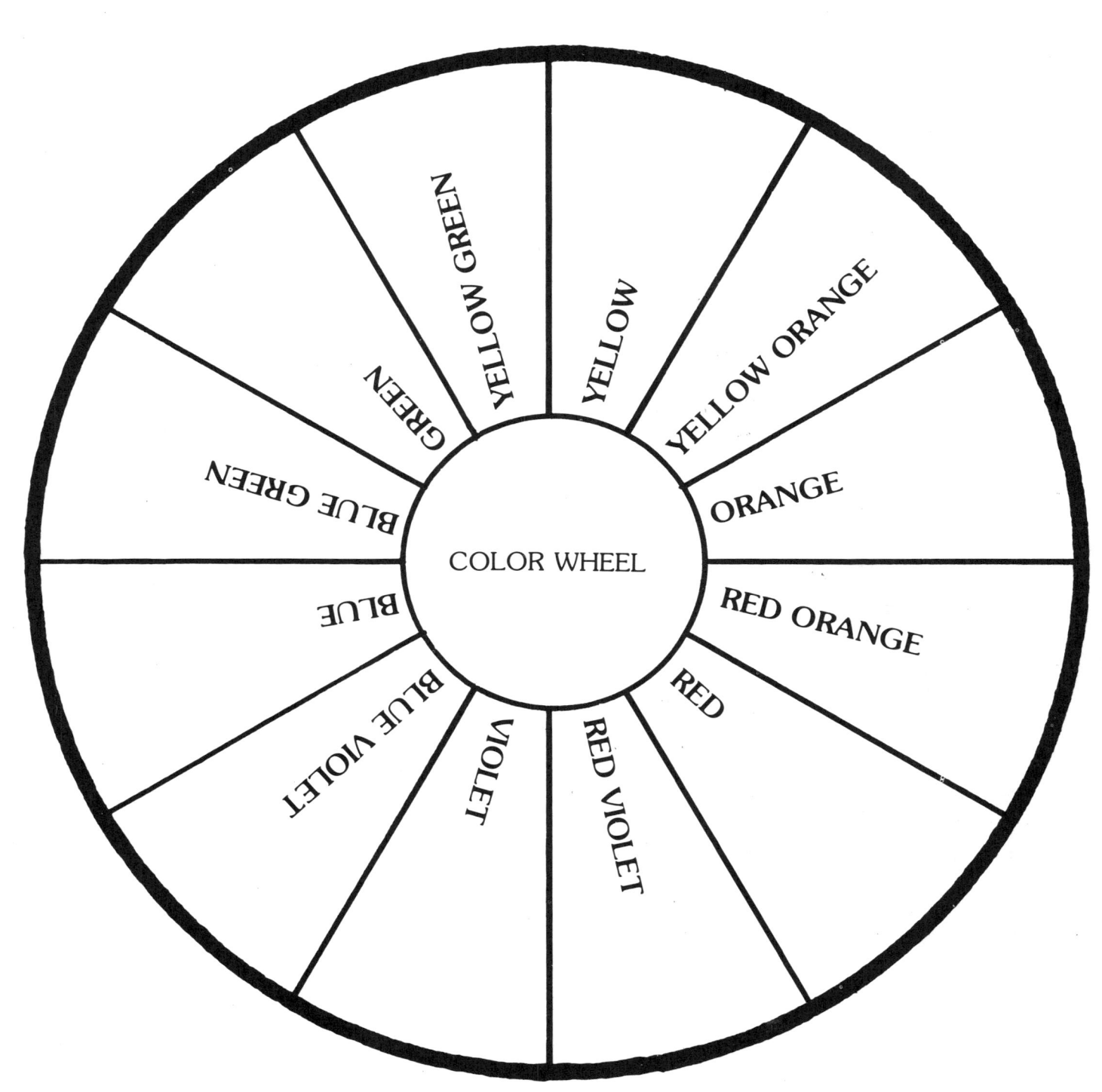

From THE HANDBOOK OF LEARNING ACTIVITIES FOR YOUNG CHILDREN', Copyright 1980 by Humanics Limited, Jane A. Caballero.

COLOR WHEEL

- YELLOW
- YELLOW ORANGE
- ORANGE
- RED ORANGE
- RED
- RED VIOLET
- VIOLET
- BLUE VIOLET
- BLUE
- BLUE GREEN
- GREEN
- YELLOW GREEN

119

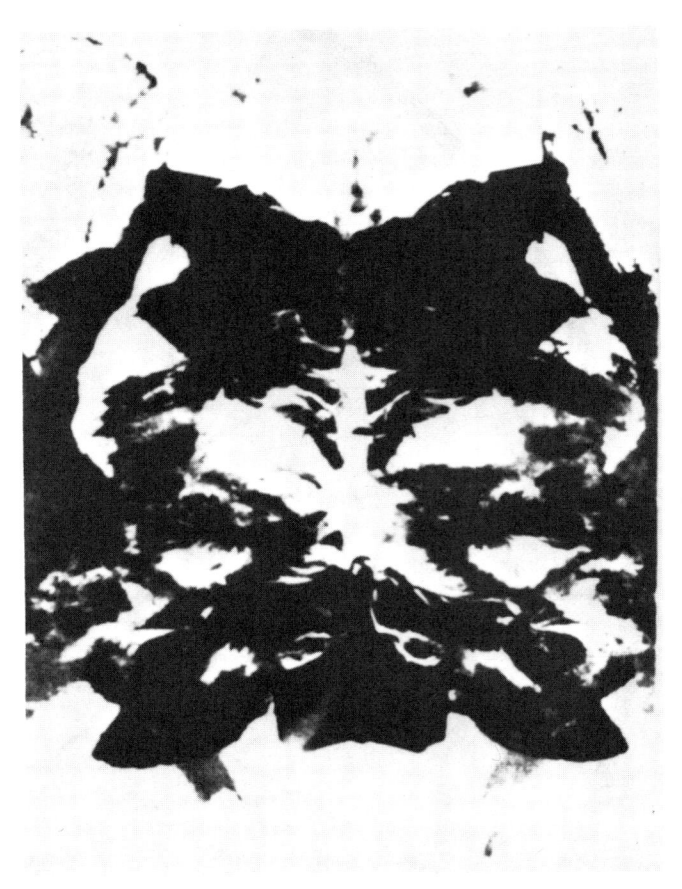

Functional Area: Cognitive (color recognition)

Purpose: The child will learn that various colors can be mixed to form another color. The blue and yellow tissue forms green as the wet tissue blends.

Functional Area:

Purpose:

Straw Blowing Painting

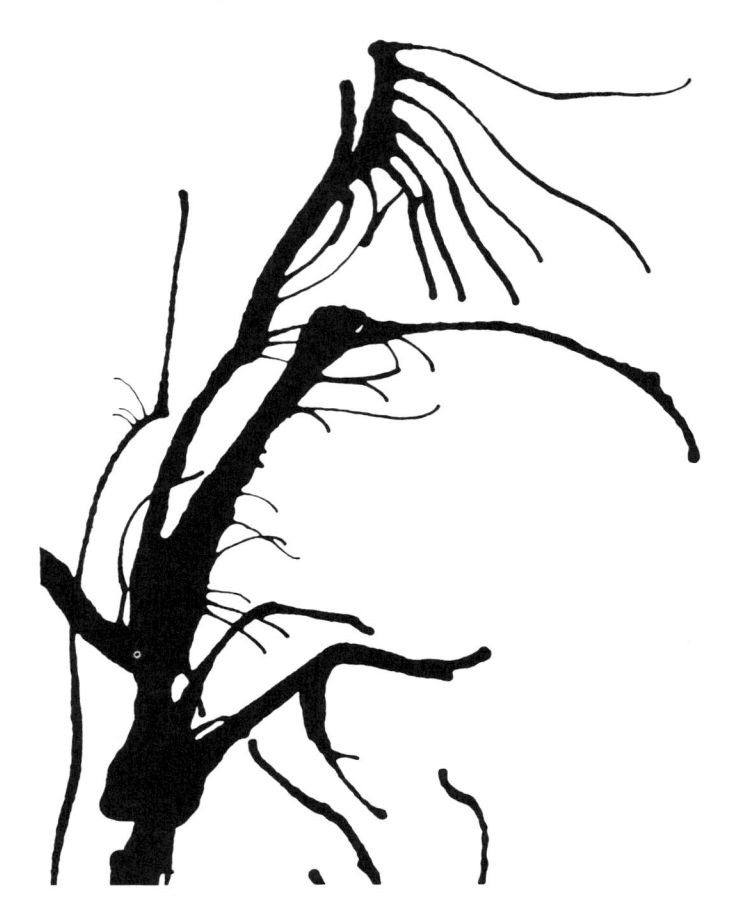

Functional Area: Physical (fine motor)

Purpose: This teaches the child control of his fine muscles as he manipulates the straw. An interesting design is created and thickness and thinness of line is emphasized.

Functional Area:

Purpose:

Blob Painting

Functional Area: Cognitive

Purpose: The child learns the idea of symmetrical balance as he creates the blob painting. (Paint is dropped in the center of the paper and the paper is folded in half.) Two primary colors dropped onto the paper will create a secondary color as the paper is folded.

Functional Area:

Purpose:

CUT AND PASTE

This is the basic beginning of paper work in art. This particular section is good in that it helps to build basic concepts of such things as fold, square, circle and triangle. A child should learn to do these basic things first.

Cutting a Square
Bring side ab of a rectangle to side bc and cut off extra piece below.

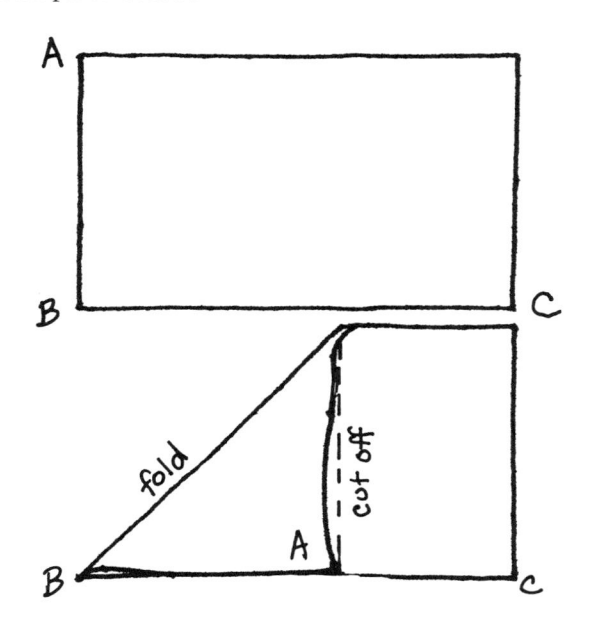

Cutting a Circle
Fold a square in half on the diagonal, forming a triangle. Fold in half again, and then in half again. Using ab as a measure, mark ac, ad and ae and cut a connecting arc.

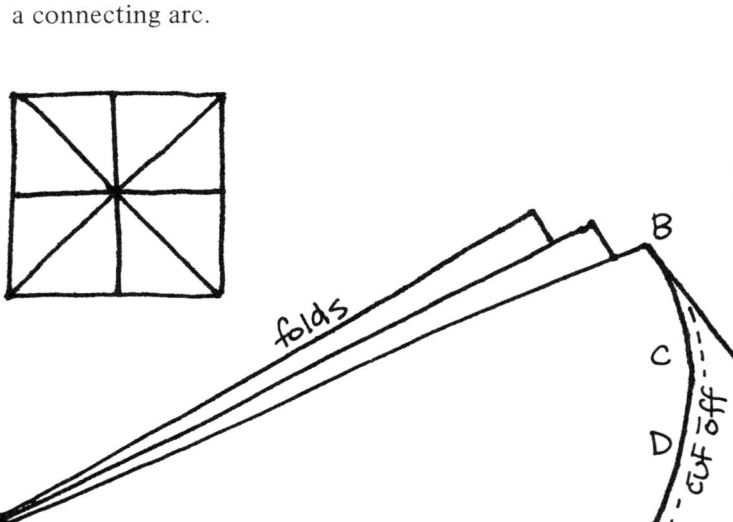

Cutting a Triangle
For an equilateral triangle, fold a rectangle in the center to get line ab. Draw a line ce the same length as cd and connect points ed. Or take the radius of a circle, ab, and mark off six times around the circumference. Connect every other point.

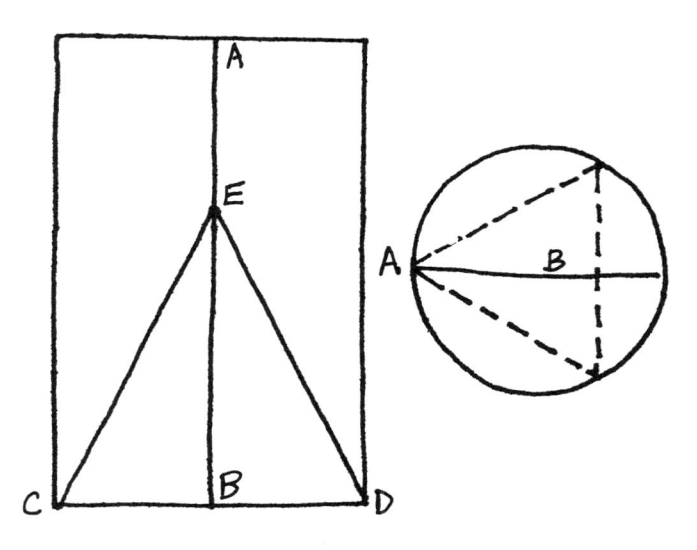

Symmetrical Cutting
A child might be interested in doing this type of activity since he could use his imagination and cut his own designs. Some of the structures can be pure in form, while others can be derived from nature, like the butterfly shape used here for a subject source

121

MAKING PAPER FLOWERS

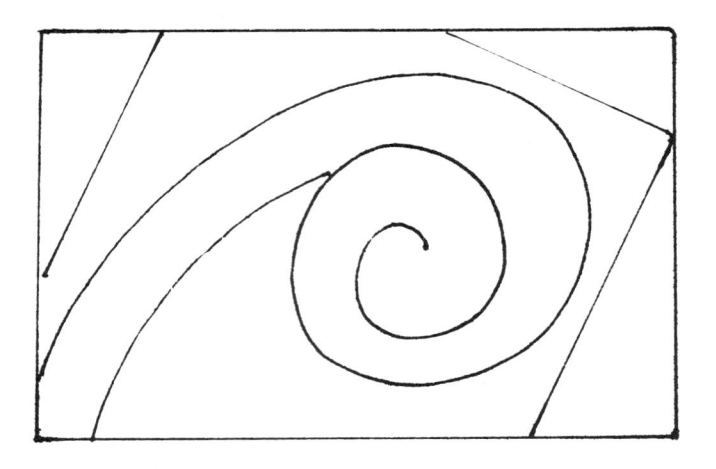

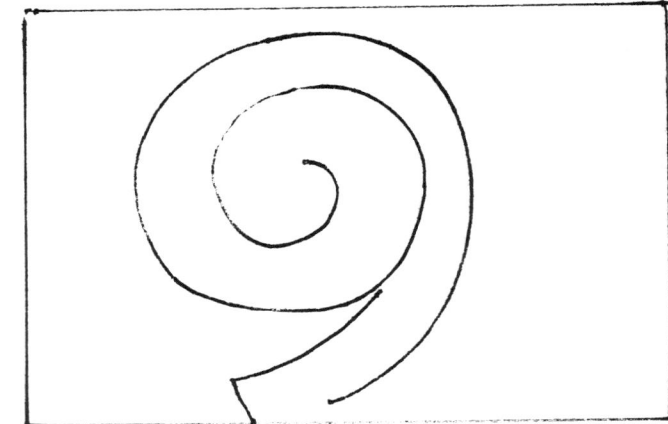

Using colorful medium paper, draw freehand a curved figure similar to the one above.

Cut out along dotted line. Take a ruler and curl with edge as pictured.

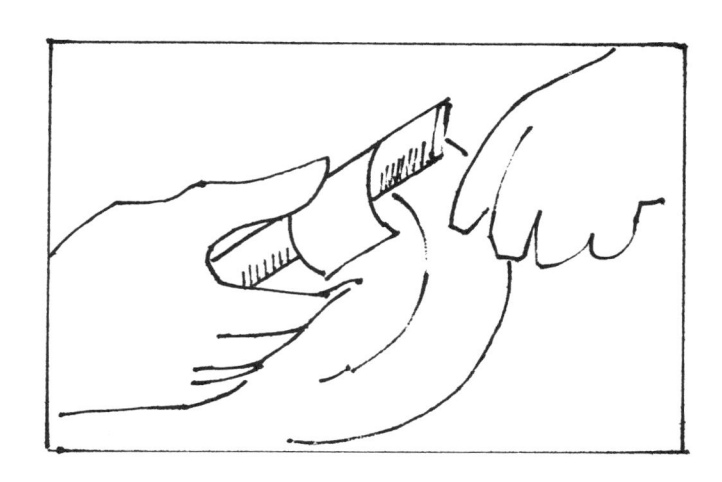

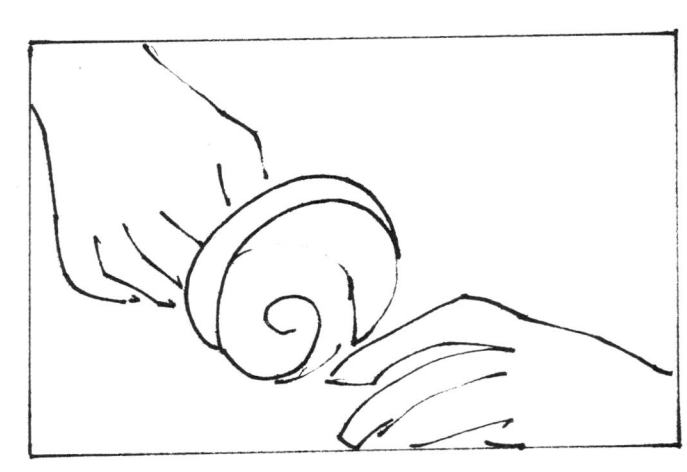

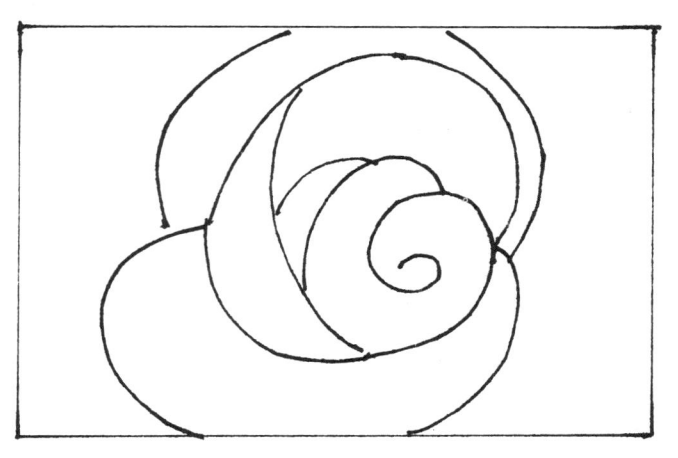

Take outside part of flower and curl together to make center part higher than outer part of flower. Tape bottom and attach to green floral wire. Suitable leaves are added by using floral wire and green floral tape.

FLANNEL BOARDS

It has been said that the child remembers FIVE times as much of that which he sees as that which he hears only.

Some of the advantages of the Flannel Board are as follows:
   Easy to make
   Inexpensive to buy
   Can be arranged, rearranged, and stored easily
   Adaptable to all ages
   Permits child participation
   Permits action
   Can be manipulated by anyone
   Attracts attention
   Stimulates interest
   Flexible in use
   Easy to use
   Improves communication — "A picture is worth a 1,000 words."

The degree of effectiveness is related directly to the skill and imagination of the teacher who decides what must be taught and how the material can best be communicated.

Self-Adhering Materials

Blotters	Corduroy
Sandpaper	Chore Girl
Rough Paper	Cotton
Emery Paper	Burlap
Flock Paper	Monks Cloth
Suede Paper	Blanket Materials
Velour Paper	Velvet
Woolen Yarns	Balsa Wood
Rough String	Steel Wool
Pipe Cleaners	Light Sponge
Rough Rope	Cellophane
Felt	Suede Cloth

BULLETIN BOARDS

Bulletin boards of the different seasons are often used in classroom situations. Students can help in the construction of the different parts. The teacher should strive to use various materials for the bulletin board.

The students also can create individual projects dealing with the bulletin board theme. For example, each student can make their own spring flowers or raindrops, as in the example.

This bulletin board is one that is used to emphasize a classroom concept. This particular example can be used for first grade classrooms to strengthen the use of the alphabet. Each student can create his individual examples to take home.

Rules and holiday theme bulletin boards are used very often in elementary classrooms. Children can take part in the production of the bulletin board and can also make holiday gifts, cards, and projects dealing with the theme to take home.

Allow children to help design seasonal bulletin boards. Various textures, colors, and lettering techniques add interest.

CLAY

Clay is a material that will give many types of learning experiences. It offers the opportunity of experimenting and positive action in changing form to suit specific needs. It can be used over and over again so that the child becomes acquainted with it. Use will not destroy it, and new and exciting possibilities appear each time it is used. It allows for experimenting with different tools; it can be used by one child or a group. It allows for self-expression and success. It stirs the imagination and its resistance is challenging. Working beside or with other children encourages communication and sociability. It extends concepts through experiences and learning of various types.

Clay is as revealing and exciting today as it was to primitive man. There is no real substitute for clay in an art program. It has a lasting influence on its creator. The manipulation of clay gratifies a basic need of children to work their hands in the same sort of satisfying way that is experienced when playing in the sand or making mud pies. Touching, pushing, pulling the pieces of clay soon develops into an urge to make something.

The organization of materials is highly important due to the untidiness connected with clay work. Water-base clay often has been ripened and worked to proper handling (clay tools, hairpins, popsicle sticks, skewer's, etc., can be used). Rags, pan of water, much newspaper for table, should be readily available. Each child should be given a mass of clay — enough to handle easily in two hands. Each finished object should be thoroughly dry before firing.

Low-fire glazes are most successful in finishing the work of children. The dry glaze should be mixed with clean water to the consistency of whipping cream. Objects should be fired before applying glaze. Two or three coats of glaze should be applied to the fired objects, being careful not to glaze the underside unless stilts are used. The pieces are then fired a second time at the correct temperature in the directions for each particular glaze. Cones and/or a pyrometer are necessary for correct firing in the kiln.

Children should learn to handle clay in simple mass forms. Subject matter is secondary to simple, sturdy form. Simple instructions should be given. The clay should be kept in mass. Legs, arms, ears, and other appendages should be pulled out of the mass of clay in the forming figures. By pinching and pressing clay from the center of the mass, simple bowls can be formed. If it is necessary to work several days on an object, it can be wrapped in plastic or moist rag so that it stays moist until finished. The finished project should be simple. An old paint brush may be washed over the wet clay object for smoothing. Allow the clay to dry slowly.

If it is possible to have the clay fired and glazed, it is most desirable. If not, it may be painted with tempera or powder painting and then given three or four coats of shellac.

Suggestions for a kindergarten class (suggestions for the teacher):
1. Use clay before giving it to your kindergarteners. Discover your feelings about using it and try to work through undesirable attitude. Find out the

best consistency for clay. Learn how much water you need to add to make it feel just right.

2. Use the back of oilcloth or plastic on the table when working with clay. Give each child wishing to participate a ball of clay about the size of an orange. Too little is discouraging and too much is wasteful.

3. If working with moist clay, children usually make a ball and stick it to another ball to make a body and a head. When these "stuck together" parts dry, they usually fall apart. You may need to help the child pull out clay to make a leg or a head. However, only a few children will be able to do it.

Finished clay pieces are sources of satisfaction and achievement. Creative projects shared by a group develop a sense of appreciation for the contributions of others. Creative art experiences pull children upward to better and better accomplishments.

Paper Mache Pulp
Ingredients:
  newspaper
  6 Tbsp. flour or 6 Tbsp. laundry starch
  1 cup liquid starch
Knead til a heavy dough consistency is achieved.

Sawdust Recipe
Ingredients:
  15 heaping cups sawdust
  13 heaping cups wheat paste
  6 Tbsp salt
  water
Put into huge container. Gradually add boiling water, stirring constantly until mixture looks like a stiff bread dough.
Makes 30 balls.

Salt Ceramic Dough
Ingredients:
  1 cup salt
  ½ cup cornstarch
  ¾ cup cold water
Mix salt and cornstarch. Gradually add cold water. Do this in the top of a double boiler, until the consistency of bread dough is achieved.
Makes enough for one student. The material can be painted and can be easily rolled flat and cut out.

Clay Dough
Ingredients:
  1 cup flour
  1 cup salt
  1 Tb. alum.
  1 cup water
  Powder or food coloring
Mix salt, flour and alum together. Add coloring and mix in water slowly. Makes small amount for one student.

PRINTING

Printmaking Activities
Printmaking ... A process in which ink or paint is spread upon a prepared surface which in turn transfers an impression upon another surface by means of applied pressure.

Vocabulary
1. Brayer — a rubber-covered roller used in inking metal plates, linoleum, and wood blocks.
2. Composition — the quality of being put together in such a way as to produce a harmonious, aesthetic whole.
3. Monoprint — a print obtained by making a single print from a plate upon which an impression has been created with paints, oils, or inks.
4. Proof — a trial print obtained from a block, plate or screen for the purpose of being studied and corrected.
5. Relief Printing — a process of printing from a raised or projected surface.

Potato Printing
This method is achieved by cutting away part of the soft raw potato. Ink is put onto the surface. The child then presses the potato onto the paper creating a pleasing print.

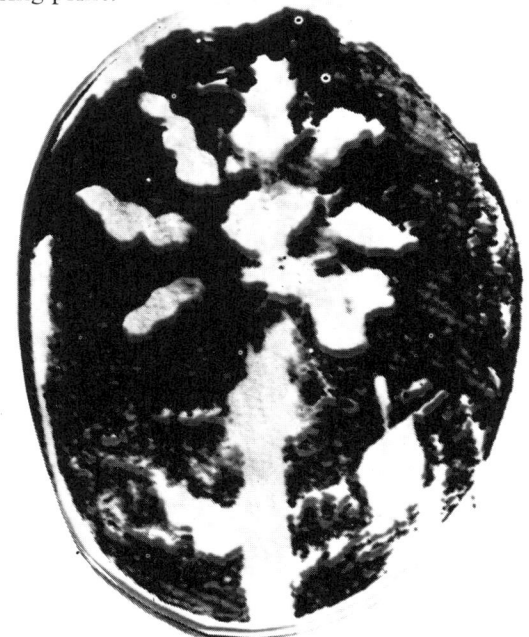

Functional Area: Cognitive

Purpose: The child learns the basic process of printing as he prints his potato design.

Functional Area:

Purpose:

Finger Printing

I. Objective:
   To allow children to use their imagination in creating pictures or designs with combined arrangements of finger prints.

II. Materials:
   1. Paper
   2. Ink pad or watercolor set
   3. Pencil or India ink

III. Procedure:
   1. Dip fingers in paing or on stamp pad
   2. Press fingers on paper
   3. Finger prints may be combined to form design or they may be drawn into individual objects with the use of India ink and pen.

Functional Area: Cognitive (basic art element: texture)

Purpose: The child learns about texture as he creates finger print designs.

Functional Area:

Purpose:

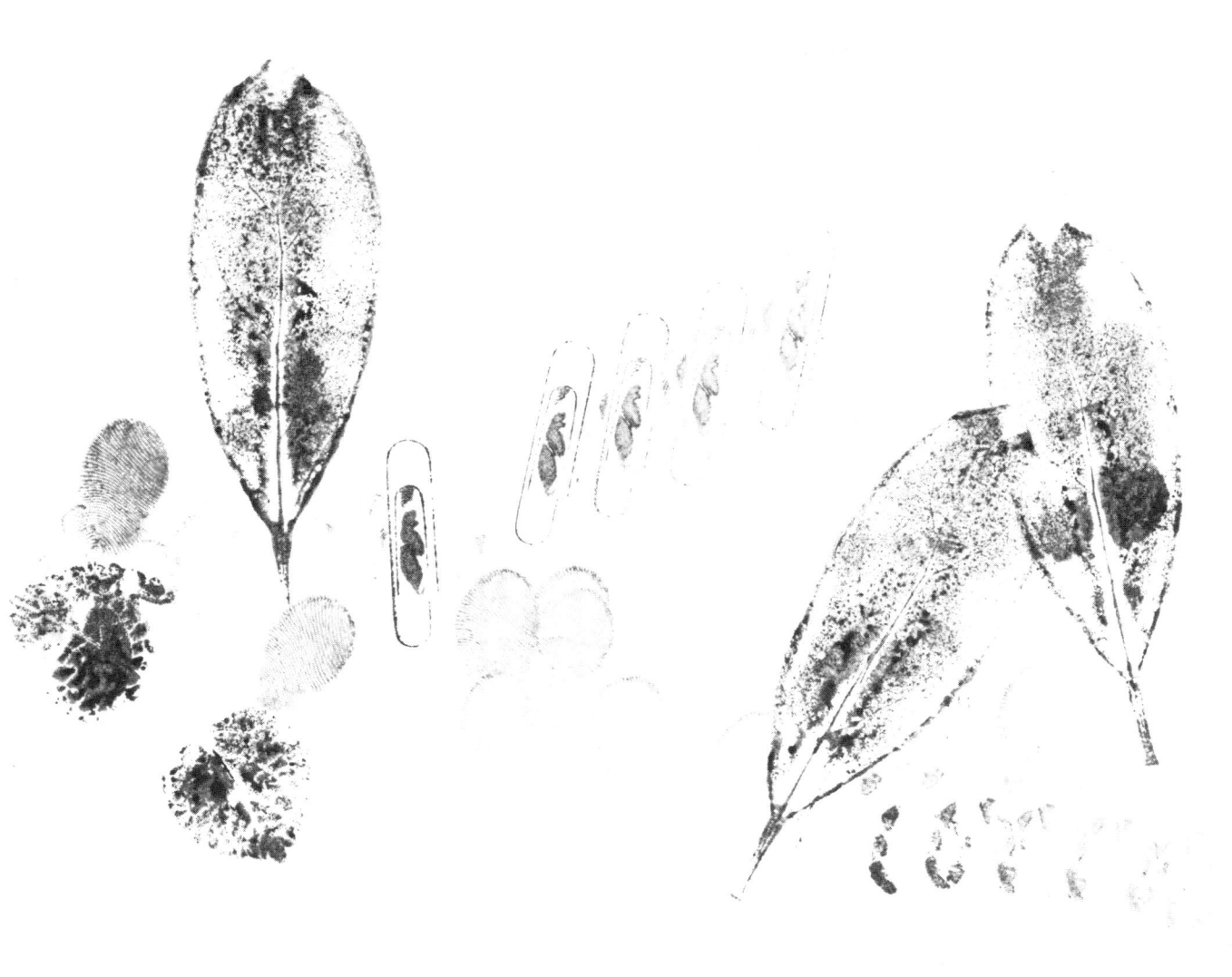

Leaf Printing

Leaf printing is one means of creating an awareness of the quality of texture in the child. Leaf printing demonstrates how to create a balanced positive and negative image from natural forms. The idea of composition is also important in order that the child be able to create a pleasing arrangement of the leaf prints.

Leaf Printing

I. Objective:
   To have children obtain an impression of the leaf on paper. Brings about awareness of texture.

II. Materials:
   1. Leaves
   2. Paint
   3. Brayer
   4. Paper

III. Procedure:
   1. Spread paint evenly on surface of the leaf or leaves.
   2. Lay painted leaf on paper (flat).
   3. Cover leaf with white paper.
   4. Roll over with brayer and print is complete.

Functional Area: Creative (compositional design)

Purpose: The idea of composition can be presented as the child creates a pleasing arrangement of his leaf prints.

Functional Area:

Purpose:

Cardboard Printing

I. Definition
   A. Cardboard printing is an example of relief printing. Relief printing is a process of printing from a raised or projected surface, also a print obtained by such a process.

II. Objective:
   A. To explain the step by step process of relief printing to the children and to let them use their imagination to obtain a pattern.

III. Materials:
   1. Cardboard
   2. Water base ink
   3. Glue
   4. Construction paper
   5. Brayer
   6. Exacto Knife and Tray

IV. Procedure:
   1. Draw desired shapes on cardboard and cut them out.
   2. Glue the shapes on a piece of cardboard.
   3. Roll the inked brayer over the shapes.
   4. Print design on paper.

Functional Area: Language

Purpose: The child will learn to follow directions as he learns the steps in cardboard printing.

Functional Area:

Purpose:

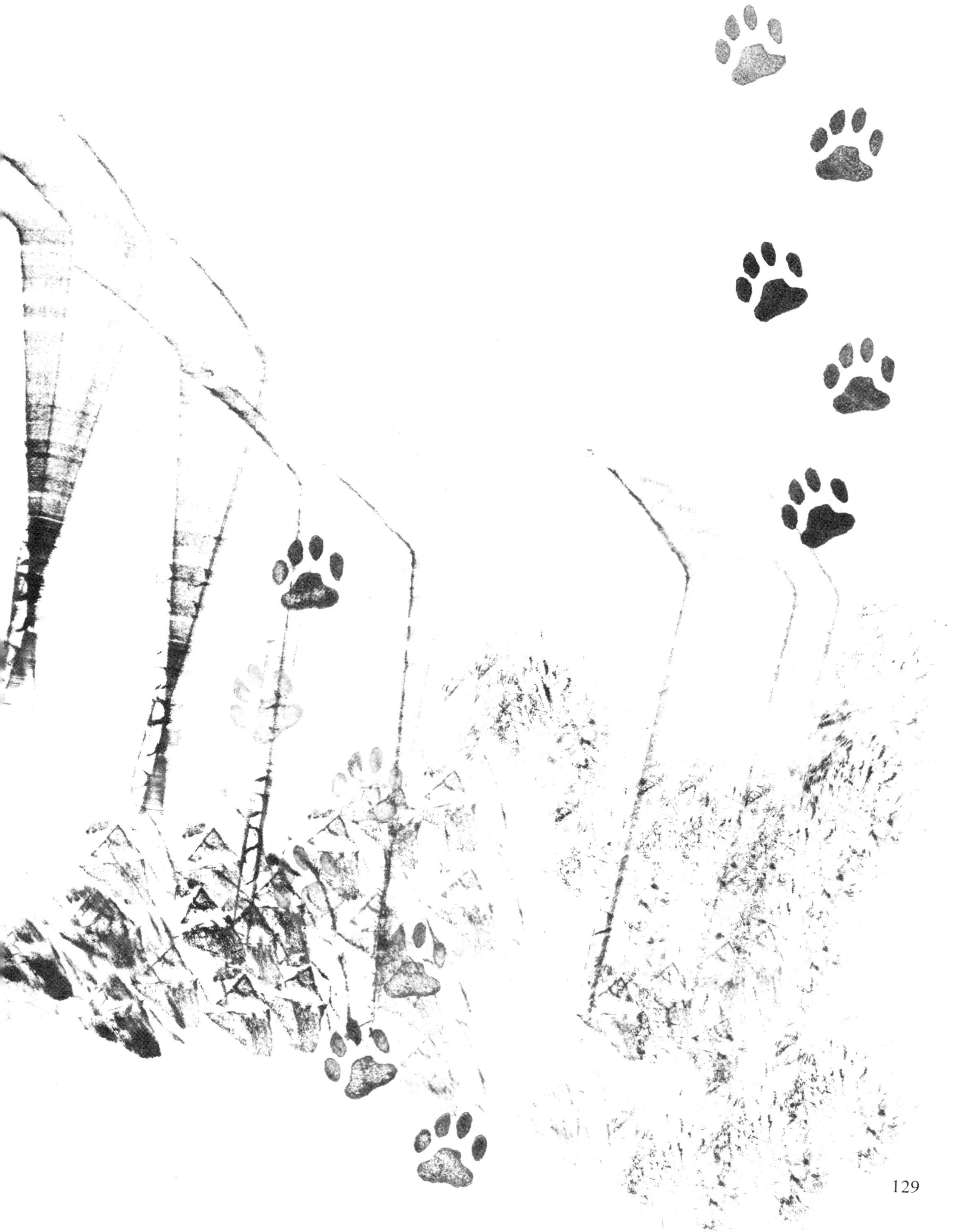

TEXTILE PROJECTS

1. Weaving
2. Collage with textile materials
3. Batik fabrics
4. Tie-Dye fabric
5. Yarn and material – sewing on paper: Big stitches
6. Yarn and material – pasting on paper

Adapt the above ideas for use in class. For example, use concepts such as:

Numbers	Animals	Families
Colors	Safety	Nature
Letters	Names	

Functional Area: Physical (left-right movement)

Purpose: The child will learn left to right movement as he weaves on his cardboard loom.

Functional Area:

Purpose:

Weaving with Yarn on Cardboard Loom

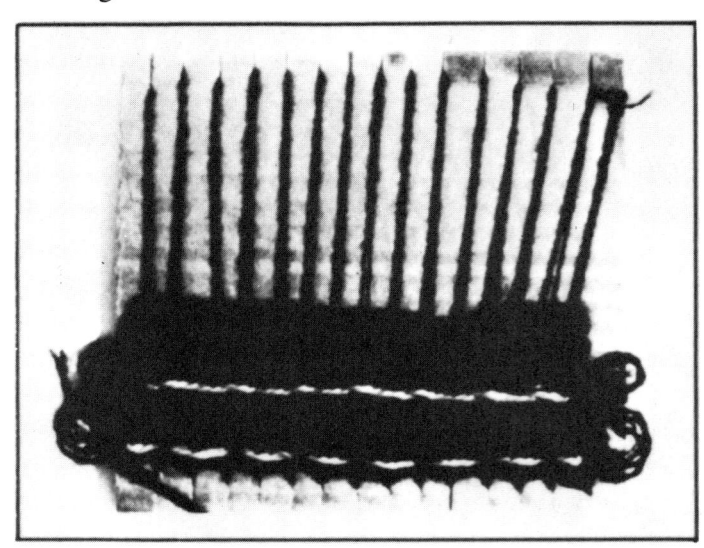

Material Collage

Functional Area: Physical

Purpose: The child will learn to cut and paste different textures as he makes the material collages.

Functional Area:

Purpose:

130

Yarn and Felt Collage

Functional Area:

Purpose:

Tie-Dyeing

Materials: Fabric, Rubberbands, Dye

Method:
1. Tie knots in fabric (secure these with rubberbands).
2. Dye fabric. Allow to stand 15 minutes.
3. Rinse fabric with cold water.
4. Remove rubberbands.
5. Allow fabric to dry and then iron.

Functional Area: Cognitive

Purpose: The child learns to follow directions as he does a simple tie dye.

Functional Area:

Purpose:

Sewing Felt on Paper

Functional Area: Physical

Purpose: Helps develop fine muscle coordination.

Batik

Materials: Wax, Dye, Fabric, Brush, Newspaper, Iron

Method:
1. Lightly pencil-sketch your design on fabric.
2. Apply melted wax to design area. It is difficult to remove wax drips if they are in the wrong area on the cloth so try not to drip. Paint the small details in your design first. Remember, every area not covered by the wax will be dyed in the background color in the final result.
3. Let the wax on fabric semi-dry.
4. Run waxed design under cold water.
5. Put the wet, waxed fabric into the prepared dye-bath. Stir slowly for 5 minutes. Allow fabric to remain in dye for 15 minutes. (You may lengthen the dyeing time if darker shade is desired.) Remember the fabric will be 2 shades lighter when the batik process is finished.

6. Take fabric out of dye and rinse in cold running water until excess dye is removed.
7. Allow fabric to dry.
8. "Sandwich" the dried fabric between newspapers. Press *lightly* with a medium hot iron to remove wax.

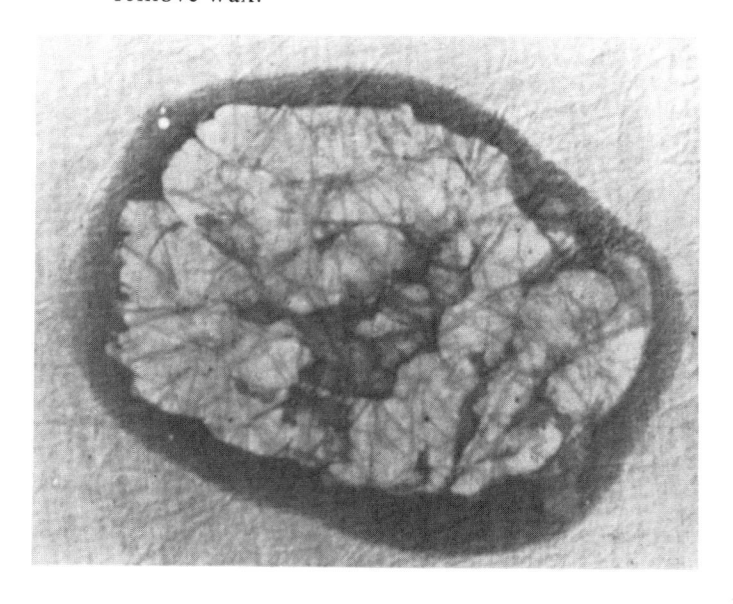

Functional Area: Cognitive (following directions)

Purpose: The child learns to carefully follow the pictures and directions associated with the step by step process associated with batik.

Functional Area:

Purpose:

1. Draw in design on fabric.

2. Paint in design with wax.

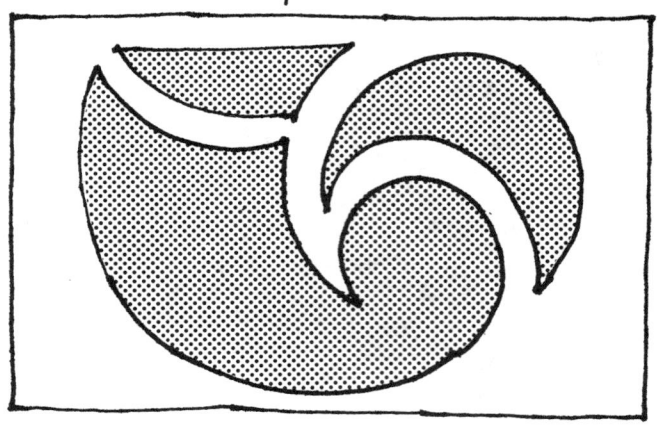

3. Dye fabric.

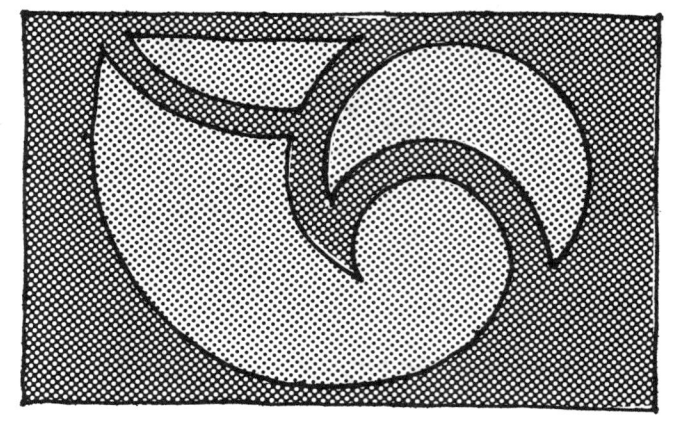

4. Remove wax with hot iron and newspaper.

PHOTOGRAPHY

The concept of photography is one which can amaze the human mind. A camera recalls more than any human eye can; therefore, children should be exposed to this "third eye."

Flip Book

Materials: small pad of paper
 crayons

Procedure:
Children decide on some action, event draw stages on successive pages of pad, make only slight changes in action each time, flip through book to see action

Functional Area: Cognitive

Purpose: The child learns the concept of basic film making by drawing his own pictures and a repetitive pattern-sequence is reinforced.

Functional Area:

Purpose:

Slides from Magazine Photographs

Materials: magazine photographs
 clear contact paper or book tape
 hot water

Procedure:
Children lay clear plastic over photograph and smooth completely to remove air bubbles, soak in hot water about 5 minutes and peel away paper, mount in cardboard frame

Functional Area: Cognitive

Purpose: The child learns that an opaque picture in a magazine can become a transparent picture after completing the process.

Functional Area:

Purpose:

Color Demonstration Slides

Materials: light cardboard, cellophane in primary colors

Procedure:
Make frames for squares of cellophane and use to overlap colors to make secondary colors.

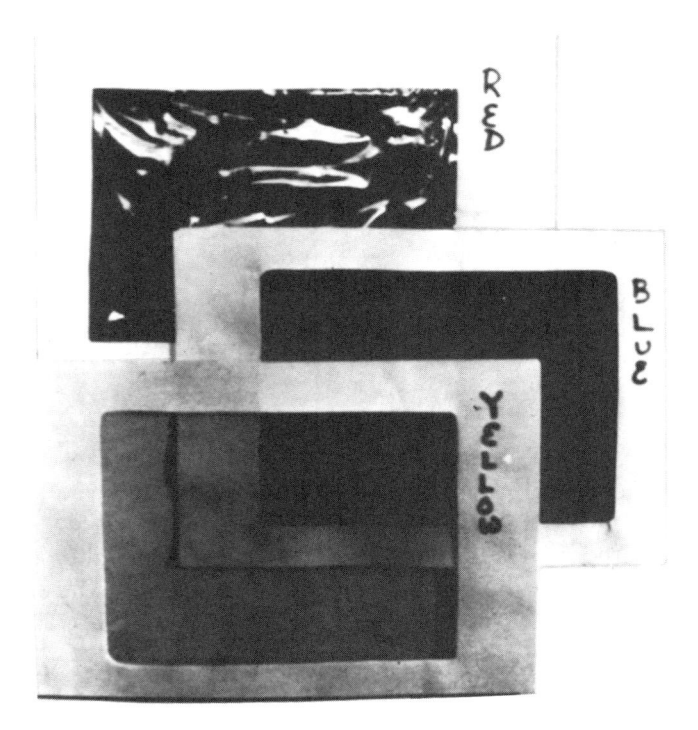

Functional Area: Cognitive

Purpose: The child learns that two primary colors can create a secondary color as he overlaps his squares of red, blue, and yellow cellophane.

Functional Area:

Purpose:

Pretend TV

Materials: cardboard box, paper, crayons, paints, cardboard rolls from paper towels

Procedure:
Read story, take trip, establish any sequence of events, children draw one event, join together in sequence and roll through TV

Functional Area: Creative (drawing)

Purpose: The child learns compositional quality of his picture as he draws a picture that occupies the entire space of the paper.

Functional Area:

Purpose:

Family Tree from Family Photographs

Materials: photographs
            crayons, paper

Procedure:
Children bring in pictures of family, arrange to make family tree

Functional Area: Self concept

Purpose: The child's self concept is enhanced as he creates his own family tree.

Functional Area:

Purpose:

PUPPETRY

Puppetry is an art. Anything inanimate, when it is given life through the imagination, becomes a puppet. They are of many shapes, sizes and are operated in a variety of ways. The urge to make puppets is nothing new. People have been creating them for thousands of years and why? People can express themselves through puppetry. It is also a means of communication, an extension of human expression.

When choosing the type of puppet with which you wish to work, you should first consider the nature and scope of each type of puppet, and the difficulties that may be met in construction and performance. You can make many different kinds of puppets from all sorts of materials.

Some Common Type Puppets
1. Hand Puppets
2. Rod Puppets
3. String Puppets
4. Paper Mache Puppets
5. Paper Plate Puppets
6. Bag Puppets
7. Stick Puppets
8. Sock Puppets
9. Hand and Rod Puppets
10. Finger Puppets
11. Flat Puppets (Shadow Figure)

Sack puppets are probably the easiest because they only require construction paper, glue and a paper bag. The child cuts out pieces from the paper and creates a character by gluing them on the bag. These are easily manipulated puppets, requiring only the use of the hand.

Stick puppets are also very simple, but aren't as fun for the child to put to use. The child simply creates a character and glues it on a stick.

Sock puppets are fun for children to make and use in puppet shows. Scraps of material and yarn or ribbons are glued on an old sock to make a character.

Paper plates can easily be turned into puppets with a little use of the imagination. Paper, yarn, felt, etc., can be pasted on the plate to create a puppet.

Papier mache puppets are relatively simple to make but require much more time, supervision, and space. Shreds of newspaper (1" x 6") are soaked with wheat paste or a flour and water mixture and are then applied to the surface of an inflated balloon. Several layers are added to create a face. The heads are left to dry and when ready the balloon is popped. Then they are painted and attached to bodies to make very nice puppets. (Remember to leave a small opening at the base of the head for your fingers!)

Some Basic Materials Needed for Puppetry may include:
1. Glue
2. Paint
3. Yarn
4. Buttons
5. String
6. Bags
7. Rods
8. Crayons
9. Sticks
10. Socks
11. Screws
12. Loops
13. Paper Mache Strips
14. Clay Forms
15. Cork
16. Wire
17. Nails
18. Cloth
19. Sewing Materials
20. Cardboard
21. Scissors
22. Anything else you want to decorate your puppet with can be used.

With the wide popularity of puppets as entertainers, those in the field of education should be aware of this medium and build upon its universal appeal. While entertainment value is important, there are greater values to be gained by making, using, and sharing puppets. The puppet makes an excellent teacher, children listen to its pronouncements and admonitions more readily than to those of a human being. Through puppets, one becomes aware of the difficulty of communication between individuals. Puppets can also help the individual to become aware of his own limitations. If a puppeteer creates a puppet who may be ugly and unpopular, perhaps he can identify with a fellow human who has this role in real life. While self-understanding is a consideration in the use of puppets, there are several concomitant learnings which aid an individual in his development. A child can develop certain manipulative skills and can achieve greater manual dexterity. Certain perceptive skills can be enhanced and the imagination can be further developed.

Thus puppets can serve as effective teachers. Teaching is not simply the outpouring of information, but the interrelationship of all who are involved in a teach-learning situation so that ideas are understood and communicated.

As individuals speak through puppets, they reveal

their understanding of the world in which they live, and thus give an indication of the concepts which they have assimilated. Thus puppets become more than activity, but rather serve to integrate many factors into the learning process. The educational values are continually being compounded as the individuals become involved in this stimulating activity.

Paper Bag Puppets

MATERIALS:
Brown paper lunch bag, newspaper, tape, glue, scrap material, yarn, buttons, construction paper, scissors, paper towel roll, tempera paint.

PROCEDURE:
Decorate the fold of the paper bag so that it represents a face.
Glue or paste on hair.
Finish up by painting, or glueing on eyes, nose, mouth and other clothes.
> NOTE: a long or big nose can be made by taking a small square of paper and wadding it into desired shape, paint and glue on to the rest of the puppet.

Popsickle Stick Puppets

MATERIALS:
Popsickle sticks, paint, glue, scrap material, construction paper, scissors.

PROCEDURE:
Cut circle for head and decorate the head in any manner. Then glue circle to the popsickle stick.

Paper Plate Puppets

MATERIALS:
Paper plates, yarn, colored paper, glue or paste, buttons, feather, and scissors.

PROCEDURES:
Take a paper plate, decorate with eyes, nose, mouth, and hair. Strands of yarn can be used for the hair. Put a stick or paper towel roll on the back by either glue or staples. This makes a handy support for the puppet. Attach 1 paper plate together with a brad to represent the head and body.

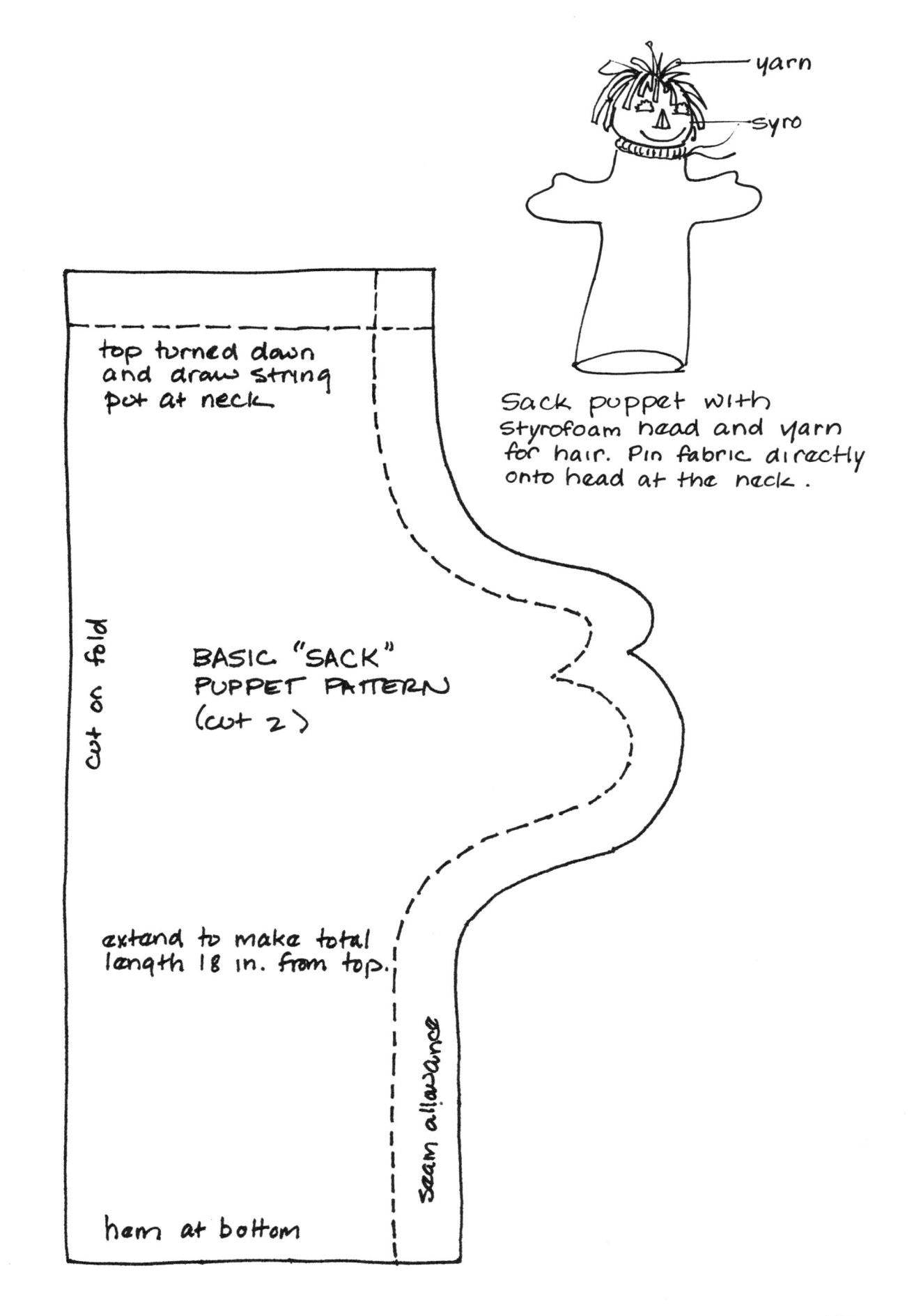

Sack puppet with Styrofoam head and yarn for hair. Pin fabric directly onto head at the neck.

- yarn
- syro

BASIC "SACK" PUPPET PATTERN (cut 2)

top turned down and draw string put at neck

cut on fold

extend to make total length 18 in. from top.

seam allowance

hem at bottom

Puppet Stages

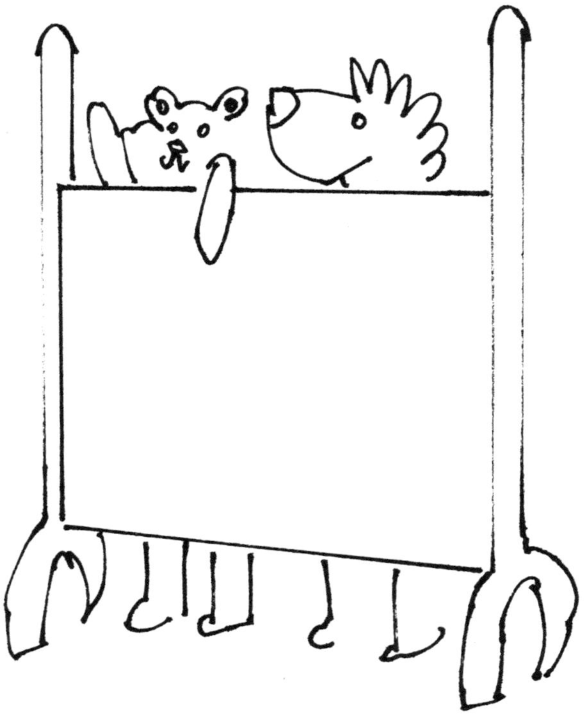

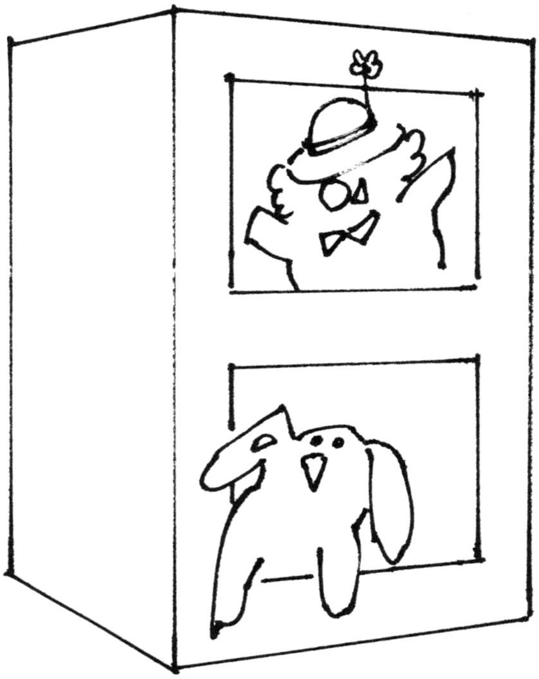

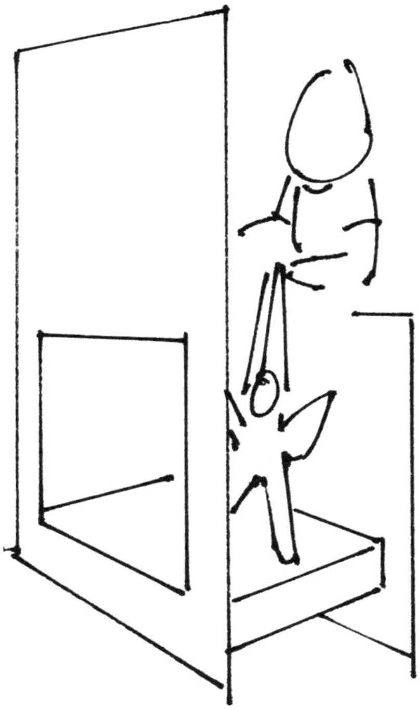

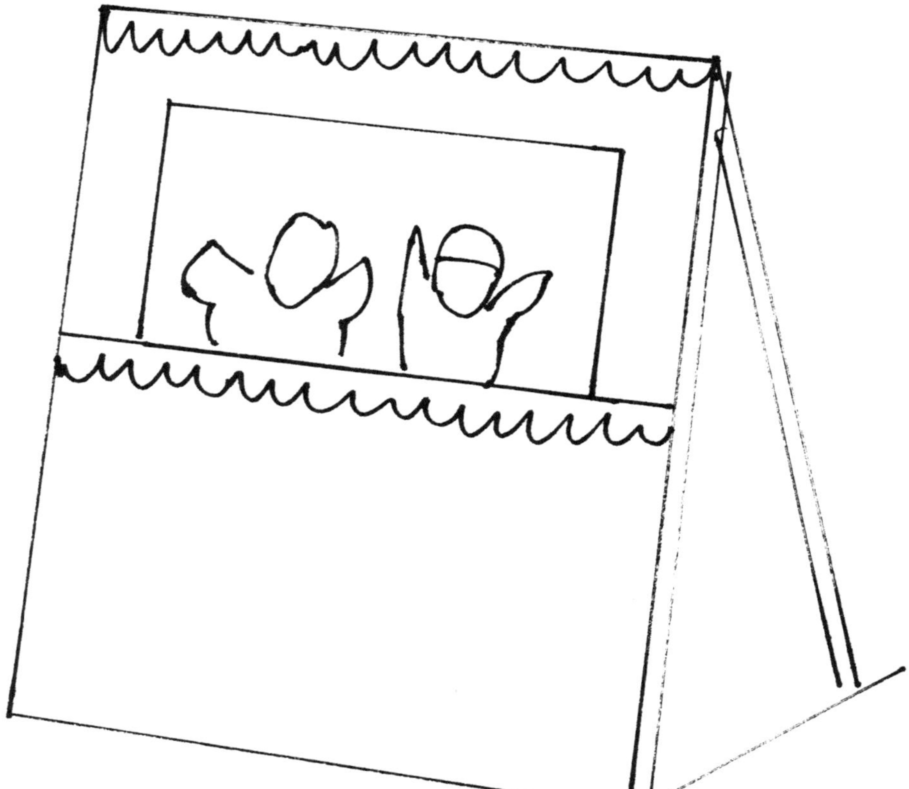

Folded Paper Puppet

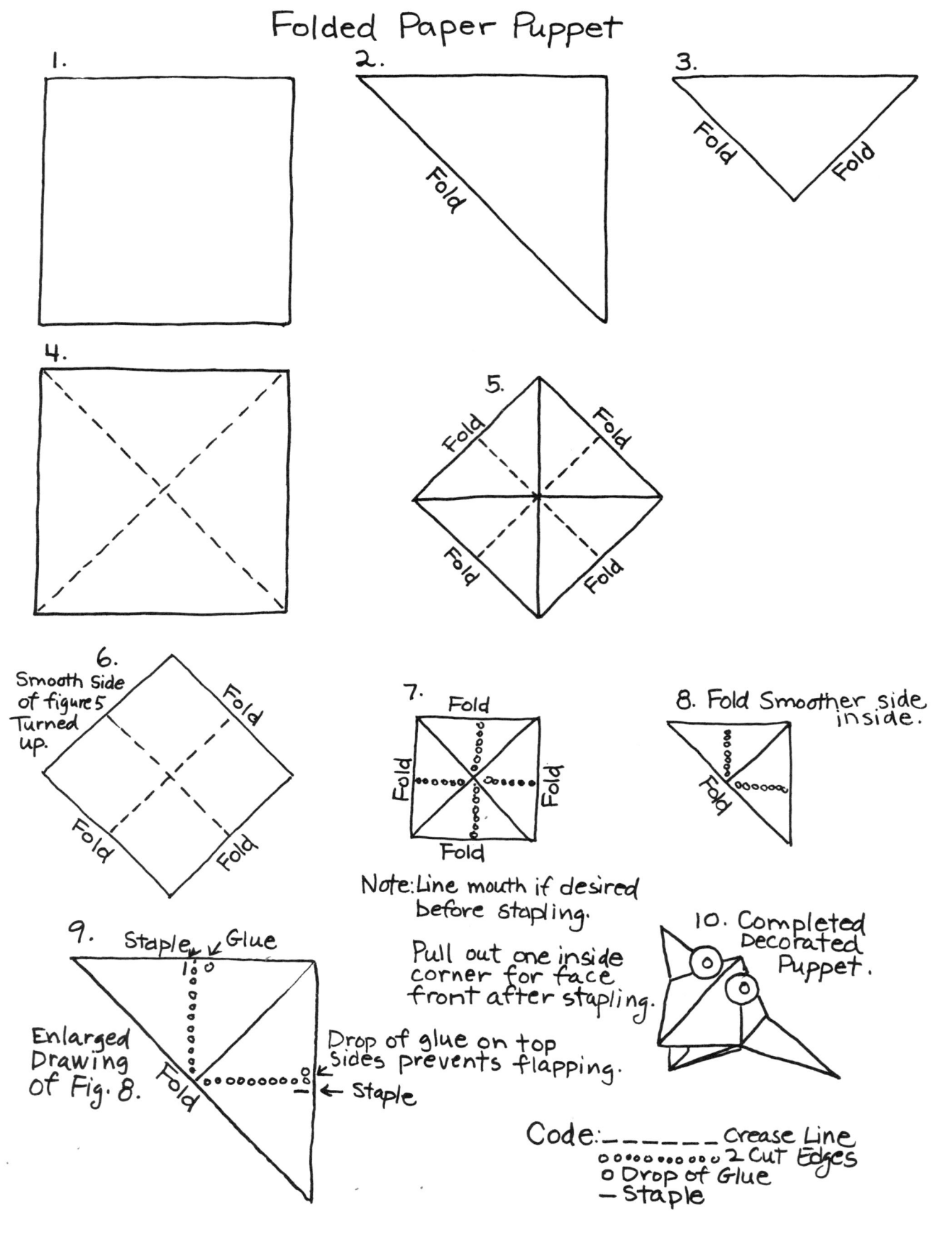

1.

2. Fold

3. Fold / Fold

4. (dashed diagonals)

5. Fold / Fold / Fold / Fold

6. Smooth Side of figure 5 Turned up. Fold / Fold / Fold / Fold

7. Fold / Fold / Fold / Fold

8. Fold Smoother side inside.

Note: Line mouth if desired before stapling.

Pull out one inside corner for face front after stapling.

9. Staple ↓ Glue
Enlarged Drawing of Fig. 8.
Fold
Drop of glue on top sides prevents flapping.
← Staple

10. Completed Decorated Puppet.

Code:
- - - - - - Crease Line
ooo•••oooo 2 Cut Edges
o Drop of Glue
— Staple

[56] The material in this chapter was taken from *Art Projects for the Young Child* by Jane A. Caballero, Ph.D. (Atlanta, Georgia: Humanics, Limited, 1979).

chapter 12
music

Music is a social art that gives each child the opportunity for social, intellectual, emotional, aesthetic, and physical growth.

Children should appreciate music. Music is a natural means of expression. We can do this through singing or playing a musical instrument. When selecting songs for children, choose a song that has a catchy tune, serves a purpose, and is within grade level.

Music appreciation is very important for the disadvantaged child. Provide the opportunity to let children pick their own song or make up their own song. You should be aware of the child's background and try to involve parents in musical activities. Remember to plan activities that are short — children's attention spans are not very long.

Objectives of music may include:
1. Promote appreciation and enjoyment
2. Encourage discrimination in the choice of music
3. Develop awareness of the sensitivity to sound
4. Develop and extend the voice range
5. Provide experience in listening

Objectives in early childhood education should include:
1. Singing — seasonal songs, poems, and finger plays
2. Rhythm — homemade and bought instruments should be provided
3. Listening skills — awareness of sounds. Include familiar songs, children's songs, and classical music. A variety of short songs should be provided.
4. Sight reading — Introduce notes through matching and other visual discrimination games.
5. Creativity — Allow the children to move and dance. Children's dances (Hokey Pokey) and ethnic dances (Mexican Hat dance) should be introduced. Allow children to be creative and experiment with instruments.

TRADITIONAL SONGS, POEMS AND FINGERPLAYS

The children will enjoy learning the following poems, songs, and fingerplays. They will develop their language and self concept. See pages 157 thru 162 for patterns that will reinforce the benefits.

Traditional

October

FIVE LITTLE PUMPKINS
Five little pumpkins growing on a vine.
Said the first little pumpkin, "Don't I look fine?"
Said the second little pumpkin, "I'll be a pie."
Said the third little pumpkin, "I'll be a lantern by
*   and by."*
Said the fourth little pumpkin, "I will, too."
But the fifth little pumpkin just said, "BOO!"

FIRST YOU TAKE A PUMPKIN
First you take a pumpkin, big, round, and fat.
Then you cut the top off, that makes his hat.
Then you cut a mouth, nose, and two eyes.
Then you have a Jack-O-Lantern, a Halloween
*   surprise!*

PUMPKIN ROUND
Pumpkin round, Pumpkin fat, Turned into a Jack-
*   O-Lantern,*
Just like THAT!

TWO LITTLE GHOSTS
A very old witch was stirring a pot. Ooooo! Ooooo!
Two little ghosts said, "What has she got?"
Tip toe, tip toe, tip . . . . Boo!

PUMPKIN SONG
Oh, once I was a pumpkin, a pumpkin, a pumpkin.
Oh, once I was a pumpkin with no face at all.
With no eyes, and no nose and no mouth and no
*   teeth.*
Oh, once I was a pumpkin with no face at all.

So, I made a Jack-O-Lantern, Jack-O-Lantern, Jack-
*   O-Lantern.*
So, I made a Jack-O-Lantern with a big funny face.
With big eyes, and big nose, and big mouth, and big
*   teeth.*
So, I made a Jack-O-Lantern with a big, funny face.

THREE LITTLE WITCHES
One little, two little, three little witches
Fly over haystacks, fly over ditches.
Slide down moonbeams without any hitches
Hi, Ho, Halloween's here.

HALLOWEEN
Hooray for Halloween, Hooray for Halloween.
Cats howl Meow, Owls hoot Ooooo.
And witches fly up in the sky.
Hooray for Halloween.

JACK O'LANTERN
Jack O'Lantern, Jack O'Lantern.
Halloween, Halloween.
See the witches flying,
Hear the wind a sighing . . . OoooooOooooo.[57]

Functional Area: Language

Purpose: Halloween poems will help the child learn to verbalize as he learns the poems and acts them out through the felt characters. (Patterns page 157-158.)

Functional Area:

Purpose:

Traditional

November

SIX LITTLE TURKEYS
Six little turkeys that I once knew — fat ones, skinny ones, fair ones too.
But the one little turkey with the feather on his back,
He led the others with a gobble, gobble, gobble.
Down to the turkey farm they all go — fat ones, skinny ones, fair ones too.
But the one little turkey with the feather on his back,
He led the others with a gobble, gobble, gobble.

INDIAN THROUGH THE FOREST GOES
The Indian through the forest goes. Softly on his tippy toes.
Step, step, step, sh, sh, sh.
Bow and arrow on his back, feather on his hair so black.
Step, step, step, sh, sh, sh.

LEAVES
Fall is here, the leaves come down,
Red, and yellow, green, and brown.

OVER THE RIVER
Over the river and through the woods to Grandfather's house we go.
The horse knows the way to carry the sleigh over white and drifted snow. O.
Over the river and through the woods, oh how the wind does blow,
It stings the nose and bites the toes, as over the road we go.

PILGRIM CHILDREN
The Pilgrim children say, "Corn is ripe, the turkey's fat
For Thanksgiving Day. Let's Thankfully celebrate and pray."[58]

143

Traditional

December

C IS FOR CANDY
H IS FOR HAPPINESS
R IS FOR REINDEER
I IS FOR ICING
S IS FOR STOCKING
T IS FOR TOYS
M IS FOR MISTLETOE
A IS FOR ANGEL
S IS FOR SANTA

GROWING UP
Sometimes you get discouraged
Because I am so small
And always leave my finger prints
On furniture and wall.

But every day I'm growing up
And soon I'll be so tall
That all those little hand prints
Will be hard to recall.

So here's a final print
Just so you can remember
Exactly how my fingers looked
In '78 . . . . December![59]

Functional Area: Self concept

Purpose: The child's self concept will be greatly enhanced as he makes his handprint out of a plaster of paris mixture and writes the poem to his parents.

Functional Area:

Purpose:

January

5 LITTLE SNOWMEN
5 little snowmen knocking at the door
1 melted away and then there were 4.
4 little snowmen playing with me.
1 melted away and then there were 3.
3 little snowmen playing with you.
2 melted away and then there was 1.
1 little snowman when the day was done.
1 melted away and then there was none.

Soapy the Snowman
Supplies: soap flakes, water, button, toothpick. Pour a box of soap flakes into a large container. Add water and mix until the consistency of paste. Roll into balls. Put 2 balls together with toothpicks. Use toothpicks for arms and buttons for features. After the child is tired of his snowman he may use it for hand soap. Psychomotor development is reinforced through this modeling activity.[60]

Functional Area: Cognitive

Purpose: Making the snowman and learning the poem will help the child follow a sequence of steps and directions.

Functional Area:

Purpose:

February

Lincoln
Edna Cobb Dutcher — W. Otto Miessner

We love the name of Lincoln, For him a song we sing; His birth today we celebrate, And grateful praises bring.

Washington and the Flag
Mabel E. Bray — W. Otto Miessner

George Washington, George Washington, We sing today of you; You fought to make our country free; You were our leader true.

George Washington, George Washington, We sing today of you, And wave on high our starry flag; Our own red, white and blue.

Valentines
Anna L. Whitmore — Franz Schubert

Valentines so bright and gay, We are sending out today, With a message, "I love you; Tell me that you love me too!"

Making a Valentine
W. Otto Miessner — W. Otto Miessner

Valentine! Valentine! Pictures bright and laces fine. Valentine! Valentine! When it's made, I'll give you mine.

Traditional

Spring

BEES
Spring has sprung, and now begun.
You see so many things,
Especially the thing that stings.
That thing will buzz, and it has some fuzz.
That thing is a bee,
And it isn't much like me.

EASTER BUNNY
The Easter Bunny runs around
Taking baskets through the town.
The Easter Bunny hops, hops, hops,
And he never ever stops
Till he's visited every house,
Then left as quiet as a mouse.

FLOWERS
Easter time is here again
Sunshine bright or dripping rain.
Flowers in the earth so deep
Waken from their winter sleep.

SPRING POSIES
Spring has sprung
The grass is riz.
I wonder where the posies is?

SAILING
A bird sails and clouds sail
   and the sun shines down so bright.
The tulips and daffodils
   are a very pretty sight.

APRIL
April, April, why do you cry
All those teardrops down from the sky?
Don't you know your little showers
Are tiny drinks for thirsty flowers?

EASTER EGGS
Easter eggs, Easter eggs. What a pretty sight.
Blue and pink and yellow, lavender and white.

PETER COTTONTAIL
Here comes Peter Cottontail
Hoppin' down the bunny trail.
Hippity hoppin', Easter's on it's way.
Bringing every girl and boy
Baskets full of Easter joy.
Things to make your Easter bright and gay.
He's got jelly beans for Tommy,
Colored eggs for sister Sue.
There's an orchid for your Mommy and
An Easter bonnet, too.
Oh! Here comes Peter Cottontail,
Hoppin' down the bunny trail,
Hippity, hoppity, Happy Easter Day.

Here comes Peter Cottontail
Hoppin' down the bunny trail,
Look at him stop and listen to him say:
"Try to do the things you should."
Maybe if you're extra good,
He'll roll some Easter Eggs your way.
You'll wake up on Easter morning and
You'll know that he was there,
When you find those chocolate bunnies
That he's hiding everywhere.
Oh! Here comes Peter Cottontail,
Hoppin' down the bunny trail.
Hippity, hoppity, Happy Easter Day.

SPRING
Birds sing in spring, Spring is a happy season
Flowers bloom, trees are green.
We like Spring for this reason.[62]

Traditional
CREATIVE MOVEMENT SONGS

THIS OLD MAN
This old man, he played <u>one</u>
He played Nick-Nack on my <u>thumb</u>,
With a Nick-Nack, paddy-wack,
Give the dog a bone,
This old man came rolling home.

REPEAT: two, shoe
          three, knee
          four, door
          five, hive
          six, sticks
          seven, Heaven
          eight, gate
          nine, spin
          ten, chin

Functional Area: Cognitive (math)

Purpose: The child can practice counting to ten as he sings this song.

Functional Area:

Purpose:

IF YOU'RE HAPPY AND YOU KNOW IT

If you're happy and you know it find a square (clap) (clap)
If you're happy and you know it find a square (clap) (clap)
If you're happy and you know it then your face will surely show it.
If you're happy and you know it find a square. (clap) (clap)

THE MUFFIN MAN

1. Oh, do you know the numeral one the numeral one the numeral one
   Oh, do you know the numeral one. It looks just like this.
2. Oh, do you know the numeral one the numeral one the numeral one
   Oh, yes I know the numeral one. It looks just like this.

POP! GOES THE WEASEL

All around the numeral 4 The monkey chased the weasel, The monkey stopped to pick up his 4, Pop! goes the weasel.

HOKEY POKEY
You put your right hand in
You take your right hand out
You put your right hand in
And shake it all about
You do the Hokey Pokey
And turn yourself around,
That's what it's all about.

Functional Area: Self concept

Purpose: Body parts are reinforced as the child does the Hokey Pokey.

Functional Area:

Purpose:

RHYTHM

Rhythm is the most important part of music. Everyone has a sense of rhythm and learning to develop it is very enjoyable. Children must learn to "feel" music. Children should be encouraged to chant rhymes that they know. They can learn to clap to the rhythms. Later they can be introduced to rhythm instruments.

Some rhythm instruments are: bells — castanets — drums — sand blocks — wood blocks — Xylophone — Maracas — tambourine — triangle — sticks — clappers

Here are some ideas for making your own instruments:

Bells — Flower pots of different sizes. Tap with a wooden stick to find their tone. Slip ropes through holes in pots and fasten to a pole laid across two chairs.

Glasses — Set thin drinking glasses (or coke bottles) in a row. Leave one empty. Pour different amounts of water in the others until their tones go up the scale as you tap with a stick.

Sand blocks — Blocks of wood, 1" x 2" x 6", sheet of sandpaper and thumb tacks or glue. Attach the sandpaper to the blocks and rub or shuffle together.

Jingles — Sew small bells to a band or ribbon and shake.

Marinbas — Put pebbles in a small tin or cardboard box. Glue cover on. Run a stick through for a handle, hold it in place with tacks. Decorate it.

Cymbals — Pot lids may be used. The child hits the lids together.

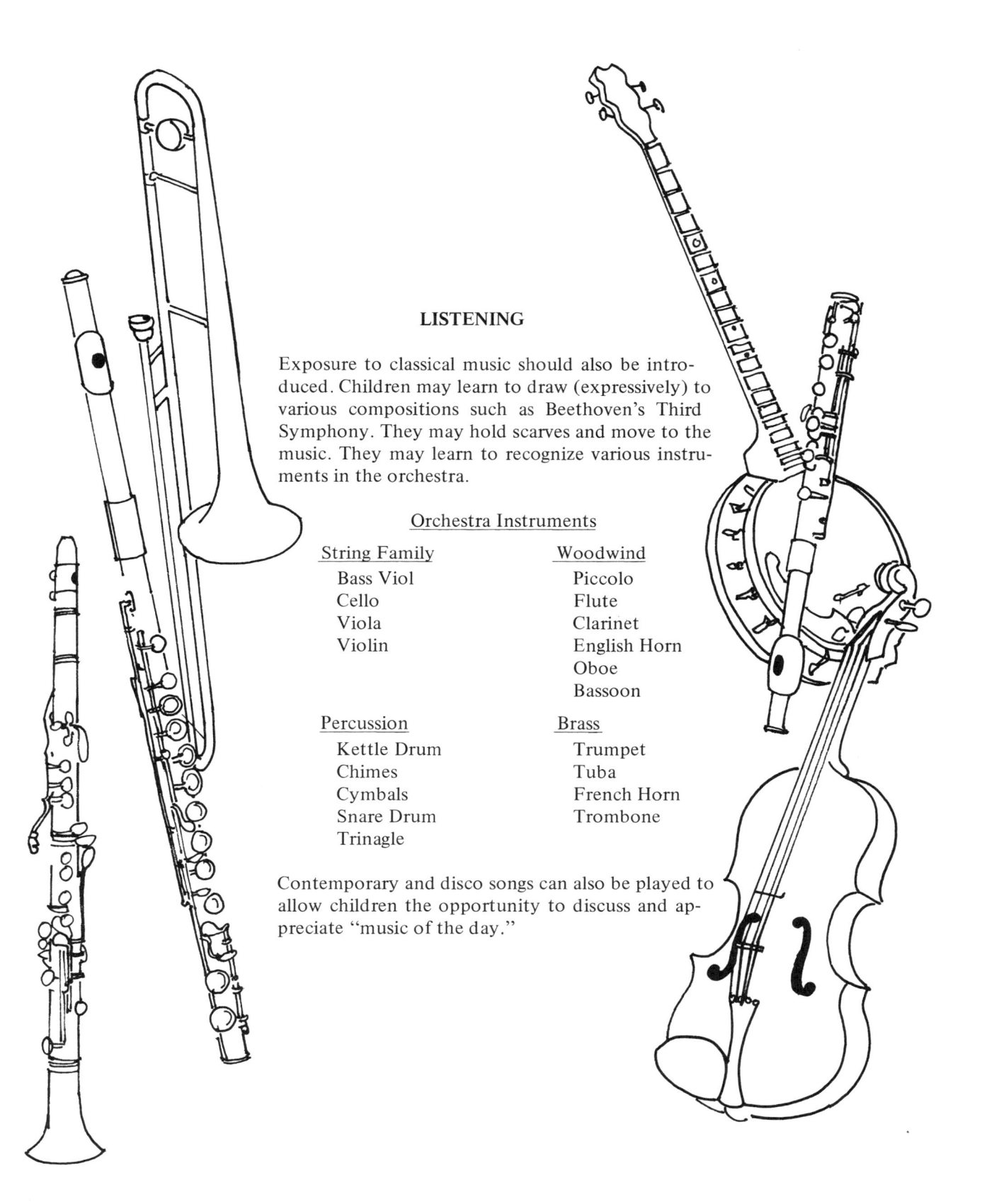

LISTENING

Exposure to classical music should also be introduced. Children may learn to draw (expressively) to various compositions such as Beethoven's Third Symphony. They may hold scarves and move to the music. They may learn to recognize various instruments in the orchestra.

Orchestra Instruments

String Family	Woodwind
Bass Viol	Piccolo
Cello	Flute
Viola	Clarinet
Violin	English Horn
	Oboe
	Bassoon

Percussion	Brass
Kettle Drum	Trumpet
Chimes	Tuba
Cymbals	French Horn
Snare Drum	Trombone
Trinagle	

Contemporary and disco songs can also be played to allow children the opportunity to discuss and appreciate "music of the day."

Records for Listening

Some excellent records are as follows:

Sesame Street, Children's Television Workshop, Columbia Book and Record Library CBS, Inc., 51 W. 52 Street, New York, New York.

Free To Be... You And Me, Conceived by Marlo Thomas, Developed and Edited by Carole Hart, Letty Cottin Pogrebin, Mary Rogers, Marlo Thomas. Ms. Foundation, Inc., McGraw Hill Book Co., New York, New York.

Hap Palmer's series, Educational Activities, Inc. Freeport, N. Y. 11520

Children can be introduced to rhythm by various approaches. The following references may be helpful:

Threshold to Music by Mary Helen Richards. Harper & Row Publishers, School Department, Evanston, Illinois 60201, 1964. (Experience Charts illustrated by Trudi Richards.)

New Rhythm Band Method. M. M. Cole Publ. Co., 251 E. Grand Ave., Chicago, Ill. 60611, 1937 (1964).

SIGHT READING

Note Bunny

To introduce the concept of "note," a bunny with hidden whole notes may be drawn. The child locates the whole notes. The drawing concept can be extended by making more detailed drawings concealing various notes and/or musical symbols. See page 151.

Functional Area: Cognitive (music)

Purpose: The child will have practice in identifying musical notes as he plays with the games.

Functional Area:

Purpose:

Music Worm

The music worm has the letters A to G on his various sections. The pieces have a staff with various notes represented. The child matches the note with its letter name. The correct letter is on the back of the piece to make the game self correcting. See page 152.

Functional Area: Cognitive (music)

Purpose: Reinforcement of the musical notes will be accomplished as the child plays with the games.

Functional Area:

Purpose:

Music Symbol Pie

The musical symbols may be placed on pie wedges. The corresponding symbol or symbol name may be drawn on the pie. The child learns to match the symbols and the words. See page 154.

Functional Area: Cognitive

Purpose: The child will have practice in learning basic music theory as he plays with the games.

Functional Area:

Purpose:

Theory Pages

Theory pages can be cut out of old music books and glued inside a file folder and covered in clear contact paper. The child can learn the treble and bass slogans, thus preparing him for note reading. See page 155.

Name _____

Find 2 whole notes on Mr. Rabbit.

Put a red ring around each whole note.

Color Mr. Rabbit BROWN.

151

152

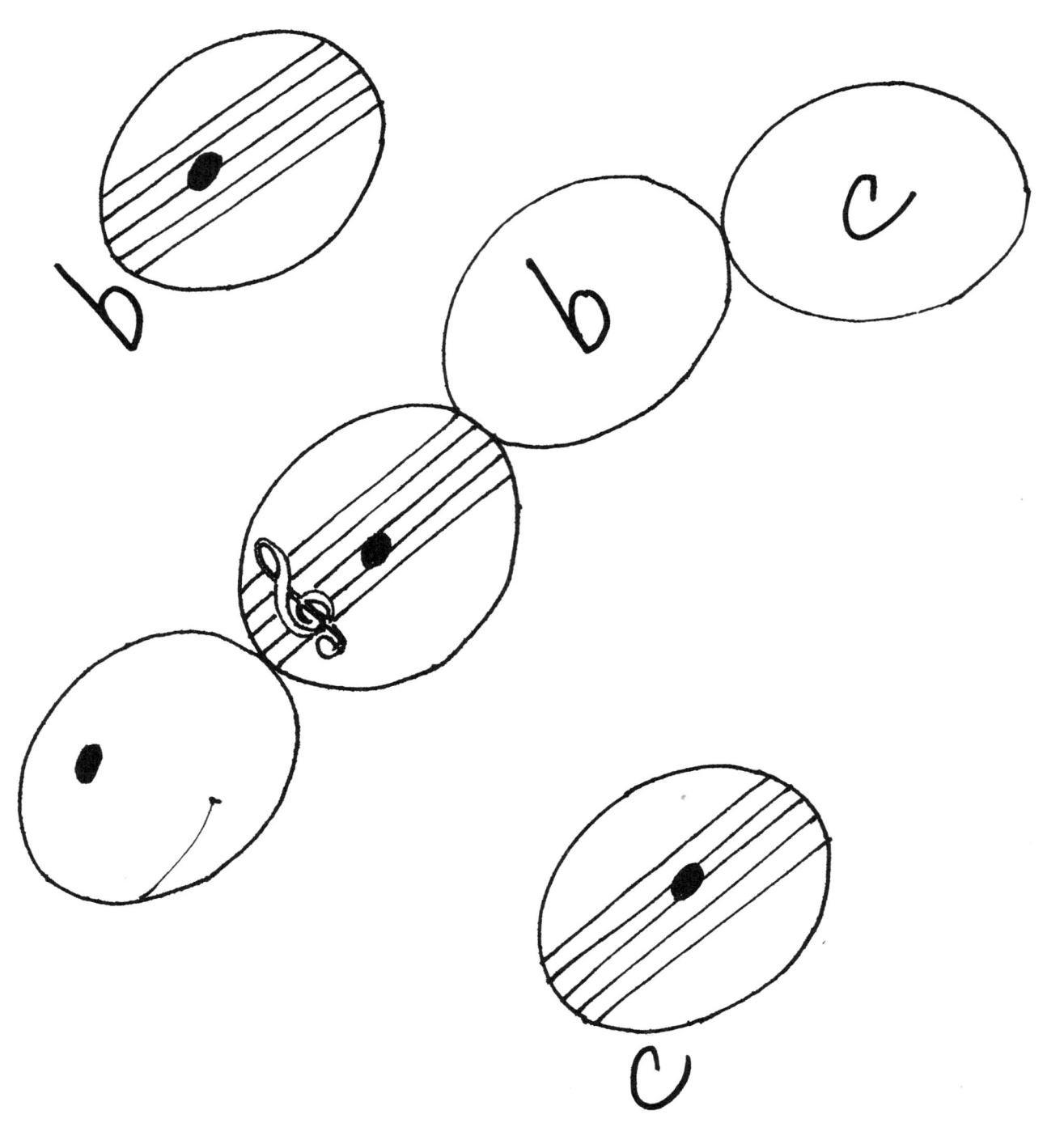

153

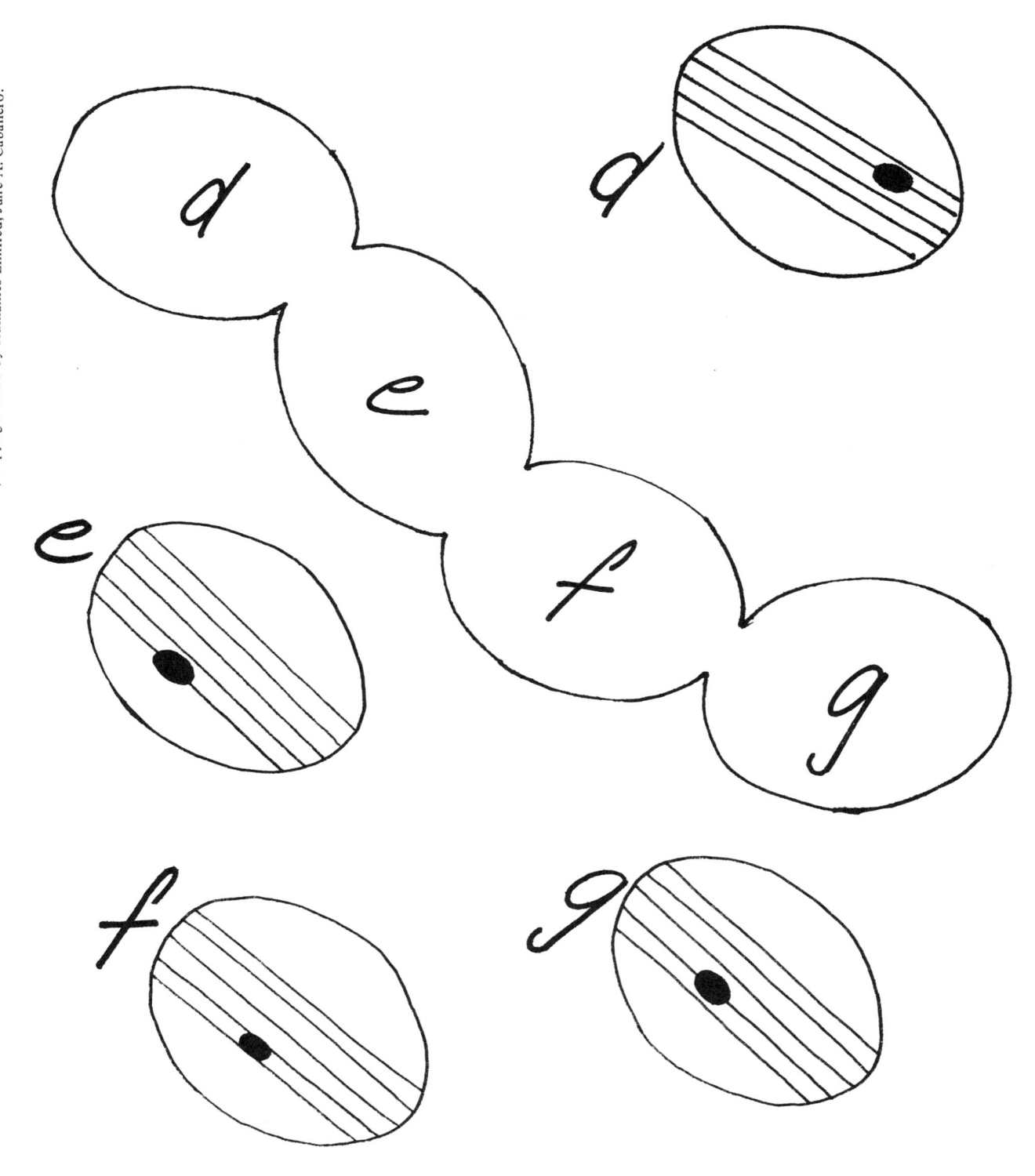

MUSIC SYMBOL PIE

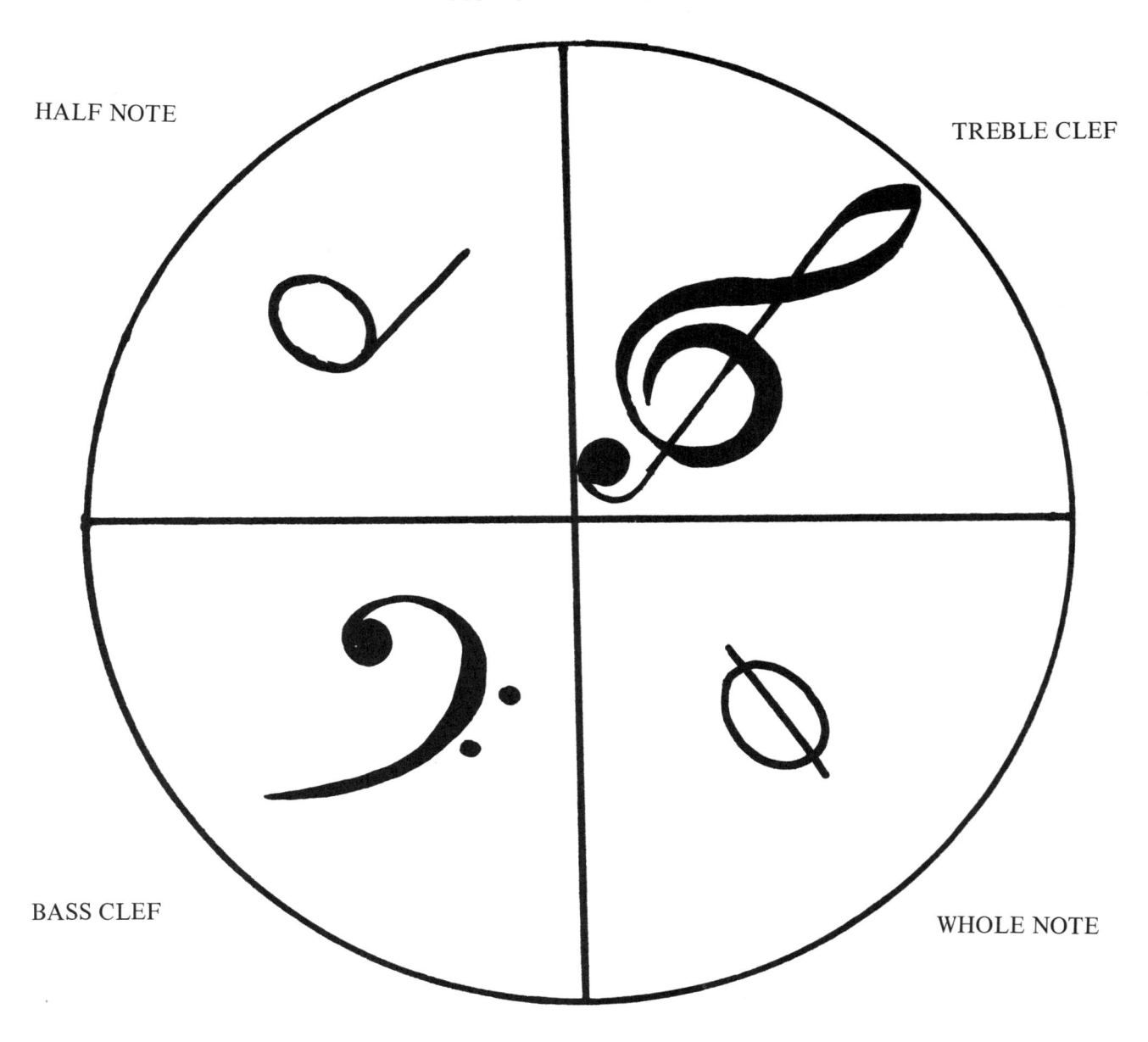

HALF NOTE

TREBLE CLEF

BASS CLEF

WHOLE NOTE

Cut out the pie and duplicate a second set of pie wedges. The child can match the two sets of symbols. Older children can name the symbols. The pie concept can also be extended by adding more pie wedges and symbols.

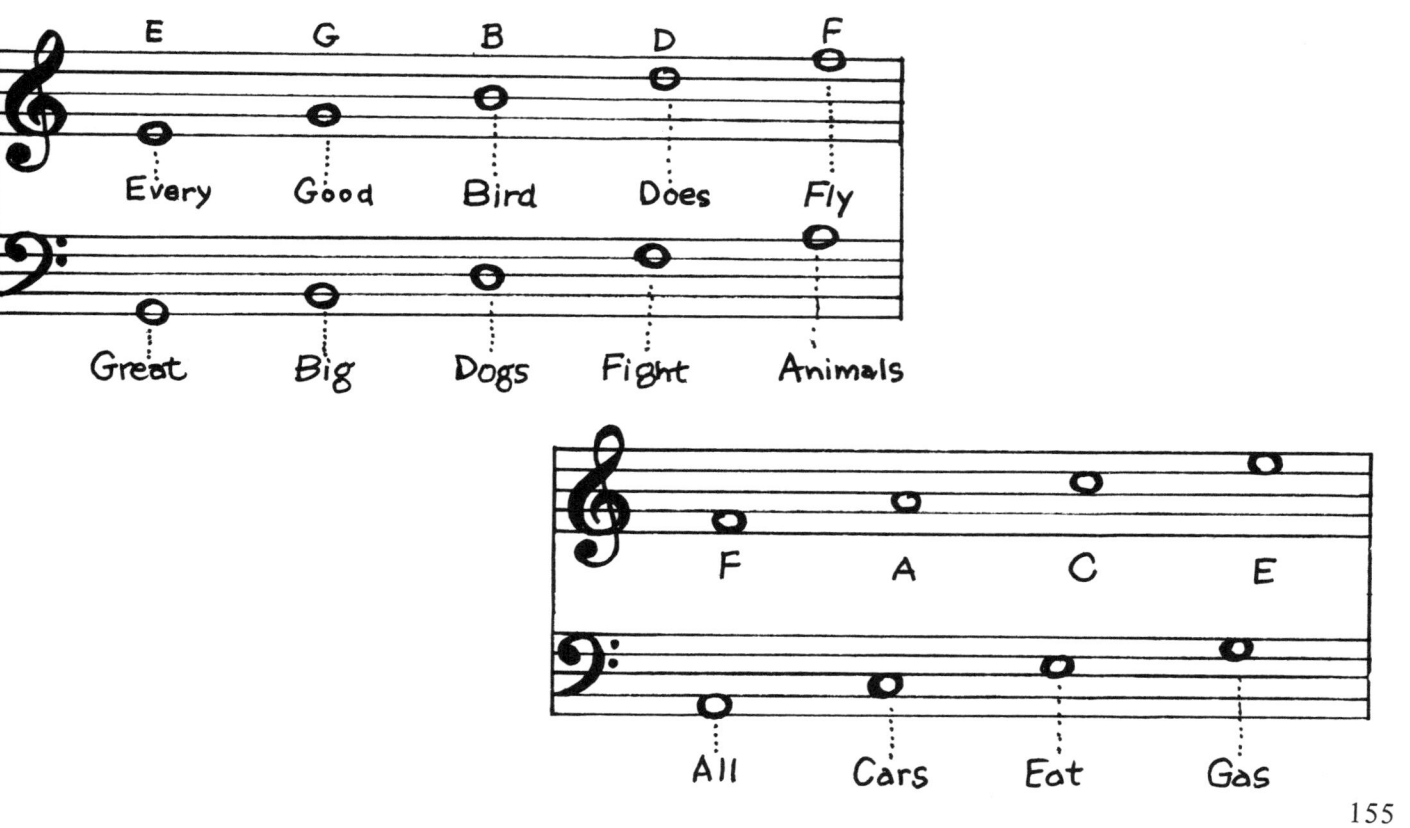

TREBLE and BASS CLEFS

155

CREATIVITY

A creative attitude toward music is always interesting for the teacher as well as the students. Children may make their own instruments or put words to music or music to words. Make up activities to get children interested. For example: Sing a song to get them all in line, all children with blue pants, all children with red pants, etc. There are a lot of records that children love that have rhythmic activities.

Ethnic dances also provide creative outlets for children. Fiestas and luaus can again provide an interdisciplinary lesson.

Polynesian Dances

The children can learn Polynesian dances and make costumes to further their study of other cultures. Coordination and fun follow the experience.

MAORIAN: Hoe a te Waka

1. Hoe ate waka e hine ma
   (3 times)
   Paddle canoe, one side then the other

2. Kia piki ai ki runga
   (2 times)
   Cross hands, palms up, raise upward, shake
   clap

HAWAIIAN: Kuu poo
(parts of the body)

Kuu poo (point to the head)
Kuu maka (eyes)
Kuu pepe iao (ears)
Kuu iho (nose)
Waha (mouth) niho (teeth)
A lalo (tongue)

Po la lima akau (right hand)
Po la lima hema (left hand)
U a pau (finish)[63]

HALLOWEEN FELT PATTERNS

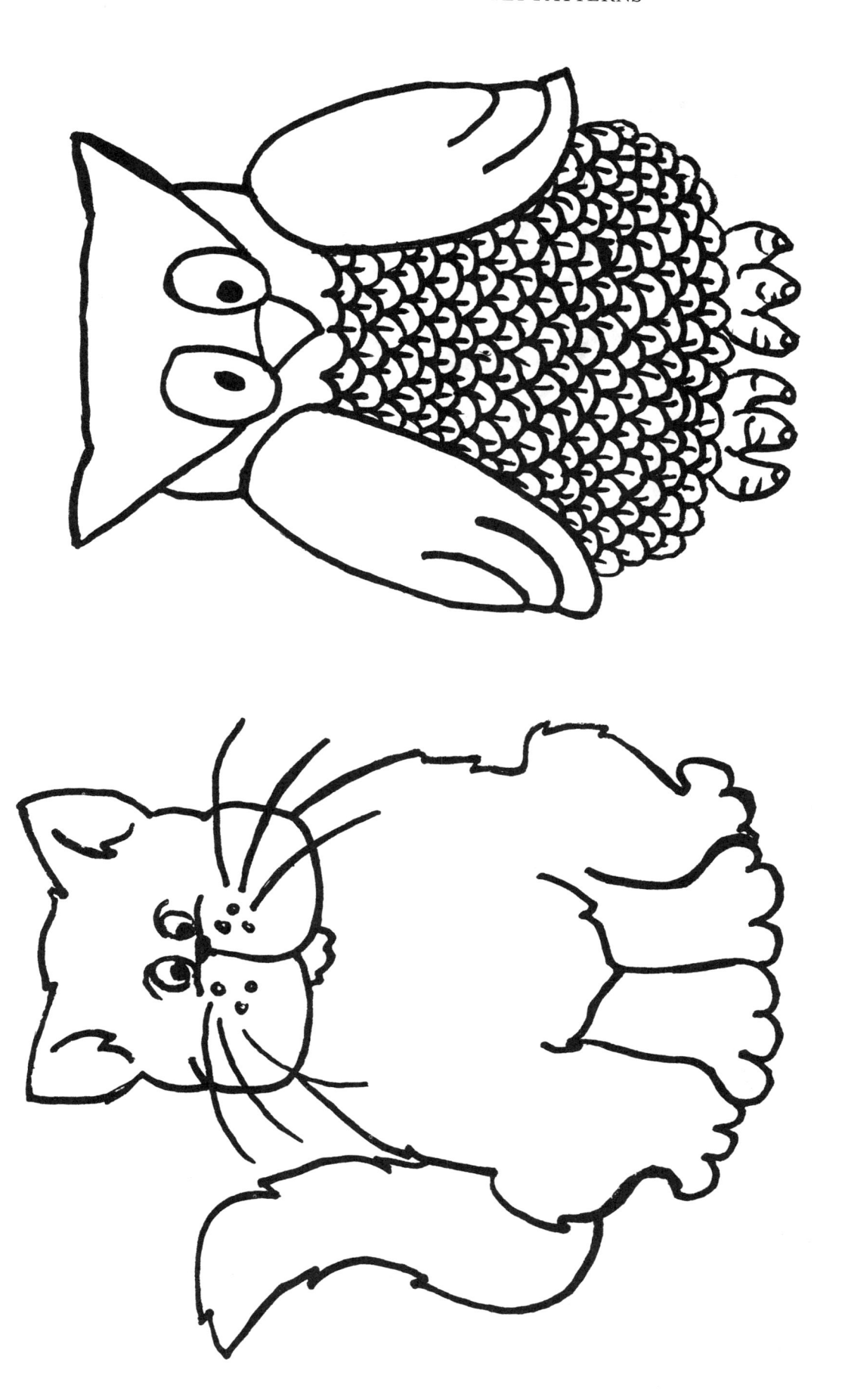

157

From THE HANDBOOK OF LEARNING ACTIVITIES FOR YOUNG CHILDREN, Copyright 1980 by Humanics Limited, Jane A. Caballero.

PILGRIM OUTFITS

GIRLS COLLAR

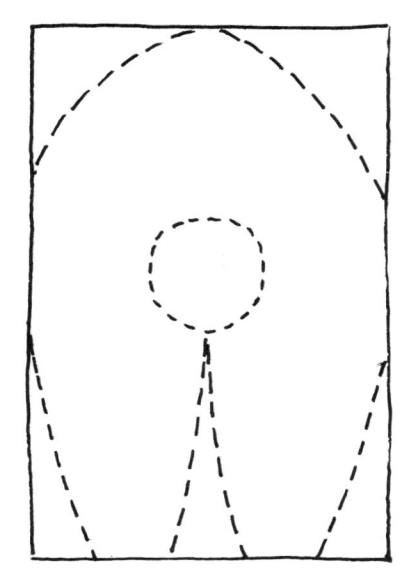

BOYS COLLAR

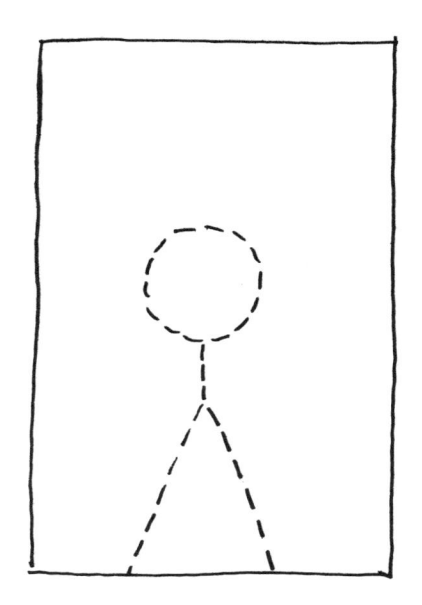

GIRLS HAT

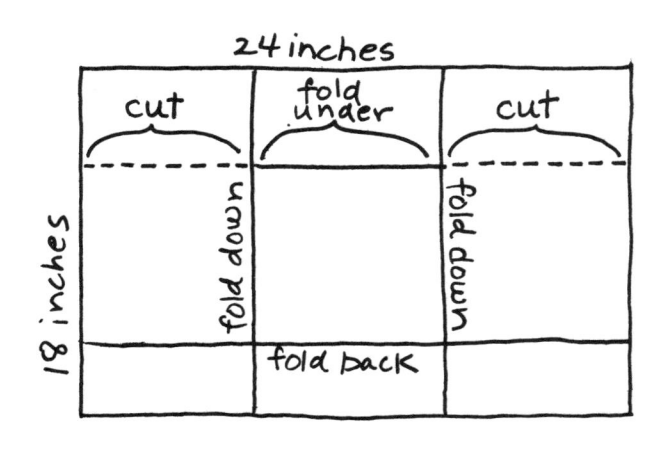

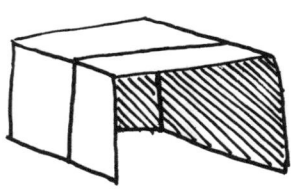

24 inches

cut — fold under — cut

fold down

fold down

18 inches

fold back

159

Staple tabs together.

extend tabs to the length that will fit around head.

EASTER BASKET

Name_____

daisy

tulip

daisy

Spring Flowers

162

From THE HANDBOOK OF LEARNING ACTIVITIES FOR YOUNG CHILDREN, Copyright 1980 by Humanics Limited, Jane A. Caballero.

part III
loose ends

chapter 13
behavior

The self-concept is the evaluation that an individual has of himself and the extent to which he feels that he is a worthy and capable person. A person establishes his self-concept through interaction with others. A positive self-concept enables an individual to use his abilities more freely. A inadequate self concept limits what the individual can do. The development of a positive self-concept is essential to children's happiness and chances for future success, both inside and outside the classroom. Perhaps the greatest responsibility of a teacher of young children is to create a learning environment which encourages children and respects their opinion and feelings. In promoting self-concepts, teachers often employ techniques. One method of encouraging a positive self-concept among young children involves the employment of affective education programs. Affective education is any program or set of activities which has growth in the affective domain as its primary purpose The affective domain includes interests, attitudes, appreciations, values, feelings, emotions, and adequate adjustment. Examples of affective education programs include Magic Circle and Values Clarification. Through such programs children are encouraged to identify and to express their feelings and ideas openly thus learning how to deal with them in a constructive, positive manner.[64]

Another method of encouraging a positive self-concept is the technique generally referred to a "behavior modification." Behavior modification involves the process of rewarding positive behaviors while ignoring or disapproving of negative behavior. A further explanation of behavior modification will follow.

BEHAVIOR MODIFICATION

Behavior—anything a person does, says or thinks that can be observed directly or indirectly
Modification—changing thus "changing behavior"

Behavior modification is a technique of changing behavior by rewarding the kind you want to encourage and ignoring or disapproving the kind you want to discourage.

Behavior modification is based on the theory that behavior is learned. You don't really have to understand why the child is behaving inappropriately. You just have to teach him new responses that will be accepted. At first the teacher reinforces the desired behavior, but the ultimate goal is to encourage the child to have appropriate self control. Intrinsic motivation is first established through external motivation.

The basis of behavior modification procedures is contingency management — in other words there is a relationship between the behavior and what happens afterwards. The teacher can respond to a behavior by: approval, withholding approval, disapproval, threat of disapproval and ignoring. It's best to try to reward the child every time he behaves correctly, at first. Then the reinforcement should be less generous. Eventually, the child should establish self-control.

The first step is to pinpoint or identify the desired behaviors. (must observe them, remember) Then you won't be tempted to label a child as troublesome, problem, bad. All behavior is learned, so our students will learn to do things that bring pleasure. Therefore, rewarding desired behavior will encourage a child to do what we want. This is referred to as a positive reinforcement — it is based on the principle that behavior which is rewarded tends to continue. This should not be confused with bribing — which occurs before the act is done, such as when a child threatens to do something bad unless paid off. Thus, in BM the reward takes place only after the child has behaved appropriately.

The child learns to avoid doing things which are ignored or bring discomfort just as he will learn to do things which are rewarded.

Punishment usually doesn't have lasting effects. Try to concentrate on positive reinforcement to mold behavior in the appropriate direction, avoiding punishment except for severe situations that could cause physical harm to the child or others or in cases of property damage.

It is very important to be consistent when using positive reinforcement to promote positive behavior. One needs to learn to catch the child being good.

As stated earlier, praise and attention are the best methods to use in increasing positive behavior. It may take a while, but persistence in catching the child being good should eventually pay off. Some positive words and actions are:

- Words: yes, good, delightful, terrific, fabulous, outstanding
- Sentences: That's good, Well done, Show us how, Thank you
- Relationships: You're a good person, You have my respect, I'd like to have that, You should be proud of that
- Symbols: Smiley faces, OK, stamps, honor roll for display
- Expressions: Look, smile, nod, grin, clap, touch on shoulder

Some behavior which should be ignored should also be known. Children are active-motor behaviors such as getting up without permission, walking or running around, moving or wiggling should be ignored. Verbal comments or noises can usually be ignored.

A general rule to follow may be: give praise and attention to behaviors which facilitate learning — tell the child what he's being praised for — reinforce behaviors incompatible with those you wish to decrease — ignore behaviors which do not threaten safety — ignoring does not work unless there is a lot of praise for appropriate behavior.[65]

Rules
Establishing rules to be followed is one of the first steps in pinpointing the expected behaviors. Formulating, agreeing and understanding rules is important for the children. Of course, you will guide them in this task. The way you'll get rules they'll be more likely to follow and you'll be teaching the democratic process. You must limit the number of rules and state them in a positive way. Be sure that they understand the rules. The idea behind good discipline is to get the child working with you — not against you. As stated earlier, catch the child being good. This will help you get started in looking for positive behavior and developing a positive climate.

One thing you will have to discover is what rewards are effective for what children. The key to using rewards effectively is finding out what turns each child on. Just remember to reward immediately after the desired behavior occurs.

Let's think a minute about why misbehavior occurs. Children are trying to achieve one of the following four goals:

- undue attention – He wants attention and service
- power – He wants to be the boss
- revenge – He wants to hurt us
- display of inadequacy – He wants to be left alone with no demands made upon him[66]

Misbehaving children are discouraged children. Encouragement and positive reinforcement is extremely helpful with them. A positive attitude toward him will definitely help – it is up to you to decide how to respond. You possess the power to make a child's life miserable or joyous. Your response to a situation may decide whether a crisis will be escalated or de-escalated and if a child is humanized or dehumanized.

The following key points may also assist the teacher in preventing discipline problems in the classroom.

1) Room arrangement and preparation is vital.
2) Boredom and frustration cause trouble.
3) Be firm, but friendly.
4) Respect for the individual child is important.
5) Harsh discipline is unnecessary, but some behavior should be forbidden. (Dangerous situations for the child)
6) Out of self disicpline comes self-control.
7) The key to discipline is the teacher.
8) Be positive – reinforce good behavior.
9) Children imitate you, so set the example.
10) Teach children to put materials up where they got them.

Prevent trouble by organizing the program, clarifying rules, and having a well supervised absorbing program with balanced play.

You, the materials, and the room should be ready before the children arrive. Don't demand instant obedience. Don't suppress intense feelings. Provide outlets – art, music, play, physical education. Establish trust.

Children's ideas are different from ours – not always right or wrong.

chapter 14
evaluation

A major concern of early childhood programs is how to evaluate and make the evaluation readily accessible and meaningful. Teachers of young children constantly evaluate their performance and group them for skill development. The evaluation may be informal and related to the parent in the grocery store, or it may be based on a more structured test and results sent home. In any case, evaluation is taking place, and it should be an integral part of the education program.

The general purpose of evaluation is to determine whether or not your goals have been accomplished. Many evaluation methods are too lengthy, specifying each color, each body part, each number, and each letter to be taught. The time involved in checking off these skills would occupy too much time; and therefore, one would not be able to teach the child. The parent does not have the time to look at each assessment test performed nor is it all parents' interest or concern. Many check lists omit the basic hierarchy of needs. Maslow presents this knowledge but sometimes one tends to assume skills are to be taught whether the child is ready or not. His hierarchy should be related to evaluation. The needs are: (1) physiological needs, (2) safety needs, (3) love needs, (4) esteem needs, (5) self-actualization.[67]

The first concern should be the actual physical readiness of the child. Health forms are available in any school or center and should be the primary concern of the teacher to identify any abnormalities in hearing, seeing, coordination, speech, and body size. Auditory, visual, and perceptual development tests should be dealt with first. The language competence-auditory, visual, and general responses to language should be determined.

Next the emotional and social maturity and adaptability of the child is to be encouraged. We know one can't teach a child with emotional problems who can't interact in the classroom. A preliminary check could be a body awareness test. Let the child draw a picture of himself and name his body parts. An indication of his self concept will be apparent to a trained teacher. The teacher can then ask the child questions about his interests, family, friends, wishes, and worries, and allow verbal interaction. Check lists asking the child if he likes different things in and out of school will also indicate insight into his self-concept. The teacher may also ask him about himself. Are you friendly, happy, sad, cooperative, mean, popular, brave, clean, and helpful? Observations of the child working within a group will be the best indication of his social cooperation. The self control and responsibility of the child would also be best assessed by teacher observation.

The third area to consider in evaluation would provide us with math concepts. Children begin counting early. The influence of such programs as Sesame Street has added to this skill. However, being able to write, match, and understand these number concepts is an area teachers and parents must look at closely. Numerous activities must be provided to allow for transfer of and understanding of number concepts. Sizes and shapes of objects must be noted.

The fourth area of evaluation may relate to shapes. The ability to draw and name the circle, triangle, square, rectangle and diamond as well as the ability to distinguish the shapes in figure-ground patterns is vital.

The fifth area of evaluation may relate to recognition of colors. The name and awareness of where these colors appear is a vital area that must not be over simplified.

The sixth area deals with the most important concepts we must develop in early childhood. It appears to be overlooked by the untrained person and must be explained to parents. This area deals with general readiness skills: left-right progression, comparison alike-different, size, sequence, position, direction, patterns, classification, sorting, matching, pairing, revisualization, and copying. These skills are developed through the games and activities provided in early childhood centers. They must be developed before reading can occur. Children must have concrete experiences and be allowed to play with games and objects that allow for the manipulative skills development. Teacher direction is needed but the materials have a vital role.

After the child has the understanding of many of the above skills, letters, sounds, and rhyming words can be emphasized. Again games and verbal interaction is necessary.

The eighth area deals with story telling. Stories must be read to the child and questions must be asked by an adult. Reference should be given to details, main idea, cause-effect, and sequence. The child should be tested for his comprehension level.

Rules, following directions, and listening skills must now be emphasized. Piaget states children aren't ready for formal rules until the approximate age of six, so these skills must be slowly integrated into the child's life.

Finally, the child is ready for reading and math computations; and therefore, his level and abilities should be determined and appropriate lessons prescribed.

Let's not forget our children don't *JUST PLAY* in early childhood centers. They are forming the basis for all later learning. We must recognize how vital these formative years are and the tremendous amount of skills we must develop in the child before he is able to begin to read.

Additional assessment tools are available from Humanics, Limited, 1182 W. Peachtree St., Atlanta, Ga. 30309. *Orientation to Preschool Assessment, Children's Adaptive Behavior Scale, and The Lollipop Test.*

READINESS CHECK LIST

Name _____ Age _____

1. General health (height _____, weight _____)
   - ☐ Visual, auditory discrimination (match alike-different)
   - ☐ Gross, fine motor coordination
   - ☐ Vocabulary, oral discussion
   - ☐ Speech development, oral communication

2. Emotional, social maturity
   - ☐ Self-concept, body parts
   - ☐ Self awareness (name, address, phone, family data, etc.)
   - ☐ Group cooperation
   - ☐ Self control, responsibility

3. Math concepts
   - ☐ Count numbers to 10
   - ☐ Write numbers to 10
   - ☐ Count, write numbers over 10
   - ☐ Match, understand number concepts

4. Shapes, able to draw and name shapes, figure ground discrimination

5. Colors, able to recognize 8 basic colors

6. General readiness
   - ☐ Left to right progression
   - ☐ Comparison, alike, different, size
   - ☐ Sequence
   - ☐ Position, direction
   - ☐ Patterns, classification
   - ☐ Sort, match, pair
   - ☐ Revisualize (shapes, letters, words)
   - ☐ Copy

7. Recognizes upper and lower case letters
   - ☐ Beginning and ending sounds
   - ☐ Rhyming words

8. Storytelling
   - ☐ Recall details, main idea, comprehension, cause-effect
   - ☐ Rules, listening skills, oral directions

9. Reading readiness
   - ☐ (Schonell Reading Inventory)

10. Math readiness
    - ☐ Addition
    - ☐ Subtraction

chapter 15
parent involvement

Parent involvement in the schools provides much value to the education of the young child. The parents bring the insight and understanding of their own child to the school. They bring a variety of skills, knowledge, and experiences which can be utilized by the teacher to enrich the learning environment for all children. As the teacher gets to know the child's parents and his home situation, the teacher can more accurately assess the experiences the child has had before coming to school. She may use his background to build upon new experiences. Through various techniques, teachers can help parents use the many hours at home with their child to further education. Teachers can help parents develop understanding necessary for enjoying their children more fully. Parents of lower economic levels get the opportunity to obtain an education that they will need to help their children at home. Parents can bring skills and knowledge to the classroom. Much parent participation will extend and enrich the school experiences. Areas in which parent participation is particularly helpful include storytelling, music and art activities, field trips, library activities, and group parties. Parents can also be resource persons in specialized areas of activities. In each group of children, there will be some parents who have special talents or hobbies who have the time and facilities to enrich the lives of all children. Benefits from parent involvement are infinite.

Contacting the Parents

There is an increasing realization that parent involvement strengthens the insights and skills evident in schools. It is important to involve parents since their influence upon the development of their children is so important. Teachers should make an effort to contact parents and involve them in the school. The following techniques can be used in helping teachers reach the parents:

1. Invite the parents to join the classroom for the day by phone call or a letter.
2. Make an effort to build a close relationship with the parents so that they feel more confident to relate to you.
3. Arrange personal conferences with the parents.
4. Have workshops that can interest the parents so that they may learn effective methods of dealing with their children.
5. Have group meetings which the parents may attend to become better informed.
6. Involve the parents in participating in special events (field trips, parties).

ACTIVITIES FOR PARENTS TO DO AT HOME

Reading: Read to your child. If you think books are interesting and important, so will he. Point to the pictures and relate them to what you have read. Sit near small children and give them your undivided attention — it *is* important. They associate your attention and closeness with reading, so reading becomes important. Don't make reading a chore — it should be enjoyable. Attention spans are short, so only read to the child as long as he is interested. Look at pictures together and make up stories about them. Suggest that he make up a new ending to his favorite story.

Speech: Try to encourage your child to use words. When you know he can produce speech at one level, don't let him satisfy his needs and wants with speech at a lower level. Make him use his best speech to get what he wants. Don't encourage baby talk. Pronounce words correctly for him. Help your child learn how to dial and talk on the telephone. Play games together and discuss them. When going for a ride in the car point out unusual sights. Watch T.V. together and discuss good and bad shows. Go for walks together and learn to look for, name, and remember things.

Commands: Be sure your child understands and can follow commands such as: show me ... point to ... give me ... hand me ... make an x on ... draw a circle around ... These commands will come later (during school), but he should know them when he starts school. Many tests given for school placement use these directions. Many children are placed in slower groups — not because they are slow — but because they couldn't follow the test directions.

Same-Different: Language concepts are based on being able to distinguish likenesses and differences. There is no way a child can learn to look at an object and correctly call it by name unless he can see that the object is different from other objects. Point out things which are alike, the same, and different. All animals may initially be called a dog until he learns the differences and begins to discriminate between dogs, cats, cows, horses, etc.

Number Concepts: A child should be able to count by rote to 10 by the time he enters kindergarten. He should be able to demonstrate that he knows how many a number is by responding correctly to a command like "Give me 4 blocks." Count his fingers and toes, plates and forks as you set the table, cars passing, or *anything* else.

Color Concepts: The child should be able to identify the 8 basic colors when he is 5–6 years old. Tell him what color his clothes and toys are. Ask him what color things are. If he doesn't know, tell him.

Spatial Prepositions: A preschool child should be able to place an object in, into, under, and on top of something else. He should be able to demonstrate that he knows beside, in front of, in back of, around, through, with, behind, over. Play "Place the Object" games.

Grammer: By 3–4 the child should be *using sentences*, stringing 2, 3 or more words together. Check to see if he uses *compound sentences* connected with "and," as "Bobby go and mama get ice cream," or "I went with Buba and we went swimming." He should, by at least 4, be using "I" as a sentence subject, "I go" instead of "me go" or "Neal go." He should be using the " – *ing*" *form of verbs*, running, going, seeing, etc. He should be *using plurals*. He may not always use the correct plural form, but his mistakes will show you that he is applying the rule, as "mans" for men or "shoo-ziz" for shoes. He should be using *past tense*. Again, his errors on irregular verbs will show you he is using the rules, as when he says "come-dad" for came or "goes" for went. He should be *asking questions*, using a helping verb, as "am I going?" or "are you ready?" and using "wh-words" and "where are we going?" and "why can't I?" He should be using *negatives*, "no, not, can't, won't," etc. Many of these things will not be completely learned until after the child is past 5, but he should at least be beginning to use them by age 4.

There are two kinds of answers to questions. There are answers which stay the same, no matter how often the question is asked, as "How many fingers do I have" and questions whose answers change, as "What time is it" or "Where are we going." A child frequently asks a question over and over when you are sure he knows the answer. He keeps asking, even when he knows the answer, until he decides what kind of answer it is. Keep answering.

Remember: a child's parents are his best teachers. Older brothers and sisters, friends, relatives and teachers can help, but if his language is to develop properly, *you must talk to him and have him talk to you.* He needs explanations when he doesn't understand. Tell him what words mean. *Talk to him and listen to him.*[68]

THE 8 BASIC TOYS

The Far West Lab for Educational Research and Development has identified 8 basic toys that can be played at home by the child with his parent. The discriptions and illustrations of the games from the Parent-Child Toy Library are based on the filmstrip-cassette presentation.[69]

Sound Cans
To teach the child to identify sounds that are the same and not the same. Put objects in several containers. Put the same objects into 2 different containers. The child shakes the cans identifying the sounds. (Spices may be substituted and the child can identify smells.)

Feely Bag
To help the child recognize shapes by sight. To help the child recognize shapes by feel. A bag is provided with various objects inside. Other objects may include paper clips, cut out numbers, eraser, etc.

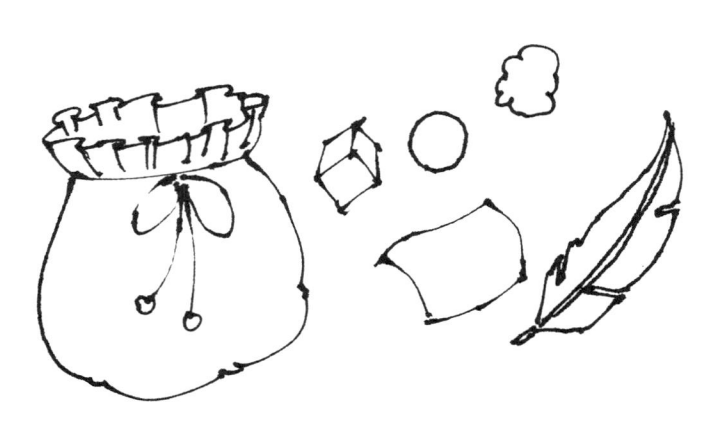

Color Lotto
To help the child learn to match a color from an example of that color. To help the child learn the names of colors. Cut up 18 squares of different colors — in pairs of the same color. Nine squares are glued on to a surface and the other 9 squares are left separated so that the child can manipulate and match the colors.

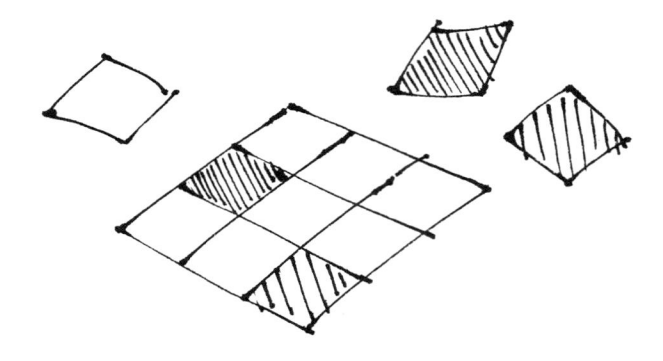

Stacking Squares
To teach same size and not the same size. To help the child see patterns and extend them. To strengthen the learning of the names red, blue, green, and yellow. Colored squares with progressively smaller areas and center holes are provided. Dowel sticks with progressively smaller centers are also provided. The child arranges the squares on the sticks.

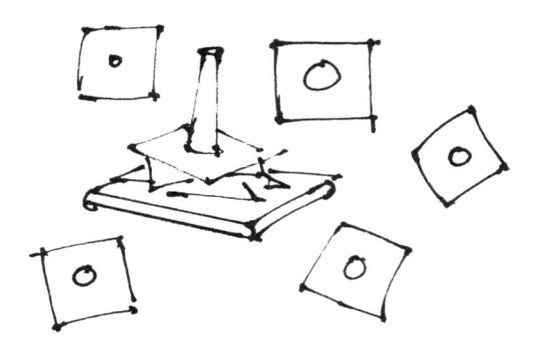

Wooden Table Blocks
To help the child learn relationships: taller, shorter, tallest, shortest. To help the child learn size relationships. Blocks representing one to ten units are provided. The child arranges the blocks in sequence.

Number Puzzle
To help the child learn to match numerals with the number quantities that they represent. To teach the child to count in sequence. Puzzles with numbers, corresponding cut out holes and pegs are provided. The child reads the number and places the correct number of pegs in the holes.

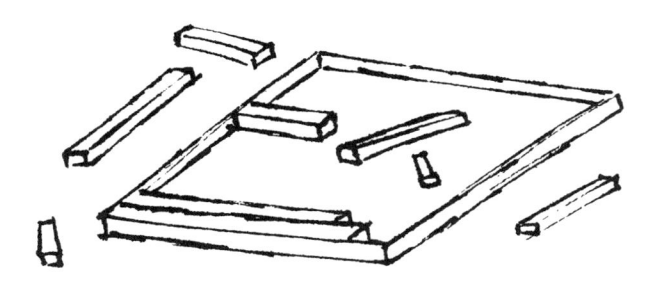

Flannel Board
To help the child learn same and not the same in regard to shape and to size. To help the child learn which colors are the same and which are not the same. Pieces of various shapes and colors are provided along with a flannel board. (Construction paper with a small piece of attached sandpaper will stick to the flannel or felt board.) The child arranges the pieces according to the objectives.

Color Blocks Read-O-Graph
To teach the child to learn words that tell where things are located. To help the child see patterns and learn to extend them. Color beads in the shapes of squares, circles, and cylinders as well as a base with attached dowel sticks are provided. The child arranges the patterns as indicated.

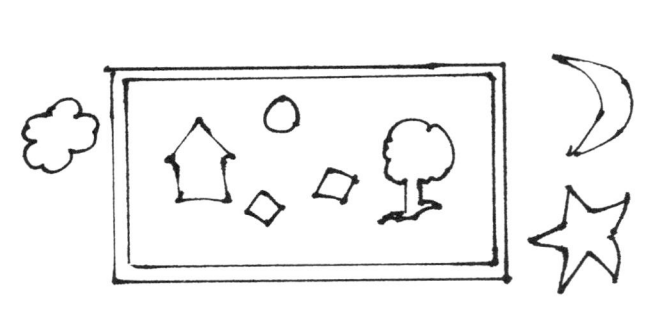

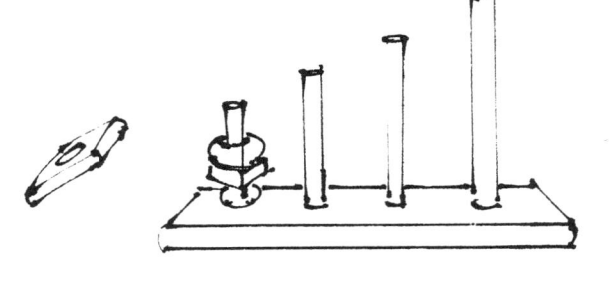

173

Tips for Parents

1. Respect the "feelings" of a child.
2. Never reject a child.
3. Never criticize or reprimand a child in front of others.
4. Use a positive approach - encourage at all times.
5. Don't make a crisis of everything.
6. Keep your voice low clear and firm. Don't shout or raise your voice to a high pitch.
7. Be fair, unemotional and calm.
8. Avoid be placed on the 'defensive' with children. Don't argue.
9. Punishment is not always the answer.
10. Don't show negative feelings toward a child. Always let him know you like him.
11. Don't make quick diagnoses.
12. Don't accuse or threaten. You may have to carry out something that is impossible or impractical
13. Listen more than you talk. You may learn something.

FILE FOLDER GAMES

The purpose of the following folder games is to provide parents, teachers, and other concerned persons with curriculum ideas that they may use and develop based on their particular needs.

The basic format is to present a picture of a completed folder to copy or adapt. Some patterns are also included. Variations of the folder are suggested. The educator can extend or simplify any idea presented; therefore, this section provides suggestions, but allows the educator to individualize the folders based on the child's developmental level.

The folders are unique because they encourage the educator to take an active role in designing the curriculum for the child. It is not a ready made kit that merely requires presentation. It requires the awareness and creativity of the user in developing the folders and extending the suggested ideas. Children readily identify with the folders and are enthused when they see their teacher involved in the actual making of the folders designed for them. They also are motivated when allowed to make their own folders. The folders are merely a stepping stone for more curriculum folders. They are not only inexpensive to develop, but are extremely practical in that they are easy to store. Children respond to the folders and learn how to learn by choosing and developing additional folders.

The success of the folders are based largely on the creativity and awareness of the educator in developing her "personalized curriculum kit."

The curriculum folders are very inexpensive to make and are designed to meet the educational objectives in the early childhood period of development, approximately 3-8 years of age. They require the minimum amount of adult instruction. Therefore, they are ideal for parent use. They require imagination and flexibility and maintain the interest level of the child. Areas of the curriculum that are covered are: general readiness, language arts, and math.

The opportunity for using this approach is endless. Parents of young children often take an active role in their child's education and are constantly seeking educational activities they can do with their child. The classroom teacher is definitely interested and in the position to use the folder games. Home-based Head Start, as well as the educational centers themselves, are in a position to benefit from the folders. The paraprofessionals in early childhood centers often become bored or frustrated because of lack of proper materials and these folders are ideal for their use. Resource teachers frequently seek out different ideas to supply their teachers based on specific objectives. Inservice ideas are always needed.

These are only a few examples of the folders which you can make. All you need are file folders and marking pens. Of course, you may add construction paper, yarn, library envelopes, and clear contact paper.

So let's begin........

[70] The folder games in this section were taken from *Extending Your Early Childhood Curriculum* by J. Caballero. More folder game ideas are available in the upcoming Humanics publication, *Vanilla Manila Folder Games for Young Children.*

Name: Seriation-Pencils, Rectangles

Skill: Seriation-putting objects in a series

Procedure: Pencils can be used to explain the seriation concept. The pencils are put in a series from short to tall or tall to short. Questions refering to the order may be asked.

Variations: Extend questions: Show me the tallest, first, last, etc.

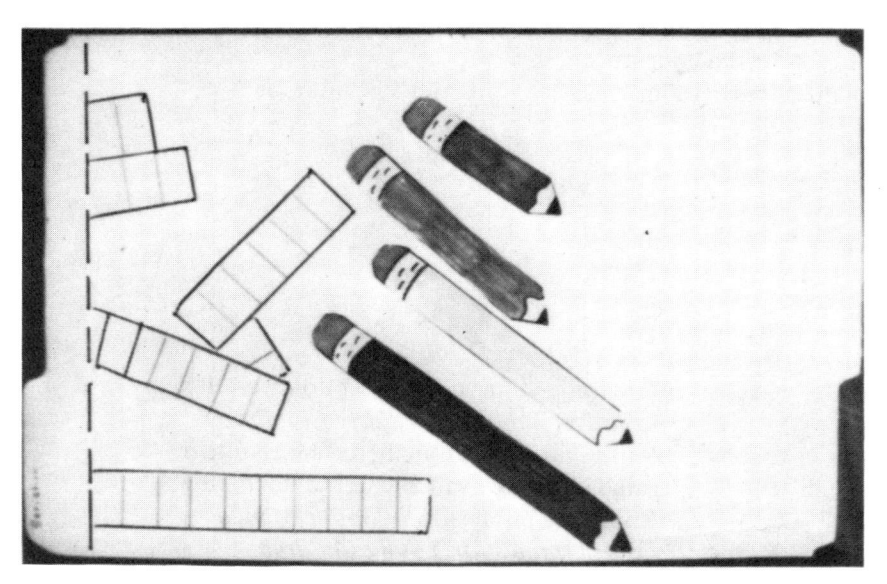

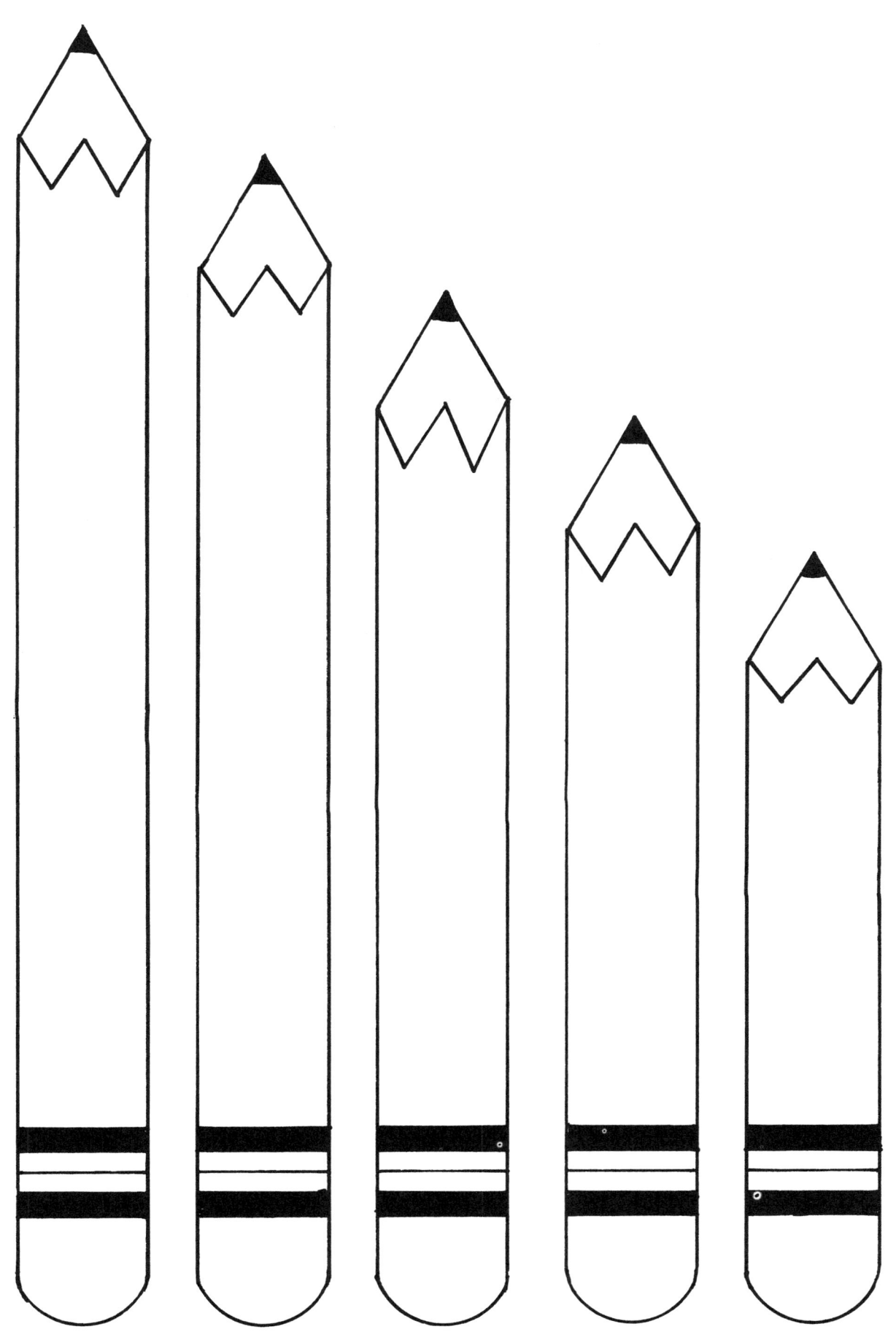

From THE HANDBOOK OF LEARNING ACTIVITIES FOR YOUNG CHILDREN, Copyright 1980 by Humanics Limited, Jane A. Caballero.

177

From THE HANDBOOK OF LEARNING ACTIVITIES FOR YOUNG CHILDREN, Copyright 1980 by Humanics Limited, Jane A. Caballero.

Name: Milkman

Skill: Counting to 10, Numeral and Set Construction

Procedure: The child reads the numeral on the door of the house, counts the corresponding number of milk bottles and places them in the slot. The numbers are in sequential order so number suquence is also reinforced.

Variations: Math combination could be substituted for the numeral and the child could count the milk bottles to obtain his answer.

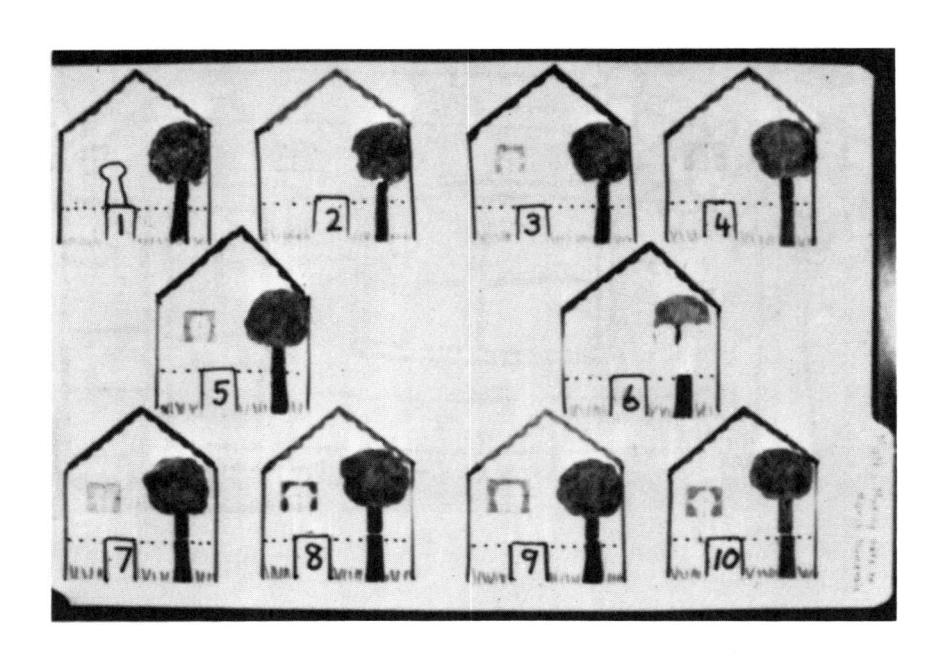

180

Name: Sequence Train

Skill: Placing Words in Sequential Order

Procedure: The engine contains the initial word and the following cars are to be placed in sequential order. The correct number is on the back of the cars.

Variations: Other sequential concepts may be noted on the train (months, days, number words.

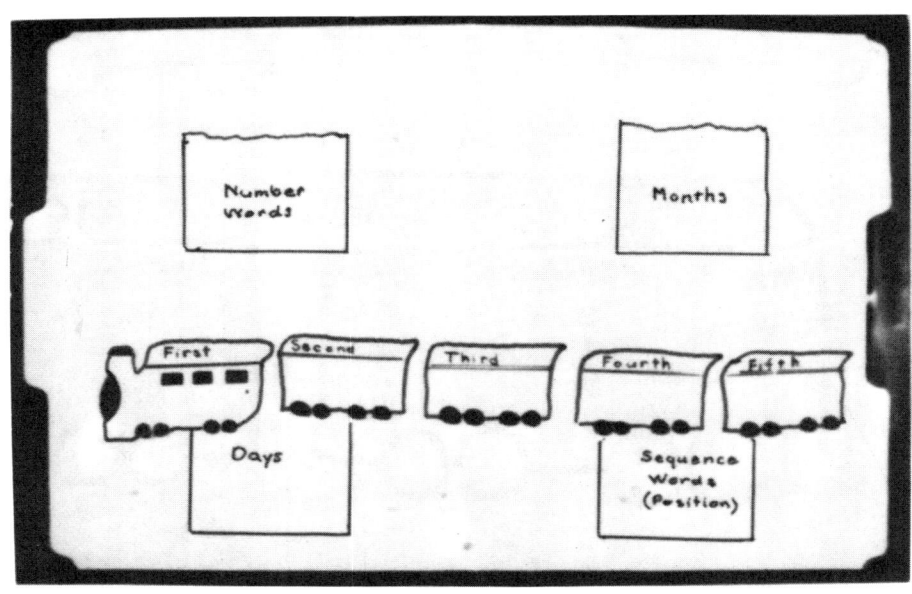

First
Second
Third
Fourth
Fifth
Sixth
Seventh
Eigth

One

Two

Three

Four

Five

Six

Seven

Eight

Monday

Tuesday

Wednesday

Thursday

Friday

Saturday

Sunday

January

- February
- March
- April
- May
- June
- July
- August
- Semptember

Name: Fishbowls

Skill: Number Sequence

Procedure: The child can place the fishbowl in number sequence-the bowl with one fish is first, two fish is second, etc. Verbal questions may then be asked, such as "Show me the biggest (smallest) fish " or "Show me the first (last) fish." The colors may also be noted.

Variations: The fishbowls can be extended and other verbal questions may be asked.

187

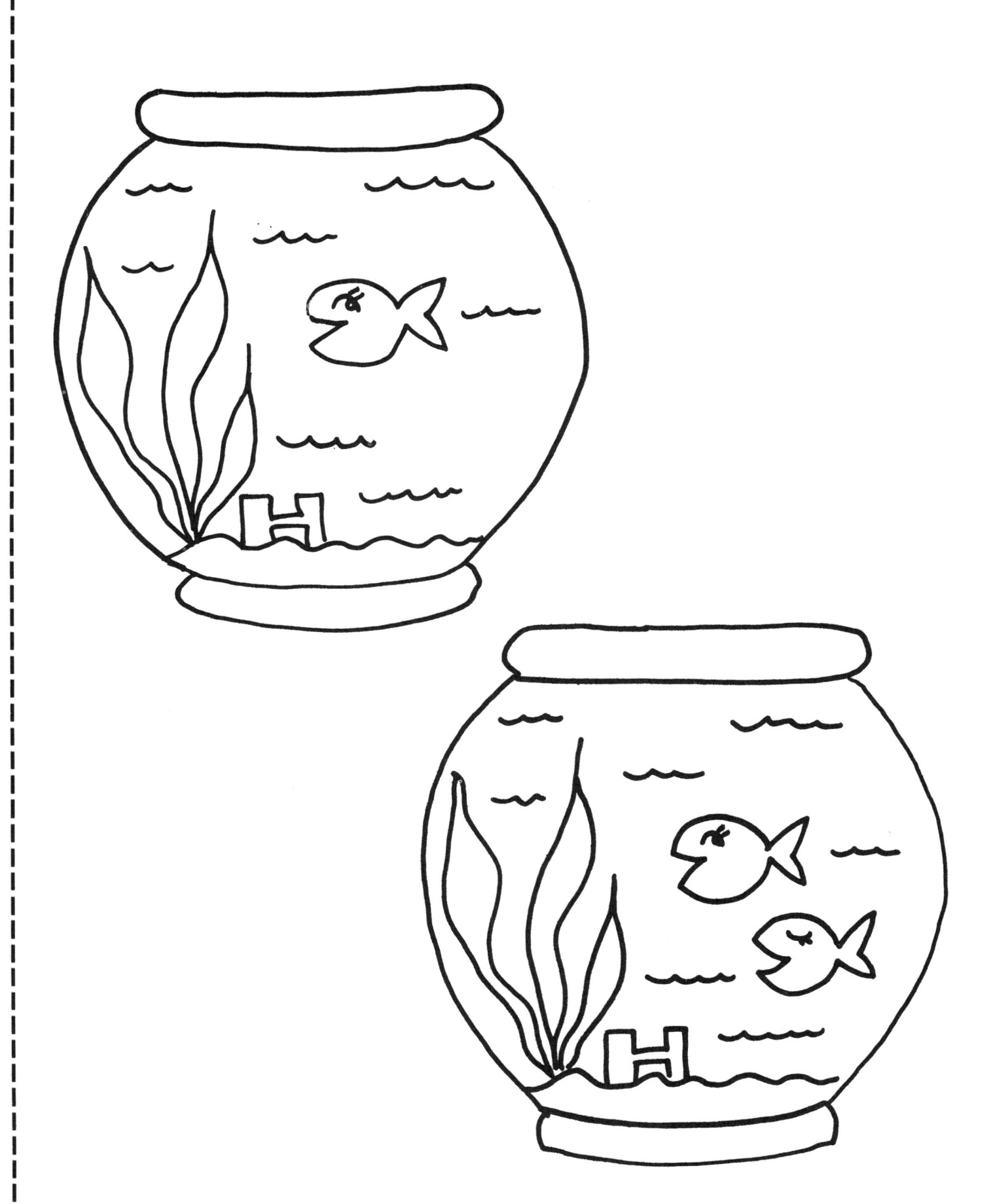

Name: Matching People

Skill: Matching Sets with Numerals 1-10

Procedure: The children with the numerals (or set of dots) are matched with corresponding number. The different children can be described to reinforce any objective such as cultural awareness, color, or dress.

Variations: The children can be used with different symbols, math combinations, or words (opposities).

Color the little people and then write the concepts you wish to teach on them.

Black hair
Brown skin

Brown hair
White skin

Black hair
Yellow skin

Black hair
Brown skin

Blond hair
White skin

Black hair
Brown skin

Red hair
White skin

Blonde hair
White skin

Black hair
Yellow skin

Brown hair
White skin

191

Name: Flower Family

Skill: Word families

Procedure: The child turns the center wheel to find new words. He learns the initial sounds and ending sounds and which combinations make words.

Variations: Any word family group may be substituted.

Cut out the flower base and circle—attach the circle to the base with a brad.

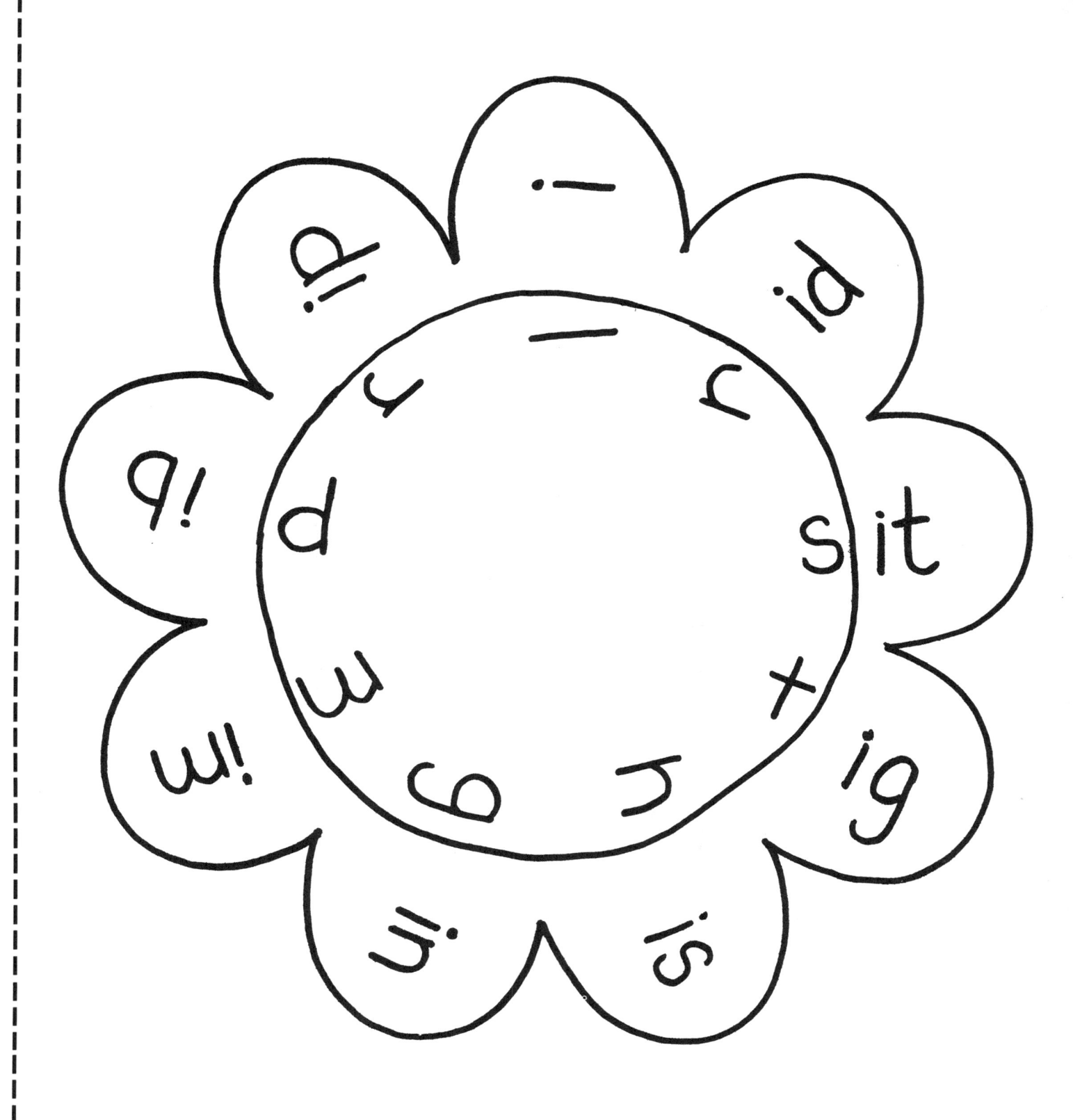

193

Name: Ice Cream

Skill: Counting and Numeral Recognition

Procedure: The child reads a numeral on a cone card and places the correct number of scoops of ice cream on the cone.

Variations: Math combinations or number words could be substituted for the numerals for a higher level task.

cut out 10-number from 1 to 10

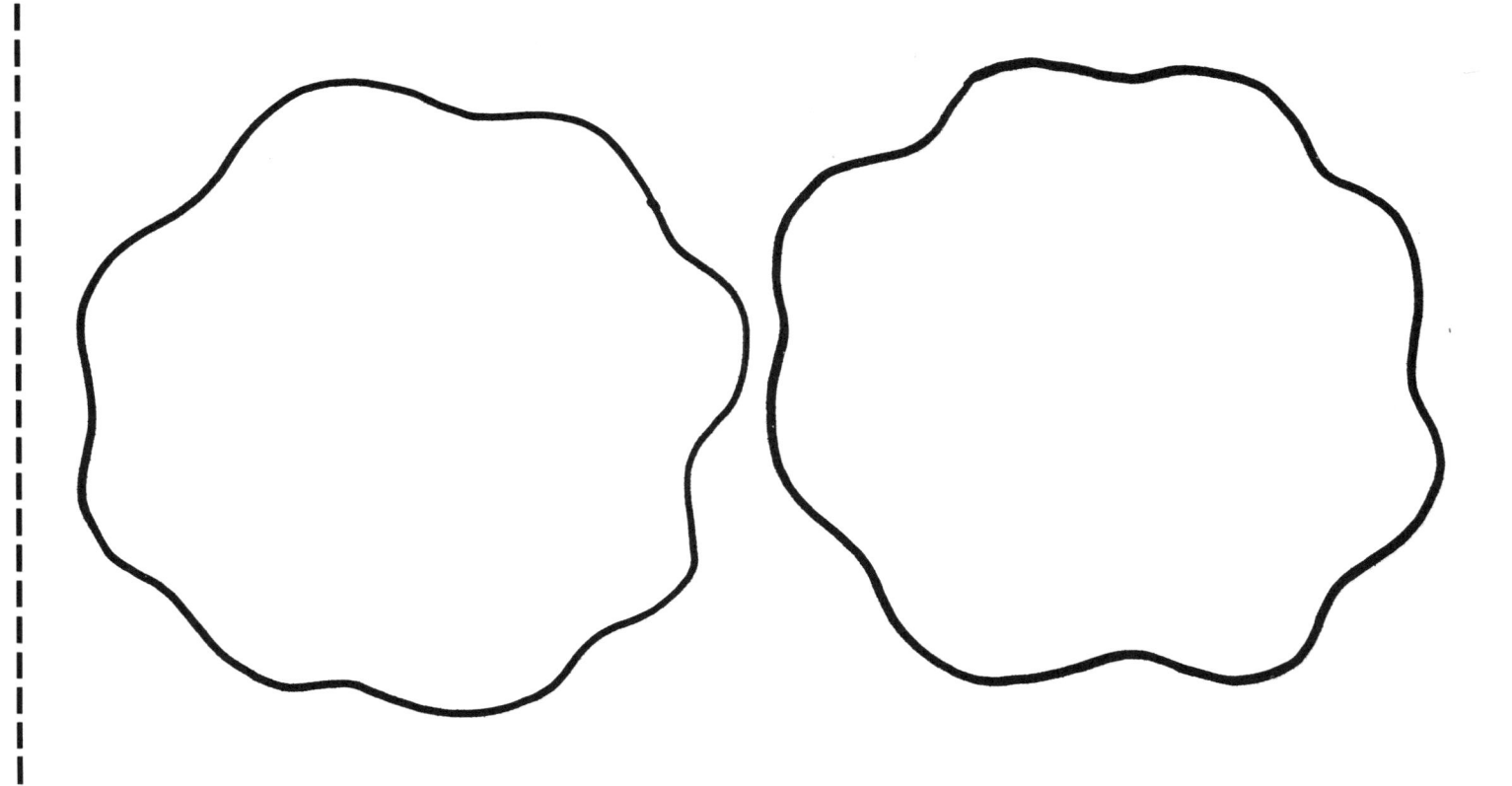

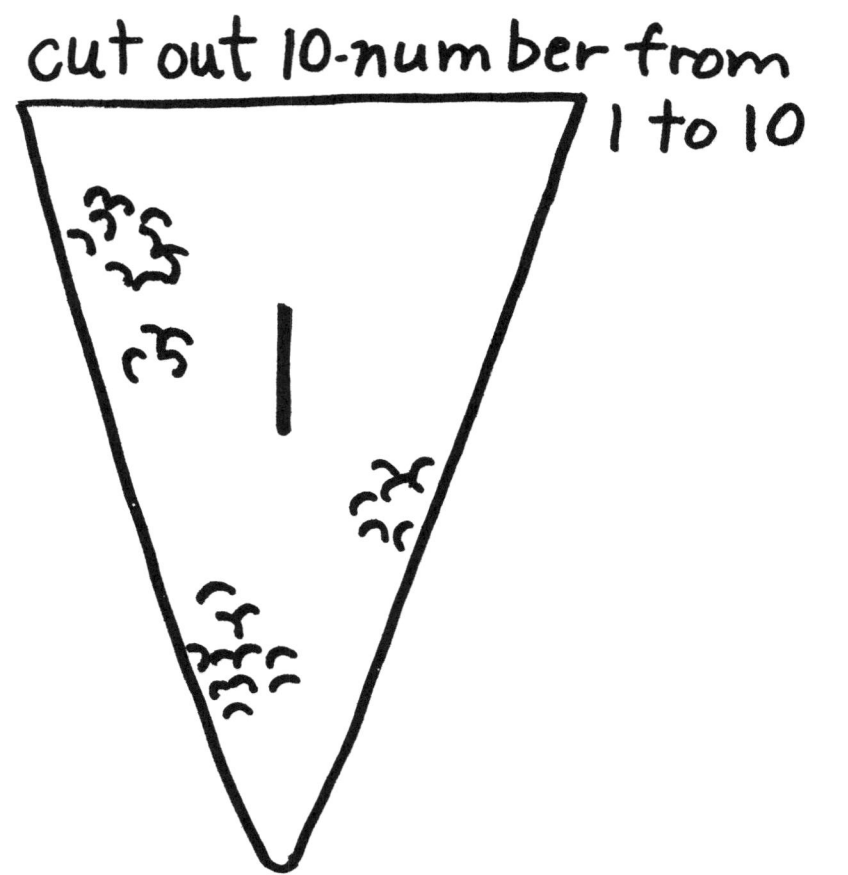

1

Name: Matching Faces

Skill: Matching Facial Expressions-Visual Discrimination

Procedure: The child looks at a face, finds the matching face on the board and places his face beside it.

Variations: Other faces with more or less detail may be made. Verbal questions regarding facial expressions may be asked.

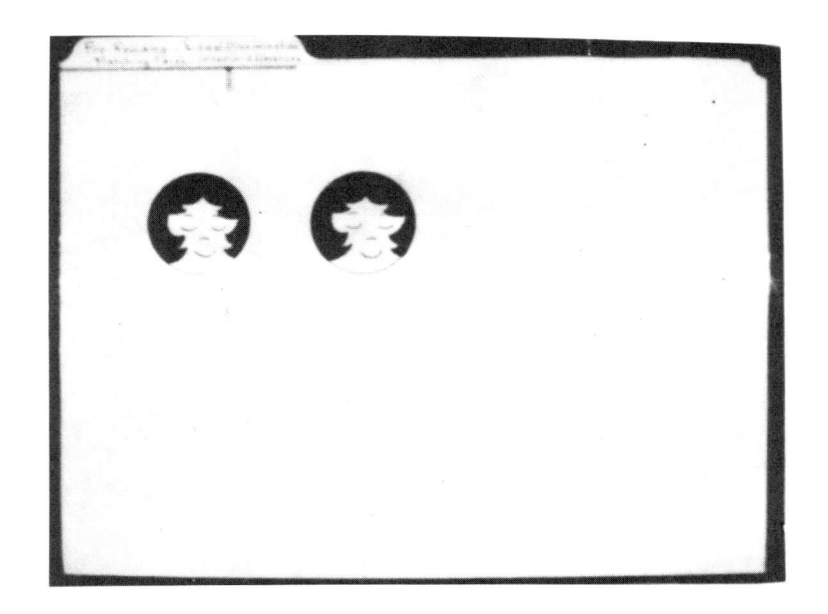

Cut out two sets of the following faces. Adhere one set to the manila folder as illustrated. Adhere the other set to tagboard and put in an envelope to use for matching faces in the folder.

197

Name: Dressing Kit

Skill: Fine Muscle Development Using Zippers, Buttons, Lacing

Procedure: The child is instructed on how to zip, button, and lace. He then uses the examples for practice and reinforcement.

Variations: Snaps, hooks and eyes, and other fine muscle fastening devices may be added.

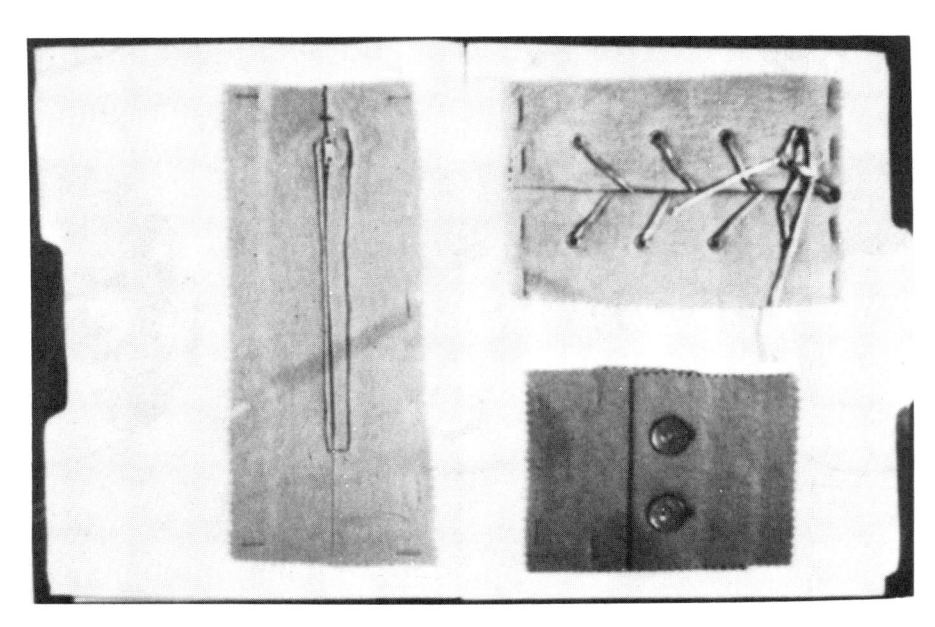

Name: Assignment Cards

Skill: Reading and Following Directions

Procedure: The child reads the directions and completes the self directed assignments.

Variations: Any self directed assignments may be listed.

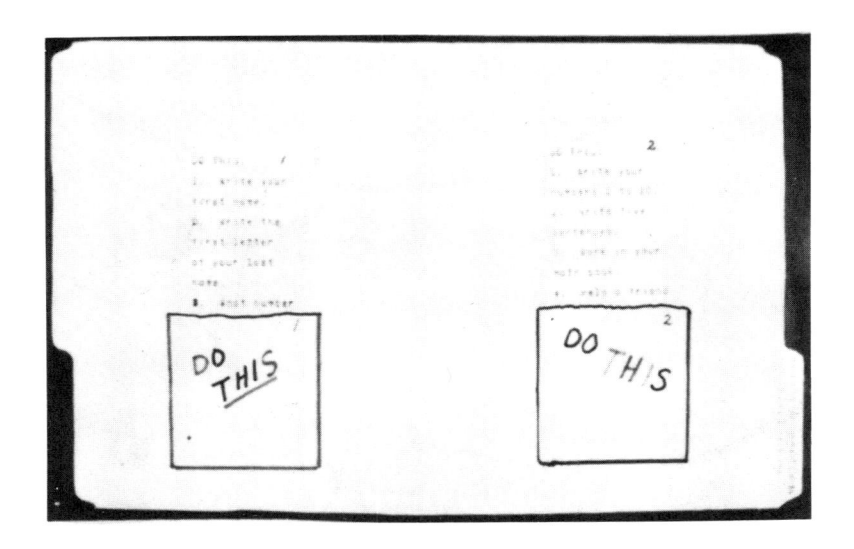

Color each section a different color.

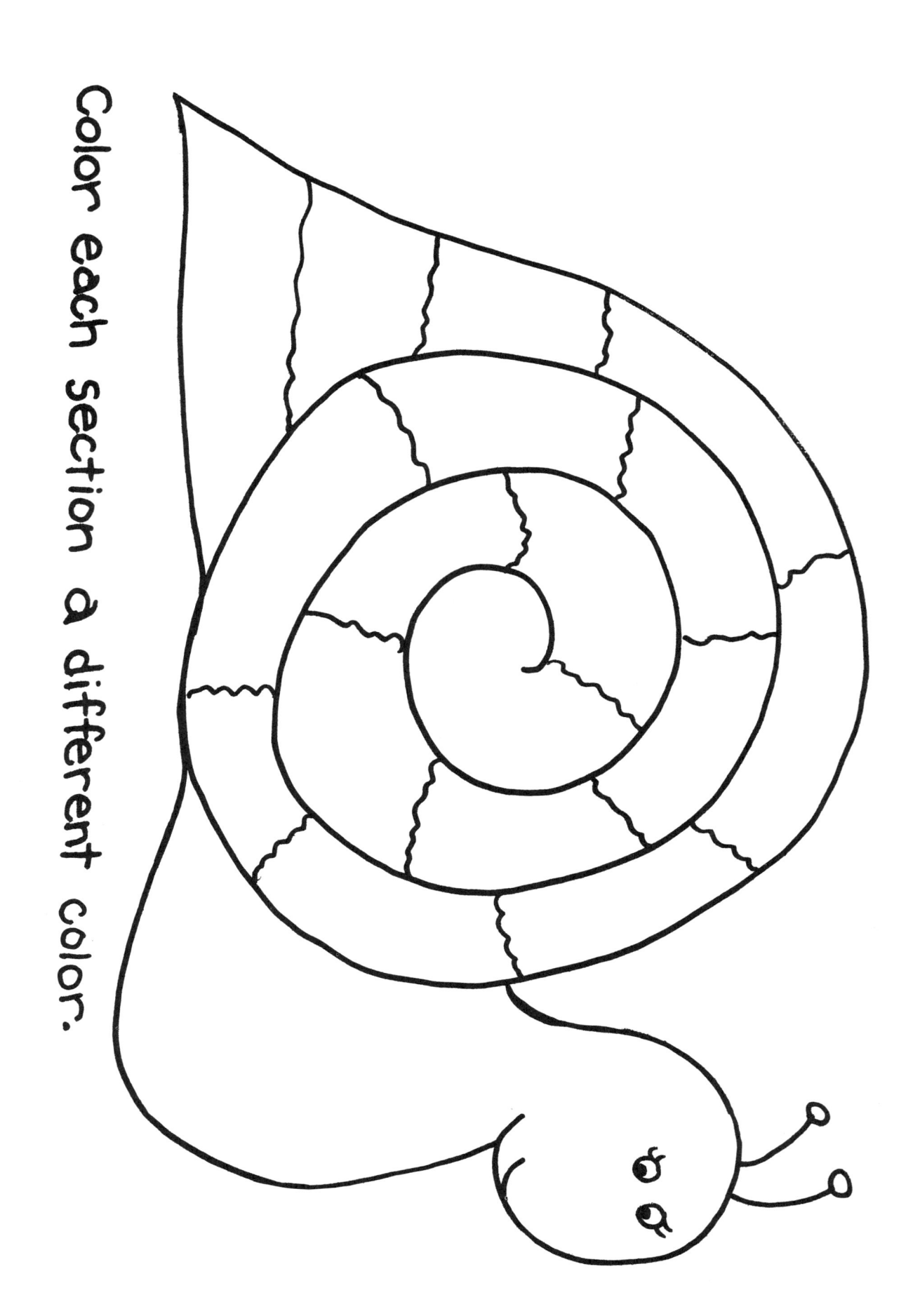

Sample Assignment Cards

Do this:

1. Write your name.
2. Write the numbers 1 to 10.
3. Draw a circle.
4. Draw a square.
5. Write a word.
6. Write a sentence.
7. Draw a triangle.

Do this:

1. Make my bed.
2. Clean my room.
3. Dust the furniture.
4. Do my homework.
5. Be very quiet.
6. Take out the trash.
7. Read a book.
8. Help Mommy.

Name : Match a Puzzle

Skill: Visual Discrimination

Procedure: Two pieces of an identical drawing are used. One is mounted and the other is cut into pieces. The child places the pieces over the identical pattern.

Variations: Use simple or complicated patterns depending on your objectives for the child. Wall paper, magazine pictures, pictures of the children may be used.

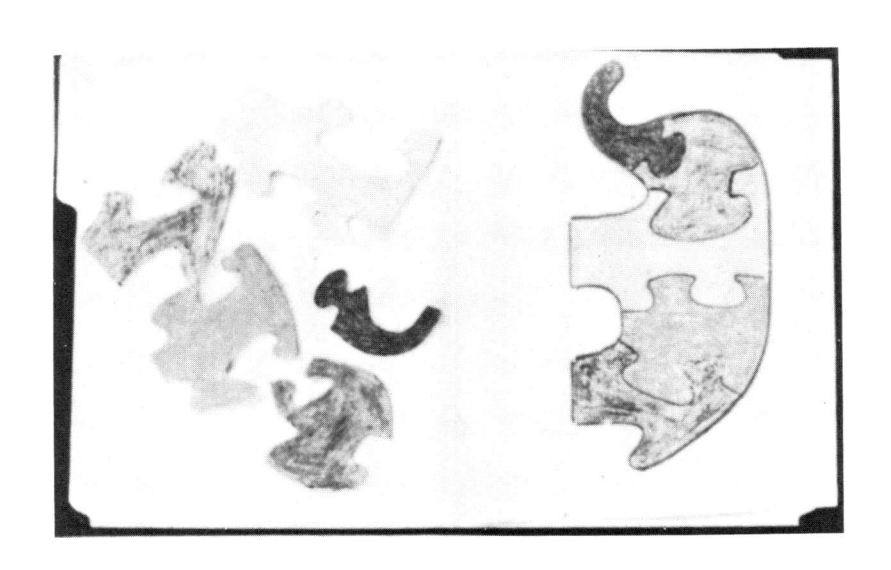

203

BIBLIOGRAPHY

1. American Automobile Association. Traffic Engineering & Safety Department: Pedestrian and School Safety Division. (Washington, D.C.)

2. Bereiter, C. and S. Engelman. *Teaching Disadvantaged Children in the Preschool.* (Englewood Cliffs, N. J.: Prentice-Hall, 1966).

3. Bloom, Benjamin S. *Stability and Change in Human Characteristics.* (New York: John Wiley and Sons, Inc., 1964).

4. Brett, Arlene, E.Ed. *Affective Education.* (Coral Gables, Florida: University of Miami, 1977).

5. Caballero, Jane A., Ph.D. *Aerospace Projects for the Young Child.* (Atlanta, Georgia: Humanics Limited, 1979).

6. Caballero, Jane A., Ph.D. *Art Projects for the Young Child.* (Atlanta, Georgia: Humanics Limited, 1979).

7. Caballero, Jane A., Ph.D. *Extending Your Early Childhood Curriculum.* (Coral Gables, Florida: University of Miami, 1977).

8. Caballero, Jane A., Ph.D. *Guidebook for the Teacher and Paraprofessional.* (Coral Gables, Florida: University of Miami, 1978).

9. Caballero, Jane A., Ph.D. "Elementary Aerospace," *Journal of Aerospace Education,* November, 1977.

10. Child Development Associate Consortium. *The CDA Credential and the Credential Award System.* (Washington, D. C.: The CDA Consortium, 1976).

11. Child Development Associate Consortium. The Local Assessment Team Guidelines. (Washington, D. C.: The CDA Consortium, September, 1976).

12. Children's Television Workshop, Sesame Street records. (New York: Columbia Book and Record Library, CBS).

13. Christman, M. L., Ed.D. "Social Studies." Unpublished paper.

14. *Criteria for Selecting Play Equipment for Early Childhood Education.* (Rifton, New York: Community Playthings).

15. Fagg, Lela. "Play Today." National Association for the Education of Young Children. (Washington, D. C.).

16. Far West Lab for Educational Research and Development. *Parent-Child Toy Library* (L4 170 18). (Morriston, New Jersey: General Learning Corporation).

17. Forgan, Harry W., Ph.D. *The Reading Corner.* (Santa Monica, California: Goodyear Publishing Co., 1977).

18. Frobel, F. *The Education of Man.* (New York: Appleton-Century-Crofts, 1903).

19. Havighurst, Robert J. *Developmental Tasks and Education*, 3rd Edition. (New York: D. McKay Co., 1972).

20. Hunt, J. McV. *Intelligence and Experience.* (New York: The Ronald Press Co., 1961).

21. Johnson, June and Clari W. Duncan, Ph.D. *Develop a Positive Classroom Environment: A Technique of Behavior Modification.* (Tallahassee, Florida: ESEA Title III, New Adventure in Learning: Demonstration/Diffusion Center, W. T. Moore Elementary School, October, 1973).

22. Leeper, Sarah H., Ruth J. Sales, Dora S. Skipper, and Ralph L. Witherspoon. *Good Schools for Young Children.* (New York: Macmillan Publishing Co., 1974).

23. Lowenfeld, Viktor. *Creative and Mental Growth.* (New York: The Macmillan Co., 1947).

24. Maslow, Abraham Harold. *Religions, Values, and Peak Experiences.* (Columbus, Ohio: Ohio State University Press, 1964).

25. McConathy, Osbourne, W. Otto Miessner, Edward Dailey Birge, and Mabel E. Bray. *The Music Hour in the Kindergarten and First Grade.* (New York: Silver, Burdett, and Co., 1929).

26. *New Rhythm Band Method.* (Chicago: M. M. Cole Publishing Co., 1937, 1964).

27. Palmer, Hap. *Learning Basic Skills Through Music* (AR 514 Volume 1) (additional albums). (Freeport, N. Y.: Educational Activities, Inc., 1969).

28. Piaget, Jean. *The Construction of Reality in the Child.* (New York: Basic Books, Inc., 1954).

29. Richards, Mary Helen. *Threshold to Music.* (Evanston, Illinois: Harper and Row Publishers, 1964).

30. Smith, Madorah E. "An Investigation of the Development of the Sentence and the Extent of Vocabulary in Young Children." (University of Iowa Studies Child Welfare, 3:5, 1926).

31. Templin, Mildred C. "Certain Language Skills in Children," Institute Child Welfare Monography Series XXVI. (Minneapolis: University of Minnesota Press, 1957).

32. Torrans, Ann, Ph.D. "Suggestions for Parents." Unpublished paper.

33. Thomas, Marlo. *Free to Be . . . You and Me.* (New York: Ms. Foundation, Inc., McGraw Hill Book Co., 1974).

34. Walton, Frances, Ph.D. "The Four Common Goals of Misbehavior. How We Can Recognize Them. What We Can Do About Them." (Columbia, S. C.: Counseling Bureau). Unpublished paper.

FOOTNOTES

1. Piaget, Jean. *The Construction of Reality in the Child.* (New York: Basic Books, Inc., 1954).
2. Havighurst, Robert J. *Developmental Tasks and Education.* 3rd Edition. (New York: D. McKay Co., 1972). pp. 262-263.
3. Bloom, Benjamin S. *Stability and Change in Human Characteristics.* (New York: John Wiley and Sons, Inc., 1964). p. 188.
4. Bereiter, C. and S. Engelman. *Teaching Disadvantaged Children in the Preschool.* (Englewood Cliffs, N. J.: Prentice-Hall, 1966). p. 42.
5. Frobel, F. *The Education of Man.* (New York: Appleton-Century-Crofts, 1903).
6. Havighurst. p. 2
7. Child Development Associate Consortium. *The CDA Credential and the Credential and the Credential Award System.* (Washington, D. C.: The CDA Consortium, 1976). p. 4.
8. Child Development Associate Consortium. *The Local Assessment Team Guidelines.* (Washington, D. C.: The CDA Consortium, September, 1976).
9. Caballero, Jane A., Ph.D. *Guidebook for the Teacher and Paraprofessional.* (Coral Gables, Florida: University of Miami, 1978). p. 110.
10. Caballero, *Guidebook*, p. 110.
11. Caballero, *Guidebook*, p. 111.
12. Caballero, *Guidebook*, p. 112.
13. Caballero, *Guidebook*, p. 112.
14. Caballero, *Guidebook*, p. 112.
15. Caballero, *Guidebook*, p. 112.
16. Caballero, *Guidebook*, p. 111.
17. Caballero, *Guidebook*, p. 111.
18. Caballero, *Guidebook*, p. 112.
19. Caballero, *Guidebook*, p. 112.
20. Caballero, *Guidebook*, p. 128.
21. Caballero, *Guidebook*, p. 128.
22. Caballero, *Guidebook*, p. 155.
23. Caballero, *Guidebook*, p. 156.
24. American Automobile Association. Traffic Engineering & Safety Department: Pedestrian and School Safety Division. (Washington, D. C.).
25. Fagg, Lela. "Play Today." National Association for the Education of Young Children. (Washington, D. C.).
26. *Criteria for Selecting Play Equipment for Early Childhood Education.* (Rifton, New York: Community Playthings).
27. Caballero, Jane A., Ph.D. *Extending Your Early Childhood Curriculum.* (Coral Gables, Florida: University of Miami, 1977). p. 17.
28. Caballero, Jane A., Ph.D. "Elementary Aerospace," *Journal of Aerospace Education*, November, 1977. p. 23.
29. Christman, M. L., Ed.D. "Social Studies." Unpublished paper.
30. Caballero, *Extending*, p. 17.
31. Caballero, *Guidebook*, p. 287.
32. Caballero, *Guidebook*, pp. 184-185.
33. Caballero, *Guidebook*, p. 245.
34. Caballero, *Guidebook*, p. 279.
35. Caballero, *Guidebook*, p. 122.
36. Caballero, *Guidebook*, p. 123.
37. Caballero, *Guidebook*, p. 242.
38. Caballero, *Extending*, p. 32.
39. Caballero, *Extending*, p. 22.
40. Caballero, *Extending*, p. 27.
41. Caballero, *Extending*, p. 21.
42. Caballero, *Guidebook*, p. 243.
43. Caballero, *Guidebook*, p. 117.
44. Smith, Madorah E. "An Investigation of the Development of the Sentence and the Extent of Vocabulary in Young Children." (University of Iowa Studies Child Welfare, 3:5, 1926). p. 173.
45. Templin, Mildred C. "Certain Language Skills in Children," Institute Child Welfare Monography Series XXVI. (Minneapolis: University of Minnesota Press, 1957). p. 174.
46. Caballero, *Guidebook*, p. 225.
47. Caballero, *Guidebook*, p. 142.
48. Forgan, Harry W., Ph.D. *The Reading Corner.* (Santa Monica, California: Goodyear Publishing Co., 1977). pp. 21-34.

49. Caballero, *Guidebook*, p. 115.
50. Caballero, *Guidebook*, p. 194.
51. Caballero, *Extending*, p. 10.
52. Caballero, *Guidebook*, p. 117.
53. Caballero, *Guidebook*, p. 195.
54. Caballero, *Guidebook*, p. 239.
55. Lowenfeld, Viktor. *Creative and Mental Growth.* (New York: The Macmillan Co., 1947).
56. Caballero, Jane A., Ph.D. *Art Projects for the Young Child.* (Atlanta, Georgia: Humanics Limited, 1979).
57. Caballero, *Guidebook*, pp. 136-137.
58. Caballero, *Guidebook*, p. 176.
59. Caballero, *Guidebook*, pp. 208-209.
60. Caballero, *Guidebook*, p. 220.
61. McConathy, Osbourne, W. Otto Miessner, Edward Dailey Birge, and Mabel E. Bray. *The Music Hour in the Kindergarten and First Grade.* (New York: Silver, Burdett, and Co., 1929). pp. 151-152, 164.
62. Caballero, *Guidebook*, p. 262.
63. Caballero, *Guidebook*, p. 284.
64. Brett, Arlene, E.Ed. *Affective Education.* (Coral Gables, Florida: University of Miami, 1977).
65. Johnson, June and Clair W. Duncan, Ph.D. *Develop a Positive Classroom Environment: A Technique of Behavior Modification.* (Tallahassee, Florida: ESEA Title III, New Adventure in Learning: Demonstration/Diffusion Center, W. T. Moore Elementary School, October, 1973).
66. Walton, Frances, Ph.D. "The Four Common Goals of Misbehavior. How We Can Recognize Them. What We Can Do About Them." (Columbia, S. C.: Counseling Bureau). Unpublished paper.
67. Maslow, Abraham Harold. *Religions, Values, and Peak Experiences.* (Columbus, Ohio: Ohio State University Press, 1964).
68. Torrans, Ann, Ph.D. "Suggestions for Parents." Unpublished paper.
69. Far West Lab for Educational Research and Development. *Parent-Child Toy Library* (L4 170 18). (Morriston, New Jersey: General Learning Corporation).
70. Caballero, *Extending*.

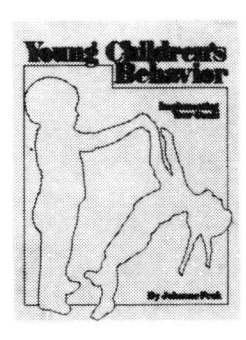

WE'LL HELP YOU TO HELP THEM.

EDUCATION

108-80 LOOKING AT CHILDREN. Richard Goldman, Ph.D.; Johanne Peck, Ph.D.; Stephen Lehane, Ed.D. Combines theory and practice, exploring such issues as language development, classification, play and moral development in children. Also includes a look at sex typing, television, single-parent families, and the fathers role in parenting. $9.95

407-80 ALTERNATIVE APPROACHES TO EDUCATING YOUNG CHILDREN. Martha Abbott, Ph.D.; Brenda Galina, Ph.D.; Robert Granger, Ph.D., Barry Klein, Ph.D. Delves into the theoretical basis behind three major programmatic approaches to education: programs emphasizing skill development; cognitive growth; and affective development. This book encourages the reader to develop his or her own theoretical and philosophical position. Each approach is discussed according to rationale and Philosophy, Curriculum Goals, Planning of Instruction, Use of Physical Space, Instructional Materials, Evaluation Methods, and the Instructional Role of the Teacher and Child. $5.95

413-80 YOUNG CHILDREN'S BEHAVIOR. Johanne Peck, Ph.D. Approaches to discipline and guidance to help the readers deal more effectively with young children. Six units focus on "Examining Your Goals," "Looking At Behavior," "Young Children's Views of Right, Wrong and Rules," "Applying Behavior Modification," and "Supporting Childs Needs." $6.95

406-80 THE WHOLE TEACHER. Kathy R. Thornburg, Ph.D. Designed for education majors and teachers of early childhood programs, this book presents a unified approach to teacher training. Topics addressed include: personal attitues, curriculum planning and development; classroom management techniques; working with volunteers, staff and parents; and professional development. $9.95

418-80 ORIENTATION TO PRE-SCHOOL ASSESSMENT. T. Thomas McMurrain. Designed for the child development center staff, this handbook presents a clear description of the effective assessment of the individual child. In addition, this manual is the user's guide to HUMANICS CHILD DEVELOPMENT ASSESSMENT FORM, a developmental checklist of skills and behavior that normally emerge during the 3 to 6 year range. Includes 5 assessment tools. $14.95

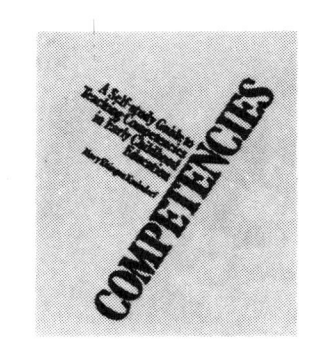

419A-80 COMPETENCIES: A SELF STUDY GUIDE FOR TEACHING COMPETENCIES IN EARLY CHILDHOOD. Mary E. Kasindorf. Divided into six competency areas and thirteen functional areas of competence as identified by the Child Development Consortium. This guide can be used to identify existing teaching skills and training needs. Designed to serve as an aid for those preparing for the C.D.A. creditial. It contains checklists of teacher and child behaviors and activities that would indicate competence and can be used in assembling a C.D.A. portfolio. $10.95

humanics
Post Office Box 7447
Atlanta, Georgia 30309

PROJECT IDEAS

416-80 AEROSPACE PROJECTS FOR YOUNG CHILDREN. Jane Caballero, Ph.D. This "first of it's kind" manual provides teachers and young students with an overview of aerospace history from kites and balloons, on to helicopters, gliders and airplanes, through todays satellites and the space shuttle. Each chapter is followed by interdisciplinary activities and field trip suggestions. $12.95

403-80 MATH MAGIC. Filled with ideas for creating a stimulating pre-school learning environment, this book encourages active participation in the learning process. Through songs, limericks, puzzles, games, and personal involvement it will help children become accustomed to basic math principles, such as classification, seriation, the development of logical thinking, as well as teaching them basic problem solving skills. Comes with "Magic Pouch" which contains full size games, puzzles, bulletin board aids and whimsical animals (17 x 24) as a supplement to the text. $12.95

Vol. I, 409-80, Vol. II, 410-80. WHEN I GROW UP. Michele Kavanaugh, Ph.D. Provides activities for expanding the human potential of male and female students, while eliminating sex-role stereotypes. Volume I contains experiences for pre-kindergarten thru 8th grade students. Volume II continues with input suitable for high school through young adulthood.
$10.95 ea.

408-80 METRIC MAGIC. Kathy R. Thornburg, Ph.D. and James L. Thornburg, Ph.D. A fun book of creative classroom activities, *Metric Magic* was developed to teach preschoolers through sixth graders to think "metric." Includes action oriented activities involving the concept of length and progress through mass, area, volume, capacity, time, speed, and temperature. $8.95

417-80 ART PROJECTS FOR YOUNG CHILDREN. Jane Caballero, Ph.D. Over 100 stimulating projects for pre-school and elementary age children, including: drawing; painting; cut and paste; flannel and bulletin boards; puppets; clay; printing; textiles; and photography. Designed for those with limited budget and time schedule. Success oriented. $12.95

400-A CHILD'S PLAY. Barbara Trencher, M.S. A fun-filled activities and material book which goes from puppets and mobiles to poetry and songs, to creatively fill the pre-schoolers day. This handbook is a natural addition to a CDA or other competency-based learning program and has been used nation-wide for this purpose. $12.95

415-80 DESIGNING EDUCATIONAL MATERIALS FOR YOUNG CHILDREN. Jane Cabellero, Ph.D. A competency based approach providing over 125 illustrated activities encompassing language arts, health and safety, puppetry, math, and communication skills. Suggested functional areas and stated purpose for each activity make this a valuable tool for the CDA candidate. $14.95

PARENT INVOLVEMENT

419-80 FAMILY ENRICHMENT TRAINING. Gary Wilson and T. Thomas McMurrain. Designed for a workshop of six sessions, this program focuses on concerns for families today including communication, family relations, discipline, and developing self-esteem. Techniques such as role playing, small and large group interaction, and journals encourage participants to develop greater understanding of themselves and others. This package includes a manual for trainers, a participants "log" and the booklet "Dialog for Parents." $9.95

102-80 PARENTS AND TEACHERS. Gary B. Wilson. Offers strategies for staff trainers or anyone involved in parent or adult education. Included are training techniques which facilitate group interaction, team building, effective communication and self awareness. Designed to build a program promoting increased parent-staff interaction, each activity includes clear instructions, stated objectives, lists of materials and time requirements. $7.95

106-80 WORKING TOGETHER. Anthony J. Colleta, Ph.D. This practical handbook includes: plans for parent participation in the classroom; alternative approaches to teaching parenting skills; ideas for home based activities; and supplements to parent programs in the form of child development guides and checklists. $9.95

107-80 WORKING PARENTS. Susan Brown and Pat Kornhauser. Designed to make a positive impact on the family life of working parents, this book presents techniques which promote constructive and enjoyable parent-child interaction without disrupting the families daily routine. $7.00

24 Hour Direct Mail Service:
404-874-2176

420-80 BUILDING SUCCESSFUL PARENT-TEACHER PARTNERSHIPS. Kevin J. Swick, Ph.D., Carol F. Hobson, Ph.D. and R. Eleanor Duff, Ph.D. Deals with the issues of parent involvement by including: an in depth examination of the changing nature of parenting and teaching in recent decades — the emergence of the two-parent working family, the vanishing extended family, the one-parent working family, and a comprehensive plan for implementing successful parent-teacher programs. $5.95

ASSESSMENT

CD-507 CABS — CHILDREN ADAPTIVE SCALE. Bert O. Richmond and Richard H. Kicklighter. A testing tool for children ages 5-10 years. Created to measure skills in the following areas: (1) language development; (2) independent functioning; (3) family role performance; (4) economic-vocational activity and (5) socialization. Useful for enabling teachers to plan remediation for the child's level of adaptive behavior. Designed to be administered directly to the child.
Manual $14.95   Student Test Booklet $.65 ea.

ADOLESCENTS

411A-80 I LIVE HERE, TOO. Wanda Grey. Designed for the teacher who would like to improve the atmosphere in the classroom by helping each student to develop a more positive self concept. Themes such as "You Are One Of A Kind," "Know How You Feel," "You And Other People," "As Others See You," and "Using Your Creativity," will foster in children a better understanding of themselves and the people around them. $8.95

414S-80 H.E.L.P. FOR THE ADOLESCENT. Norma Banas, M.Ed. and J. H. Wills, M.S. Explores the underlying causes of the problems of the high school underachiever or potential dropout. Useful tests, programs and reading references are included to help identify "learning weaknesses" and promote "learning strengths." $5.95

humanics
Post Office Box 7447
Atlanta, Georgia 30309

SOCIAL SERVICES

302-80 ASSESSING STAFF DEVELOPMENT NEEDS. Gary B. Wilson, Gerald Pavloff and Larry Linkes. Provides a step-by-step methodology for determining the training needs of child development programs and planning their resolution. Tear-out worksheets and staff questionnaires will help clarify job descriptions and goal definitions, in conjunction with the needs assessment. $3.00

206-80 A SYSTEM FOR RECORD KEEPING. Gary B. Wilson, T. Thomas McMurrain and Barbara Trencher. Designed for family oriented social service agencies. This handbook is an integral part of HUMANICS Record Keeping System and should be used as a guide to proper use of the HUMANICS Record Keeping Forms. $5.95

201-80 INTERVENTION IN HUMAN CRISIS. T. Thomas McMurrain, Ph.D. Clearly presented intervention strategies based on an evaluation of crisis intensity and the response capacity of the individual or family. Rights, risks and responsibilities of the helper are also discussed. $6.25

MAINSTREAMING

404S-80 NEW APPROACHES TO SUCCESS IN THE CLASSROOM. Norma Banas, M.Ed. and J. A. Wills, M.S. A companion volume to Identifying Early Learning Gaps, designed for mainstream children in kindergarten through third grade. Includes activities structured to inspire the student who has experienced repeated failure and to help him or her acquire learning skills in the areas of reading, writing and arithmetic. Can be used in the classroom for the entire group or for a small group. $7.95

412S-80 LATON: THE PARENT BOOK. Mary Tom Riley, Ed.D. Presents a training plan for parents of handicapped children, designed to acquaint them with the resources, facilities, educational opportunities and diagnostic processes available to help them raise their children. This easy to read book will encourage parents to get involved. $12.95

New Publications

REALTALK: EXERCISES IN FRIENDSHIP AND HELPING SKILLS. George M. Gazda, Ed.D., William C. Childers, Ph.D., Richard P. Walters, Ph. D. A human relations training program for secondary school students including student text and instructor manual. REALTALK includes training in getting along with others, making and keeping friends, leadership, helping others deal with their problems, and learning how to talk with practically anyone about practically anything.

THE LOLLYPOP TEST: A DIAGNOSTIC SCREENING TEST OF SCHOOL READINESS. Alex L. Chew, Ed.D. A lollypop loved by all. Children will enjoy taking this test for school readiness, educators will appreciate the easy quick, and significant results. Purpose of the test: (1) to assist the schools in identifying children needing additional readiness activities before entering first grade (2) to identify children with special problems and (3) to assist schools in planning individual and group instructional objectives. Culture-Free.

SPECIAL INTRODUCTORY PRICE
$14.95 each

ORDER FORM

ORDER NO.	TITLE/DESCRIPTION	QUANTITY	PRICE

Subtotal ....
Ga. residents add 4% sales tax .....
Add shipping and handling charges .....
TOTAL ....

humanics

Make checks payable to:
HUMANICS LIMITED
P. O. Box 7447
Atlanta, Georgia 30309

Ship to:

NAME _____

ORGANIZATION _____

ADDRESS _____

CITY _____ STATE _____ ZIP _____

_____
(AREA CODE) TELEPHONE NO.

Institutional P.O. No. _____

Date _____

Shipping and Handling Charges

Up to $10.00 add	$1.25
$10.01 to $20.00 add	$2.25
$20.01 to $40.00 add	$3.25
$40.01 to $70.00 add	$4.25
$70.01 to $100.00 add	$5.25
$100.01 to $125.00 add	$6.25
$125.01 to $150.00 add	$7.25
$150.01 to $175.00 add	$8.25
$175.01 to $200.00 add	$9.25

Orders over $200. vary depending on method of shipment.